Advance praise for "Fire Call!"

"The 'fire call' stories are absolutely riveting. I can't get enough of them. Inspired me. Made me want to do something – either look into becoming a fireman myself or at least write the guys in my community a bigger check."

**Joe Kita, author of "Accidental Courage:
Finding Out I'm a Bit Brave After All"**

"Fire Call!" is billed as a firefighter's memoir, but it often reads more like a fast-paced action novel. First time in my life I have read an introduction that is actually gripping and exciting, and I'm 82!"

Gene Logsdon, author of "The Contrary Farmer"

"An emotional roller coaster ... wiping tears one minute, smiling the next. If this book doesn't make you want to be a volunteer first responder, it'll sure make you want to hug one."

**Joel Salatin, farmer, author of "You Can Farm" and
"Everything I Want To Do Is Illegal"**

FIRE CALL!

SOUNDING THE ALARM
TO SAVE OUR
VANISHING VOLUNTEERS

by GEORGE DeVAULT

Design: Kenneth Kleppert
Copyeditor: Alice Perry
Text: Minion
Front cover: George DeVault/Columbus Dispatch
Back cover: Mitch Mandel/Rodale

Manufactured in the United States of America
ISBN 978-0-9909236-0-2 Hardcover
ISBN 978-0-9909236-1-9 Softcover
ISBN 978-0-9909236-2-6 E-book

With love, for Melanie, my guardian angel
And for all firefighters, and their families, everywhere

"I can think of no more stirring symbol
of man's humanity to man
than a fire truck."
Kurt Vonnegut
(volunteer firefighter Badge #155, Alplaus, NY)

The first fire truck in the village of Vera Cruz, Pennsylvania, a 1939 International
with a 500 gallon per minute surplus Civil Defense pump. Photo circa 1950.
UPPER MILFORD TOWNSHIP HISTORICAL SOCIETY

CONTENTS

Introduction

It's 4 o'clock in the morning. Suddenly, you're wide awake. You smell smoke. Your house is on fire!

You flip on the bedside lamp and see smoke curling out from under your bedroom door. You call 911, right away. You want to warn the rest of your family, but your bedroom door is already hot to the touch. You don't dare open it. After just a few breaths, you'd pass out. Worse, the added air from the open door would feed the fire like a bucket of gasoline. A smoke detector screams in the hallway. You pray it's enough to wake everyone.

You scramble out a bedroom window, hoping, praying that help will arrive before it's too late. As you hit the ground, the fire siren atop the firehouse half a mile away roars to life. You wait … for what seems like forever. Then you wait some more. The firehouse siren goes off, again, calling local firefighters a second time.

Eventually, you hear fire truck sirens. Thankfully, they're growing closer. The fire department is finally on its way. But something weird is going on. The sirens are coming from the opposite side of town, from a firehouse that's three miles away. Your nearest firefighters aren't responding yet. Why?

Could be many reasons. Maybe they don't have a driver. Maybe the 30-year-old fire truck just won't start, again.

That fictional scenario is not as far-fetched as it might sound. It's based on grim reality. Throughout the United States, our volunteer firefighters are getting fewer, older and more burned out. Between 1984 and 2012, the number of volunteer firefighters in the United States fell by 13 percent, while the number of emergency calls nearly tripled.

"The volunteer emergency services … is a tradition in danger of weakening and possibly even dying out," the United States Fire Administration (USFA) reported back in 2004. "Many fire departments across the nation today are experiencing more difficulty with recruiting and retaining members than ever before."

Pennsylvania, for example, had some 300,000 volunteer firefighters in 1977. By 2014, that number was closer to 50,000.

"Sooner or later, somebody's going to dial 911 ... and the 911 center is going to dispatch a fire department, and nobody's going to show up. That's where we're headed," Pennsylvania State Fire Commissioner Edward Mann testified before the state legislature in February 2014. Pennsylvania is not alone. "Vanishing volunteers" are a serious problem, nationwide.

"The causes of the problems are similar in all 50 states," said the USFA. "No single region of the country is dealing with problems that are significantly different than those found in other regions. On a regional level, the Northeast has seen the greatest decline in volunteers because it has traditionally been protected by volunteers more than other regions. Four states (New York, Pennsylvania, Delaware and New Jersey) that have historically been served by large numbers of volunteers have all experienced a major volunteer decline.

"Fire departments can no longer count on the children of current members following in their parent's footsteps. Nor can they count on a continuous stream of community people eager to donate their time and energy to their local volunteer fire department. Adding to the problem, departments cannot rely on members staying active in the volunteer fire service for long periods of time."

In its "Third Needs Assessment of the U.S. Fire Service" in 2011, the National Fire Protection Association (NFPA) said, "Fire service needs are extensive across the board, and in nearly every area of need, the smaller the community protected, the greater the need."

That should scare us all, because in 2014, fully 69 percent of our firefighters — seven out of every 10 firefighters — were volunteers. That's 783,300 volunteers out of the estimated 1,129,250 firefighters in the country, according to the nonprofit National Volunteer Fire Council (NFVC) in Washington, D.C. An estimated 30,000 to 40,000 of those volunteers are women; unfortunately, no one keeps close track of their numbers.

Every year, volunteer firefighters save American taxpayers an estimated $139.8 billion, not to mention countless lives.

Around the world, volunteers are the backbone of fire protection in many countries. Australia has some 175,000 volunteers, France about 190,000. Volunteers account for the majority of firefighters in Austria, Germany and Switzerland. Canada has some 127,000 volunteers. Chile's 40,000 firefighters are all volunteers. In Japan, a whopping 920,000 firefighters are volunteers.

Surprised? Most people are blown away by such statistics for the simple reason that the volunteer firefighter's story is seldom told. Volunteers, and what we really do, are something of a well-kept secret. The firefighters you see in hit movies ("Backdraft," "The Towering Inferno," "Ladder 49") or read about in popular books ("Report From Engine Company 82," "Fighting Fire," "Working Fire") are almost always from the big cities, Chicago, Los Angeles, Baltimore, New York City, San Francisco and Oakland, respectively, in the case of those movies and these books.

Why? For starters, volunteer firefighters don't "work" regular hours at the firehouse, or have scheduled days off from firefighting. Volunteers have day jobs. And families. When we're not answering fire calls, we're busy trying to catch up on normal lives delayed by fire calls. But it's not my intention to widen the already deep divide between volunteer and paid firefighters. That historic split is way too big as it is, and for no good reason at all. The way I look at it, a "firefighter" is a firefighter is a firefighter. Period. End of discussion.

I've fought fires for free; I've fought fires for pay, as a part-time employee of the Borough of Emmaus, Pennsylvania. And on more than 5,000 fire calls, no one ever asked me as I stepped off of a fire truck, "Are you guys paid or volunteer?" In an emergency, such thoughts never cross anyone's mind. All people care about is that we're there and we're doing everything humanly possible to make things better. Discussions about pay and "working conditions" usually come long after the fire is out. "You couldn't pay me enough to do that," someone nearly always says. Sometimes, a very different voice chimes in: "You're a damn fool!" A time or two, I must admit, I've had to agree with that assessment. Bottom line is a paycheck — or the lack of it — makes no difference to the fire. The dangers are the same. That's why some unions and municipalities forbid their firefighters from volunteering in the smaller towns where many of their paid firefighters live: They don't want anyone to get hurt or killed.

Then there's the long-standing "tradition" that strictly forbids volunteers from talking much about what we do. We're "Iron Fireman," as it says on my first fire department T-shirt. We can take it, whatever "it" may be. We suck it up and tough it out. What happens on the fireground stays on the fireground. If we talk openly about what we do, see and feel, the conventional thinking goes, people will think we're either macho braggarts or a bunch of bellyaching softies.

Convention be damned! Such thinking is as outdated as bucket brigades. It's as dangerous as riding on the tailboard of a fire truck, and as self-destructive as going into a burning building without wearing an air pack. It's just not done in the 21st century. But, as Mark Twain said, "The less there is to justify a traditional custom, the harder it is to get rid of it."

While the stories you are about to read come from my 30 years (1982 to 2012) as a volunteer firefighter in southeastern Pennsylvania, nationwide fire insurance ratings by the Insurance Services Office say the two fire departments I ran with are typical of the vast majority — nearly seven out of 10 — fire departments throughout the United States. So the stories in "Fire Call!" are coming soon to a firehouse near you. In fact, many have already played in your hometown, maybe right down the street from where you live. You just didn't know about it because no one was talking.

Some hidebound firefighters may curse me for writing this book. So be it. That's their problem, because they're the same ones who are the very first to complain that the public doesn't understand or appreciate volunteers enough to make even a token contribution to the annual fundraising drive. Seriously? Can you really blame people? If the public doesn't know what we do, why should people support us? Refusing to explain our training and activities only works against the fire service. It's what creates ignorant couch potatoes who believe that all volunteers are just "playing fireman." They don't know, for example, that:

* About half the firefighters who die in the line of duty every year are volunteers. Of the 97 firefighters who died in the line of duty in 2013, fully 41 were volunteers, and 25 were career firefighters, according to the NFPA. The other 31 were seasonal, federal, state or municipal contractors or employees. One was a prison inmate. While their median age was 40, the fallen ranged in age from 17 to 76.

* Fewer and fewer volunteers are in their late teens, 20s or 30s. More and more are in their 40s and 50s. In our smallest communities, the number of volunteers who are 50-plus has nearly doubled. No wonder heart attacks are the biggest killer of firefighters.

* About 9,000 fire engines were at least 30 years old in 2010. Nearly two-thirds of those were owned by volunteer departments serving populations of less than 2,500. Up to 2,000 more fire trucks turn 30 every year.

That's a national disgrace, and also a clear and present danger to the security of our families, our homes and our nation.

It's also why I wrote this book. I had three goals in mind:

1. Inform people about the benefits of having volunteer firefighters as well as what it really means to be a volunteer.

2. Let volunteer firefighters know that it's OK — no, it's mandatory — to talk about what we do.

3. Encourage greater financial and other kinds of support for the volunteer fire service.

I'm not alone in that. Since 2000, comedian-actor Denis Leary has raised more than $10 million through his nonprofit Leary Firefighters Foundation (LFF) to benefit firefighters in New York, the Boston area, New Orleans, and Detroit. Leary "played" the deeply troubled New York City Firefighter Tommy Gavin on the hit FX Network TV comedy-drama

"Rescue Me" from 2004 to 2011. His commitment to firefighters, however, comes from real-life personal tragedy. Leary's 38-year-old cousin, Jeremiah Lucey, was one of six firefighters killed in the catastrophic Worcester Cold Storage and Warehouse fire in Worcester, Massachusetts, on Dec. 3, 1999. Also killed was Lt. Tommy Spencer, Leary's childhood friend and high school classmate. Spencer was 42. The fire was started accidentally by a homeless couple "squatting" in the abandoned 6-story warehouse when they knocked over a candle. The firefighters became trapped while searching for the homeless couple, who had already left the building. The 2004 movie "Ladder 49," starring Joaquin Phoenix and John Travolta, was loosely based on the Worcester fire. An LFF program named after Lucey awards grants of $25,000 to $50,000, but "only to non-volunteer, union-affiliated uniformed fire departments."

I mourn the loss of the six Worcester firefighters. I also applaud the work of Leary's foundation. All firefighters deserve our fullest support. I don't have Leary's money, celebrity and contacts. I'm just a firefighter. But I do have an IRA. I'm dipping into my modest retirement savings to publish this book, because the story of our "vanishing volunteers" needs to get out — now. On fire calls, minutes matter. Our volunteers are in trouble.

So, I am publicly pledging a portion of the proceeds from the sale of "Fire Call!" to benefit volunteer firefighters around the country. With volunteers accounting for nearly 70 percent of our firefighters, there's no reason a grassroots effort on their behalf couldn't produce results similar to Leary's.

People want to know what we do. They have a right to know. And they need to know, because volunteers have been the backbone of the fire service for almost 300 years now. The volunteer tradition is older than the country itself. It all began on Dec. 7, 1736, when Benjamin Franklin founded the first volunteer fire company in Philadelphia. The list of volunteer firefighters from around the 13 colonies is a who's who of our founding fathers:

* George Washington
* Thomas Jefferson
* Samuel Adams
* John Hancock
* Paul Revere
* Alexander Hamilton
* John Jay
* John Barry
* Aaron Burr
* Benedict Arnold
* James Buchanan
* Millard Fillmore.

They paid for their leather buckets and other firefighting gear out of their own pockets. Our first president even bought a fire engine for Alexandria, Virginia.

For the next 115 years, ALL firefighters in the United States were volunteers. The first paid fire department didn't appear until 1851 in Cincinnati. That's why today we still have monuments to our rich volunteer heritage in the very heart of some of our largest cities. Take San Francisco, for example. San Franciscans and tourists from throughout the world know and admire Coit Tower atop Telegraph Hill. But few people know that the tower was named for — and was paid for by — a volunteer firefighter.

Her name was Lillie Hitchcock Coit (1843–1929). Actually, she was an "honorary" firefighter because she was a woman. She was also a socialite and an heiress. "Fire engines" of her day were little more than light wagons loaded with hose or a pump. They were pulled by men, not horses. One day in 1858, three rival fire companies were racing to a fire on Telegraph Hill. Because it was short one man, Knickerbocker Engine Co. No. 5 was falling behind. That's when 15-year-old Lillie purportedly threw down her school books and joined the firefighters on the ropes pulling No. 5. As she did, she turned toward bystanders and yelled, "Come on, you men! Everybody pull and we'll beat 'em!" The sidewalk fire chiefs pitched in. Knickerbocker won the race, and Lillie won a place in the hearts of San Francisco firemen. For the rest of her long life, she signed her name "Lillian H. Coit 5" and always wore a solid gold "5" pin on her dresses.

That's ancient history now. Modern day volunteers with names that may surprise you include:

* **Sam Springsteen**, the son of rock musician Bruce Springsteen. In 2014, when 20-year-old Sam Springsteen passed Firefighter I certification at the Monmouth County Fire Academy in New Jersey, the amount of time required for Firefighter I coursework had risen to 188 hours. Sam is a member of the Colts Neck (New Jersey) Fire Department, which averages about 400 fire calls a year.

* **Brian Williams**, anchor of the "NBC Nightly News." As soon as he was old enough, Williams joined the volunteer fire department in his hometown of Middletown, New Jersey.

"Firefighting isn't for everybody, but for me, it was the most pleasing act of volunteerism. It was tactile, tangible, and it paid huge dividends. It ties directly to your community and your neighbors," Williams wrote in *USA Today* in 2011.

As a young volunteer, Williams was wearing an air pack and crawling around on his hands and knees inside a burning house. He rescued a 3-week-old puppy. As a reminder of those glory days, Williams said he keeps his old fire helmet in his office at NBC world headquarters at 30 Rockefeller Plaza in New York City.

 * **Kurt Vonnegut**, author of "Cat's Cradle," "Slaughterhouse-Five" and "Breakfast of Champions," among many others. The blend of satire, gallows humor, and weird science are all ingredients that he probably first experienced as a volunteer firefighter in Alplaus, New York.

Nearly 50,000 fire departments throughout the United States are constantly and carefully studied and then rated by risk assessment experts at the for profit Insurance Services Office (ISO) to determine how much communities will pay for fire insurance.

"Class 1" is exemplary; "Class 10" is so minimal that it's considered no protection at all. (Nationwide, more than 1,700 fire departments are rated Class 10.) Only 17 states have at least one Class 1 fire department. New York state has just two, and California seven, while Texas has the most with 18. The Borough of Emmaus, where I first became a volunteer firefighter, has an ISO rating of Class 3. The neighboring rural Citizens' Fire Company of Upper Milford Township (aka "Vera Cruz," the name of the village where it's located), is rated Class 8a. I joined Vera Cruz in 1987. Emmaus has a population of about 12,000 and is blessed with hundreds of fire hydrants. It answers about 400 fire calls a year. In the township, where only 7,300 people live spread out over 18 square miles, we haul all of our water in tank trucks and answer about 150 fire calls yearly. Included in the broad spectrum between ISO Class 3 and Class 8a are nearly 33,000 fire departments, roughly seven out of every 10 fire departments in the country.

"Virtually all U.S. insurers and businesses use ISO's Public Protection Classifications [PPC] in calculating premiums. In general, the price of insurance in a community with a good PPC is substantially lower than in a community with a poor PPC, assuming all other factors are equal," said ISO's website. That's why fire departments fight to maintain the best rating possible. As a result, up to 20 percent of ISO ratings are under appeal or review at any one time.

That's also why many fire departments spend more time raising money to buy new and better equipment than they do answering emergency calls. It's an "incessant quest," in the words of a 2014 report by the Pennsylvania Senate Veterans Affairs and Emergency Preparedness Committee. "Studies show that volunteer firefighters spend 60 percent or more of their available hours on fundraising. And less than 20 percent of today's citizens donate to their fire company," the committee report said. Costs are skyrocketing. An air pack that sold for $900 in 1984 cost $5,000 in 2014. Over the same 30 years, the price of a pumper truck shot up from $100,000 to about $500,000. That's one reason Illinois, Pennsylvania and other states are finally raising the limit on the amount of money volunteer fire departments can borrow.

"Although the shortage of volunteers, money, equipment and training existed 40 years ago, these challenges have reached 'emergency status.' Some experts predict that the problems are hitting such a feverish level that volunteer firefighting will go the way of the dinosaur by 2020," the Pennsylvania Senate committee report concluded.

After 143 years, the Emmaus Fire Department ceased to exist as a "volunteer" organization on May 15, 2014. That was the date a Pennsylvania Labor Relations Board hearing examiner ruled Emmaus firefighters are not "volunteers" but are "employees" of the borough, because "there is substantial evidence that the borough exercised control over the firefighters' appointments, wages, hours, working conditions and discipline, establishing an employer-employee relationship between the firefighters and the borough." As employees, firefighters are entitled to seek union representation. Six days after the ruling, firefighters voted to do exactly that. The result, so far, has been appeals and counter-appeals, the filing of an unfair labor practices complaint, and unbudgeted expenses of $102,529 — mostly for legal fees — coming out of the fire department budget. The borough talked of disbanding the fire department and contracting with neighboring fire departments to provide fire protection. Few see how that could work, since those neighbors sometimes have trouble finding enough volunteers to answer their own fire calls. The borough plans more appeals. The case may well end up before the state supreme court. It's a real mess, for everyone — for firefighters, who want to begin collective bargaining; for the borough administration; for surrounding municipalities facing similar issues with their volunteer fire departments, and especially for Emmaus residents, who are anxiously waiting to see how it will translate into their tax bills.

The longer our nation waits to address the well-documented problems decimating the ranks of our volunteers, the more solutions will cost in the future. "We simply cannot sit by and do nothing at all," warned Pennsylvania's Commissioner Mann. "We face a public safety crisis."

But wait … Why take just the experts' word for it? Why not go see for yourself?

Pretend you're a volunteer firefighter. The fire siren is wailing again. You have another fire call. Now, make mental tracks for the firehouse. You don't have to go far — just to the next page. Be warned, though, you never really know what's going on until you answer a fire call, and even then things keep changing. So, be safe.

PART 1

My Secret Life

CHAPTER ONE

Moment of Truth

Jan. 11, 2008 — On a good day, our biggest fire truck carries a crew of five. Today is not a good day. It's a weekday, the time when the fewest volunteers can respond to a fire call. We're heading to a roaring house fire with a crew of two.

Answering a fire call with just two people is risky, and not recommended. Why? Because the driver of the fire truck is also the pump operator. The driver must always stay with the truck to supply water and regulate pressure in the hoseline. That leaves only one firefighter to actually carry the hose and attack the fire. That's not something we want to do or like to do. It makes a dangerous job even more dangerous. But when enough volunteers just aren't available and lives are at stake, we don't have much choice.

"Working dwelling fire — with entrapment," says the county dispatcher.

Any "worker" is bad enough. But a "working dwelling fire — with entrapment" is as bad as it gets. That means someone is trapped in a house that's filling up with deadly smoke and burning down around them.

The fire is a few miles into a neighboring fire district, which is covered by our sister fire company, Old Zionsville (Station 19). The fact that both Station 19 and our Station 28 are being dispatched at the beginning makes this an automatic two-alarmer.

It's a Friday. A handful of us are cleaning up from a luncheon after the funeral of Claude F. Rauch Jr., a lifetime member, when our pagers go off. Claude joined the Citizens' Fire Company of Upper Milford Township (aka "Vera Cruz") just a few months after its founding in 1942. He was 85 when he passed away of natural causes.

We're in the Social Hall, right across the street from our engine room, one mile west of my home. I'm sinking a plastic fork into my second piece of chocolate cake when the call comes in. The cake can wait. Suddenly, minutes matter. They could spell the difference between life and death. Being at the station gives us a big head start that could reduce our response time by as much as 10 minutes.

Trouble is we have just one firefighter, me, and three drivers. Two of the drivers are well into their 70s. They haven't worn an air pack or manned an attack line in decades. Still, there is no hesitation from anyone, not with a working fire and a person trapped inside.

We run across the street to the firehouse. The doors of the engine room go up. I hustle into my bunker gear. Driver Gary Mohr tosses his gear into a side compartment. It's a lot easier to drive in street clothes than in bulky bunker pants and heavy fire boots. We scramble into the cab of the "War Wagon," 2821, a combination pumper/tanker. Black smoke belches into the engine room as the giant diesel engine rumbles to life.

"Should we roll, or wait for a crew?" Gary asks.

A loaded question. It sums up the constant conundrum of a volunteer fire department in just eight words. We know some volunteers have to be responding from work or home by now. At least we hope they are. God knows when they'll get here. And who will they be? Our most experienced interior firefighters? Or a carful of kids who just joined the department and aren't yet trained or allowed to do much of anything? God knows, but isn't telling.

At the time, I'm fire chief in Vera Cruz, so it's my call. Normal procedure is to wait. But this isn't a normal situation. Most of our volunteers are just now getting back to work after the morning's funeral. If they can leave work again — and that may be a pretty big "if" after having half a day off for the funeral — it's going to take most of them a good 10 minutes to reach the station. The person trapped in that burning building doesn't have 10 minutes. It's a crapshoot.

A hundred other thoughts flood my mind in a single second. The more experience you have in the fire service, the worse the process of making seemingly "snap" life-and-death decisions becomes. That's because you can play out scores of possible scenarios. You know from hard-won personal experience the dire — sometimes deadly — consequences of a bad decision.

Iowa State University (ISU) knows how it goes. "Firefighters with a high level of experience, who we expected to be faster decision makers and have a lower stress level, did not. In fact, the opposite occurred," the website FireRescue1 quoted ISU professor Ner Keren as saying of his study of 62 firefighters taking virtual reality tests. "The experienced firefighters took significantly longer to make decisions, and their stress levels were at least as high as novice firefighters, if not higher."

It's Station 19's call, I remind myself. Chances are good that at least some of its people will be in the area and available. Weekday calls are always iffy. But the first truck out of their engine room will be a pumper. That truck carries only about 750 gallons of water. If they hit the fire with their deluge gun, as they often do, it could completely empty their water tank in less than one minute. With two hose lines, their water will last only a few minutes longer. They're going to need more time — and a lot more water — to knock the fire down enough to safely search for a person trapped somewhere inside. Our pumper/tanker, on the other hand, carries 2,000 gallons of water. That's nearly three times the amount of water that Station 19 has on its pumper. They may have the personnel, but we have the water.

"Let's roll!" I tell Gary.

"*2821 responding*," we radio county.

We're the only fire truck responding, so far.

Gary usually drives our tankers, but he also has basic training on the pumper/tanker. As Gary flips on the flashing lights and reviews the location of all the controls on the dashboard, I slip my arms through the straps of an air pack clipped in the back of the officer's seat beside him.

Gary eases the truck up to the end of the firehouse driveway. Entering the highway at the station is always tricky. The view is almost blind to the left because of the Pennsylvania Turnpike bridge. It's only a little better on the right because a sweeping curve still hides oncoming traffic until the last few seconds. The speed limit is 30 miles per hour, but people often drive 40, 50, or faster. We look both ways — twice. I lay on the air horn and siren. Gary floors it. The truck roars through the Turnpike underpass and begins slowly climbing a long hill.

Gary's 78-year-old firefighter father, Cyrus, will follow with our 3,300-gallon tanker. There are no fire hydrants out here in the country. We have to bring all of our water with us. Whenever more firefighters finally make it to the station, Firefighter Bill Stahler will roll with our second pumper. He fires up the 25-year-old Hahn pumper and pulls it onto the pavement in front of the station to wait for a crew. Cy and Bill are brothers-in-law. Combine their years of service, and they have been active firefighters in Vera Cruz for 109 years.

The radio crackles with chatter. Station 19 Chief Joe Kernick is heading directly to the scene. Other Old Zionsville officers make for their firehouse. An ambulance is on the way. State police are en route. All the while, the fire rages, unchallenged.

A dispatcher comes on the radio: A car belonging to a young woman who lives in the house is parked in the driveway. Neighbors say the woman is still inside the burning house.

We can only go so fast. Main Road West is a narrow, hilly two-lane road with no shoulders and lots of curves. Gary pushes it as much as possible within the limits of safety. We don't want to cause any more problems by having a wreck on the way to the fire. The main thing is to get there, safely, so we can do our job.

While Gary drives, I run the sirens and radio. Then something tells me I will need to be "combat ready" — completely geared up and ready to attack the fire the instant I step off the truck — when we finally reach the scene. I finish putting on my air pack. We have three miles to go, so I have plenty of time to properly adjust the straps on my air mask for a tight fit, pull my Nomex hood up, and buckle my helmet with the earflaps down. I reach behind me and open the valve on my air tank all the way. Every second counts now.

The traffic light at Chestnut Street is red. We slow almost to a stop, siren and air horn blaring. Cross traffic screeches to a halt, and we roar through the busy intersection. Two miles to go.

Chief Kernick is on the scene now. He radios that one end of the house is fully involved in flames. Topping a hill, we see a big column of smoke from a mile away. Finally, we reach the scene.

Gary parks the truck on the side of the road at the end of the driveway. We are at least 75 feet away from the burning house, yet heat slams into us as soon as we open the doors. The fire is roaring, crackling. Bright orange flames leap high into the sky.

I go around the front of the truck and pull the 150-foot hose on the side facing the fire. It's already connected to the pump. All it needs now is water. Chief Kernick pulls a second hose from the opposite side. He circles around in the parking area to the far corner of the garage while I loop my hose through the front yard. We have the blaze in a crossfire.

Gary puts the mighty pump in gear. Our usual hose pressure is 100 pounds per square inch (psi). But, for a few seconds, Gary pumps somewhere around 300 pounds as we open our nozzles. The pressure slams both Chief Kernick and me to the ground. And Gary becomes an instant legend — the only pump operator in the history of our fire department to knock two fire chiefs flat on their butts in a single pump operation.

Gary quickly dials the pressure back to a manageable 100 psi. I pick myself up out of the snow and drag the hose toward the house. Where the garage joins the house, a tall window has already been broken out by the heat of the fire. It provides the perfect opening for an attack. About 15 feet from the house, I yank the nozzle wide open and begin ripping the fire up and down, back and forth with a solid stream of water. I'm cutting the advancing fire off from the house as Chief Kernick blasts it from the opposite side. My goal is to kick the fire in the teeth, knock it back on its haunches just long enough to allow a quick search of the house. We gotta find that woman!

Macungie Paramedic Chris Greb says the neighbors insist she's still inside. He points out her bedroom window. It's on the lower level, sandwiched between the front door and the blazing garage.

I drop the hose and kneel beside the window. It's dark and smoky inside. I can't see much. I bang on the window and yell. There is no sound or movement in the bedroom. All I hear is the roaring of the fire to my right as it starts building back toward full fury. I don't have much time. Neither does anyone who might be inside.

This is a moment of truth, a question of life-or-death. Maybe I can save a life. Maybe I will meet my death. It's a coin toss. And I have to "call it," right now. Do I play it safe and wait for backup? Or do I take a big risk and try to get her out on my own? Suppose I wait. Suppose she dies. Can I live with myself, knowing that I might have saved her?

What would you do?

It's a question you can never answer with any degree of certainty until it suddenly stares you in the face.

I know what the book says I should do. Since 1995, the federal Occupational Safety and Health Administration (OSHA) has held that four firefighters must be assembled outside a burning building before two firefighters in bunker gear and air packs may safely go inside to attack the fire. It's called the "two-in, two-out" rule. In theory, it's fantastic, a real lifesaver. At least that's what it's meant to be. In reality, it's a royal pain, especially for volunteer fire departments that often have a hard time coming up with two pair of fully trained firefighters in air packs in the middle of a workday. Still, a quick search might be OK because technically, I wouldn't be "attacking" the fire. I'm leaving the hose outside. But I'm splitting hairs here — and running out of time.

I'm no fire science expert. I'm just a firefighter. For serious technical guidance, firefighters depend on outfits like the International Association of Fire Chiefs (IAFC) and its "Rules of Engagement for Firefighter Survival." The goal is to keep firefighters from unnecessarily risking their lives, as tradition demands, by automatically and aggressively searching burning buildings for people who are probably already dead.

"Fire in a building today is not what it was 50 years ago," the IAFC warns. "Today's fires are hotter and flashover occurs quicker. Flashover can occur in less than five minutes and reach a temperature of 1,100 degrees. Flashover can occur as the first fire companies are arriving on the scene. In such cases, the survivability of any victim … can be very limited or non-existent. Victims die sooner than what occurred a few decades ago." A flashover occurs when a room and everything in it reach ignition temperature and simultaneously explode into flames.

Why the change? In a word, plastic. Blame the way we now furnish our homes and offices. While burning a pound of wood produces just 8,000 British thermal units (BTUs) of heat, burning a pound of plastic really turns up the heat, pumping out a scorching 19,900 BTUs, the IAFC says. Plastic almost triples the heat of a fire. But it gets worse. Burning plastic also produces more deadly gasses, such as cyanide. High levels of carbon monoxide and cyanide, can kill — in less than one minute. While victims of carbon monoxide poisoning may sometimes be successfully resuscitated, there's no help for the organ damage caused by cyanide.

"Search and rescue and the related removal of any trapped victims from a fire building takes time, and most of these operations are occurring while conditions continue to deteriorate, sometimes rapidly. This situation decreases the possibility of victim survivability while increasing the risk to firefighters," the IAFC says.

"A fire in a home in the middle of the night, with fire showing out a rear window and modest smoke throughout the rest of the building, may allow victim survival," the IAFC says. That is, of course, if the victim is not in a room full of fire.

"A fire in the same home in the middle of the night, with significant fire showing, from several windows and dense smoke, under pressure, pushing out of nearly all openings, may not allow any victims to survive the heat, toxic environment and the time required to search and remove them." If the whole house is full of fire, forget it. Put the fire out before searching for any victims, the fire chiefs advise.

"Search efforts must be based on the potential to save lives," admonishes the IAFC.

This fire is roaring back to full fury. It's eating its way into the upstairs bedrooms above me. But it hasn't broken through to the woman's basement bedroom. Not yet. It will soon, though. At this moment, chances are excellent that she may still be alive. But we're quickly running out of time. And she may be dying inside a room just 10 feet away from me. I have the training, protective clothing and air pack required by the NFPA to possibly save her life. But I don't have any backup.

What should I do?

What would you do?

More firefighters are responding, I know. But it will be at least three, maybe five, more minutes before they reach the scene. Anyone inside that burning house doesn't have three to five more minutes. She may already be out of time — and air.

"I'm going in," I tell Chris, the medic. He says he'll watch my back and tell the next firefighters to arrive where I am. That'll have to do.

I try the front door. Locked. With a pick-head fire axe, I smash the glass in the front door, reach inside and open the door.

The foyer's dark, smoky. A short flight of stairs to the right leads down toward the woman's bedroom. The smoke thins a bit as I move to the lower level. Still, it's not a good place for anyone to be without an air pack. Cut off from the pale winter daylight, the lower level is even darker. I see a doorway on the right. It has to be the door to her bedroom. I knock hard on the door a few times, turn the knob and crawl inside, yelling behind my air mask.

"Anyone here? Hello? Fire department! Where are you?"

There is less smoke inside the bedroom, but it's still dark and gloomy. I see a bed against the outside wall near the one small window. It doesn't look like anyone is in the bed, but I run my hands through rumpled bedding, feeling for a body. Nothing. Nobody.

"Where are you? Say something!"

Still yelling, I drop down to the floor and look under the bed with the flashlight clipped to my bunker coat. Then I reach under the bed as far as I can, sweeping my arm back and forth, just to make sure I'm not missing anything in the murky light. I open a closet at the foot of the bed and rummage through the piles on the floor. There is a desk, some other furniture and more piles in the rest of the room. I search through, under and around them. Nothing. Nobody.

That's a relief, sort of. Where is she? What am I missing? I open the bedroom window. Chris is standing right outside, his blue jumpsuit a welcome sight. "Bedroom's clear," I yell. Chris says I have the right room and more firefighters are pulling up beside the house.

"Good! I'm coming out." I yell through my mask. As I close the bedroom door, I see another door to my right. Maybe she's in there, I think. That's the wall against the fire. The flames haven't broken through the wall into the house, yet, at least not on the lower level. I can feel heat and hear crackling from above. Fire conditions may be much different on the floor above me.

There is no one in the closet. Crawling back toward the stairs, I see an open door opposite the bedroom. It's a laundry room. Better check it out. I crawl inside, feeling through piles of clothes and cleaning supplies in the darkness. Nothing. Nobody.

Then I hear something that makes my heart soar. It's the unmistakable sound of a metal air cylinder slamming against a wall directly above me. There is shouting muffled by air masks. Help is finally here! Other firefighters are now inside the house. The way it sounds, they're attacking the fire in the bedroom above me next to the garage. It's time for me to get out.

My new best friend, Chris, the medic, is right there as I lurch through the front door. I'm whipped. My heart is racing, I'm breathing heavily. Sweat soaks my dress uniform shirt inside my heavy gear. Once sparkling white, the shirt is now a dingy gray. Tiny carbon particles, the kind that clog your lungs in an instant, are permanently embedded in the cuffs and collar.

"You OK?" Chris asks.

Firefighters douse hot spots in the house where neighbors
insisted a woman was trapped.

PHOTO BY JIM MARSH

I am now. More hoses crisscross the front yard. Firefighters are everywhere. Besides Old Zionsville and Vera Cruz, firefighters are rolling in from
Emmaus (pronounced E-MAY-us), Macungie, South Whitehall Township,
and even Hereford in neighboring Berks County. Emmaus is the designated
"Rapid Intervention Team," the OSHA-mandated "two-out" guys. Their job
is to rescue any firefighters who get into trouble. South Whitehall is refill-
ing air bottles. Macungie Ambulance has three squads on the scene. Medics monitor the pulse and heart rate of every firefighter coming out of the
burning house. Vera Cruz and Macungie Fire Police control traffic, keeping
everyone and all of the trucks safe. In the next township, firefighters in the
village of Limeport are on standby at their station in case there's another
emergency call anywhere nearby.

Water shoots out of garage windows and holes in the roof as firefighters
attack the fire from different directions. I hear the whack of an axe. A chain
saw roars to life around the corner. Metal ladders clang against the eaves.
The sound of the fire is dying down. I unbuckle my helmet, peel off my
hood and air mask, and drop down to one knee in the front yard. Fresh air
is delicious.

"Take a break," Chris says. "They're setting up rehab out by the road. Go get checked out."

He doesn't have to tell me twice. I grab my helmet, gloves and mask and head out of the yard. Halfway to rehab, I see a knot of people. Some fire officers and medics are talking with a disheveled young woman. She's crying, her body shaking as she tries to speak. Her face is white, eyes wide with disbelief.

"She's the woman you were looking for," Chris says. "She was at a friend's house."

"God! Am I ever glad to see you!" I say to the woman. "I was looking for you all over the place." I want to wrap my arms around her, squeeze the stuffing out of her, but I'm covered with soot and soaking wet.

Her response is a blank stare. She has absolutely no idea what I'm talking about. She's in shock. All she knows is that her house is on fire, her life is in ruins. The rear window of her Ford Explorer is a pile of jagged chunks of glass, the victim of intense heat. Her bumper and taillights are molten masses of dripping plastic.

Nothing I can say is going to change that. There is only one thing to do. We break down our hoses and start packing up our gear. After all, it's Station 19's call. Chief Kernick and his crew can finish off the hot spots, investigate the cause of the fire and secure the building. That's one of the few good things about away games.

Turns out our timing is perfect. Just as our trucks parked out on the main road are ready to roll, our pagers go off again. We have another call back in our own district. It's an auto accident — with injuries.

CHAPTER TWO

Close Call

April 9, 1984 — A pot of black coffee is the perfect start to my workday. But this morning, after just a few sips, the coffee — along with everything and everyone at work — is going to have to wait. A house is on fire. Someone's trapped inside. The fire chief's calling for help. I'm a rookie volunteer firefighter. See ya later. I have a fire call!

The fire call this Monday morning is a working dwelling fire near where I live in the small town of Emmaus about 60 miles north of Philadelphia in southeastern Pennsylvania. A careless smoker accidentally set his basement recreation room on fire. Now, volunteer fire departments from throughout the area are rushing to the scene. This fire call will escalate to six alarms before it's all over.

The fire has a huge head start.

As thick smoke fills the townhouse, one of the three men living there runs out the front door. Another man bails out of a second floor window. But the third man refuses to leave until he's sure his little dog is safe. By the time he saves his dog, heavy smoke traps the man in a second floor bedroom. He leans out of a window and drops the dog to neighbors gathered below. Other neighbors run for a ladder. The man is still conscious, but barely. Smoke is really getting to him. A ladder goes up against the front of the house. Finally, the local police chief carries the man down the ladder — over his shoulder.

As our ladder truck pulls up in front of the burning building, the three men are on stretchers in the front yard. Medics are giving them oxygen, checking pulses and other vital signs. Everyone's attention is on the three men. No one is fighting the fire. Two fire hoses lie tangled in the yard, unmanned.

We connect our air packs and pick up one of the hoses. Four of us crawl inside through the front door. Heavy smoke pumps out above us.

"Basement door's on the left," says a cop.

That's good to kno w. If we don't knock the fire out soon, we stand an excellent chance of losing the entire six-unit building. So we crawl straight for the basement door as fast as we can hump the heavy, water-filled hose down the hallway.

A firefighter from another department leads the hose team. An air mask hides his face, but I don't think I've ever seen this guy before. His bunker gear is a different color. His size and movements are foreign to me. He has the nozzle, the business end of the hose. I'm right behind him, ready to hold the hose and relieve the back pressure once he opens the nozzle to attack the fire. Next on the hose is Emmaus Fire Chief Robert Reiss (pronounced "Rice"), my chief. Behind him is another firefighter I don't know.

Just before we reach the basement door, the nozzleman stops. He doesn't move for a second. He's kneeling. It almost looks like he's praying. Then, in one smooth motion, he rises to a half-crouch, turns around and runs toward the front door. He almost steps on us in his mad rush to get out of the burning building.

He says something as he runs by, but the tight-fitting air mask muffles his words. No one catches what he says. I just watch in horror and disbelief as our nozzleman bails out on us. I only have two years in the fire service at this point. This is one of my first really bad fires. But it's been drummed into my head countless times that you just don't do stuff like that. Firefighters don't run! We especially don't run out on each other. The first one in is always the last one out. Always. We never leave anyone behind. We work together as a team. We go in together. We come out together. Sometimes, we die together.

Is that what's about to happen? Is this going to be the day I die? I push such thoughts out of my mind and focus on the nozzle. The only thing I can think of is that nobody is on the nozzle. We are totally defenseless.

Instinctively, I launch my upper body forward from a kneeling position. I'm on my belly now, my long arms fully extended. I pounce on the nozzle like a drowning swimmer clutching a lifesaver.

Being facedown on the floor gives me a totally different view. I don't like what I see. Something is rising from the ugly orange carpet in front of me.

Is that smoke? No, it's steam. Our nozzle dribbled some water on the floor. It's so hot now where the nozzleman was kneeling seconds ago that the water is turning to steam. That's when I realize what the nozzleman was yelling as he ran away. "Floor's going!"

Suppose the floor does suddenly go out from under us, plunging the three of us left on the hose into the fiery basement below. Will we have minutes — or seconds — to live? The basement stairs probably burned away long ago. I wonder, can I shinny up our fire hose like the thick rope in high school gym class? It has to be hot as hell down in the basement. How long will it take the guys on the outside to get a metal ladder down into the hole to us? Can we last that long?

I don't know. The only thing I'm sure of is that we're directly above the inferno, the most dangerous place you can be in a fire, and something is terribly wrong. I push on the carpet with my fingertips. Even through my heavy leather gloves I can feel the floor give easily. I push harder. The floor feels soft, crunchy, crumbly. Locking my fingers out straight, I stab my right hand into the floor. My whole hand disappears through the floor up to the wrist.

I hook my fingers and rip the soggy carpet and flooring back toward me. Tiny yellow flames dance around the edges of the hole in the floor. Now the floor feels crunchy under my knees. I scoot back a few feet, stretch my arms out and jam the nozzle into the hole, opening it all the way. The hose bucks. Water gushes into the blackness below. Desperate now, I start whipping the nozzle in a tight circle, hoping to knock the fire back. I can't see where I'm aiming or even if I'm coming anywhere close to the seat of the fire. Time is running out. For all I know, it may already be too late.

But the firefighters behind me are eager to press the attack and hit the fire head-on. They want to get to the basement door and fight our way down the basement stairs, even though heat and flames will be roaring up the stairway like it was the chimney of a blast furnace. That's why basement fires are just plain awful. The other firefighters keep pushing the hose forward. They push the nozzle right out of my hands. It disappears down the hole. I claw at the hose, but my wet gloves just slip off of its canvas jacket.

"Pull the fucking hose back!" I yell at the chief. His eyes go wide inside his air mask. I don't usually scream at the chief. He knows something is wrong, very wrong. "I lost the nozzle. Back it out!"

The team hauls the nozzle back within my reach. I give the fire a few more licks, then signal the team to retreat. No one argues. Moving as one, we swivel around on our hands and knees and quickly crawl out the front door, dragging the hose behind us.

We spill outside onto the green grass in a pile. Off come our helmets, hoods and air masks. We open our heavy coats. Warm sun and a light breeze hit our sweat-soaked bodies. For a moment, I want to track down the nozzleman who deserted us. I'll wring his neck, break every bone in his body. But I don't know where he is. I don't even know who he is. But I do know this: He's going to have to live with the knowledge that he left three men inside a burning building to possibly die in a fiery pit every minute of every day for the rest of his miserable life. I wish him a long life, then go back to greedily gulping fresh air as I sprawl in the thick grass. It's a joy to be alive. Fresh air never tasted so good.

A minute later, a firefighter summons us back to the front door. "Look," she says, motioning inside. The floor we had just been crawling around on is completely gone.

CHAPTER THREE

If Not You, Who?

Hours later, I dragged myself back to the office. I was beat, but elated. I was also late for a business lunch with some out-of-town visitors.

"Where have you been?" my boss asked. Strange question for a firefighter's boss to ask a firefighter after a bad fire call and a narrow escape. But my boss was not who or what you might expect. He wasn't a fire chief. He wasn't even a fellow firefighter. My boss was a vice president at Rodale Press, a publishing company best known for its health and healthy living books and magazines such as *Prevention, Men's Health, Runner's World* and *Organic Gardening.*

Remember, I didn't fight fires for a living. I was a volunteer firefighter. I did what I could, when I could. I had a day job that paid the bills. In real life, I was a magazine editor. Now I was back at my day job, where everything was nice and quiet and safe — until someone dialed 911 and the pager on my belt went off again.

But our visitors didn't know anything about my "secret life," as some call it. Where did they think volunteer firefighters come from? They didn't. Almost no one does. And that's exactly the problem. Like most of us, our visitors to the office took volunteer firefighters completely for granted: Just call 911, and someone automatically — almost magically — materializes out of nowhere with big red trucks, flashing lights and screaming sirens, breathing gear that looks like a space suit, and an arsenal of firefighting tools. But where do these modern minutemen and women come from? From the firehouse, of course. We sit around the firehouse all day, drinking coffee, shooting pool, scratching our backsides and waiting for a cat to get stuck in a tree. Right? Yeah, right.

Where were we *before* the firehouse? What were we doing? Whatever it was, we instantly dropped what we were doing, and rushed from the factories, farms and fields. We regularly left our dinner tables, family gatherings and loved ones, and our warm beds or hot baths on cold, wet nights. We scrambled from job sites, churches, classrooms, grocery stores, and even the dentist's chair the instant there's a fire call. Depending on the time of day and the season, volunteers might show up at the firehouse in swimsuits and flip-flops or insulated coveralls and knee-high rubber chore boots. Younger women might sport flannel jammies and blue fuzzy, bunny-eared bedroom slippers. Suits and coats ranged from sweat suits to business suits, from white lab coats to blaze orange hunting coats. Few things were worse than having the pager go off when you were in a tree stand, sighting in on an eight-point buck.

The logo of the nonprofit National Volunteer Fire Council (NVFC) in Washington, D.C., puts it all into graphic perspective with a silhouette of a running man with a map of the United States in the background. Half of the man is dressed in a business suit. He holds a briefcase in his left hand. But the right half of his body is clad in firefighting gear. A fire helmet sits atop his head. He holds the nozzle of a fire hose in his outstretched right hand.

Our business guests were clueless. And, so, they were naturally intrigued by my boss' question. Where *had* I been? A flip answer came to mind. "Oh, nowhere special. Just out trying to get myself killed ... by almost falling through the floor in a burning building." But this wasn't the kitchen at the firehouse. It was the executive dining room at a well-respected business. And this was, after all, a "business meeting." So I behaved myself and canned the firehouse wisecracks.

"On a fire call. We had a nasty basement fire in a townhouse in Macungie. It went six alarms. Five people, including two firefighters, went to the hospital. Four were treated for smoke inhalation, one for a shoulder injury. It took 50 firefighters three hours to put the fire out. Damage is somewhere around $100,000," I said as I plopped down in the only vacant chair at the lunch table. The empty chair just happened to be right beside my boss. He looked skeptical.

Immediately, my boss leaned toward me. He stuck his nose against my soggy dress shirt and took a deep breath. Our visitors held their breath. They had never seen a performance quite like this before. Finally, my boss announced his verdict: "You're OK. You smell like smoke." The visitors relaxed.

Actually, I was a lot more than OK. *I was alive! Unhurt!* But that was not why I was smiling. Answering serious fire calls during business hours was an unwritten part of my job description. It wasn't always that way, though.

Employers don't have to let volunteer firefighters cut out of work to answer fire calls. Never mind that someone's house is on fire, or that there's a gravely injured person to cut out of a wrecked car. When you're at work, you're supposed to work and do the job you're getting paid to do. That's why they call it "work."

Now, if you're late for work because you were out half the night on a fire call, that's a different matter. Under Act 83, Pennsylvania law says you can't be fired or disciplined for coming in late because of a fire call, providing you have a proper excuse signed by your fire chief. A "note from your Mommy," firefighters call the excuse slips. Your employer also can't discriminate against you if you're injured in the line of duty and file a workman's compensation claim. But once you're at work, none of that applies. You're there to do your job, not to "play fireman," as some ignorant people describe volunteering. At most businesses, once you clock in, you're not allowed to leave unless the boss says OK.

When I joined the Emmaus Fire Department in 1982, barely a year after starting work at Rodale, company policy on this was anything but clear. So, before long, a rival editor tried to advance his cause by raising the sticky question of my leaving work to answer fire calls. His timing was perfect, or so he thought. It was during another business lunch with my boss and my boss' boss — the owner of the company — sitting at our table.

My boss immediately started squirming. He obviously didn't like being put on the spot in front of his boss. He was not wild about the idea of someone leaving work — for who knew how long — whenever there was a fire call. He stammered, trying to come up with an ironclad reason to say, "No," as he thought a good company man should. Then the owner of the company spoke up.

"Do what you have to do, George," said Bob Rodale, chairman and chief executive of the international publishing house bearing his family name.

My boss looked surprised. The rival editor, too. My boss breathed a sigh of relief. Suddenly, he was out of the hot seat. A difficult decision had been made for him, and by the highest authority. He had been spared.

Bob Rodale then turned to my boss and explained his reasoning: "It might be *my* house. It might be *your* house."

No one argued with Bob, and not just because he owned the company. Bob was a man of strong convictions. He believed in putting his money where his mouth was, whether he was fighting to save 15 acres of the scenic Lehigh Parkway from a greedy developer with political connections or preserving prime farmland or the disappearing wildlands atop South Mountain. When the Emmaus Fire Department needed money to consolidate three antiquated firehouses into one modern Central Station, Bob's company contributed thousands of dollars to the classroom part of the project.

Bob had an uncommon amount of common sense, especially when it came to protecting public health and safety. And his logic was flawless. He answered the question at such a deeply personal level that no right-thinking person could argue another side: "It might be *my* house. It might be *your*

19

house." How much plainer could it get? It was as straightforward as the old fire department recruiting poster that showed a pair of empty fire boots sitting in front of a fire engine. The caption read, "If not you, WHO?"

EMMAUS HISTORICAL SOCIETY PHOTO

CHAPTER FOUR

Just Another Day at the Office

Thankfully, the emergencies that followed never involved Bob Rodale's house or my boss' house, although the house directly behind my boss' house atop South Mountain burned down some years later. Over the years, there were so many fire calls in the immediate area that it almost seemed like South Mountain was jinxed. I fought no fewer than seven house fires there, five wildfires, two chimney fires, and a few vehicle fires; took part in a water rescue; and responded to multiple medical runs, ranging from a drug overdose to diabetic shock, a suicide, a search for a lost child, and scores of auto accidents and downed wires and trees on the mountain.

Oddly, the very first time I was allowed to ride a pumper to a fire call, there was a major Rodale connection. It was at the home of Rodale President Bob Teufel. He had just driven back to Emmaus from New York City. Bob had parked a company-owned station wagon in front of his house. Not long after he went inside, heavy smoke started rolling out from under the hood. As car fires go, it wasn't much of a fire. The veteran firefighters on the hose line had it out in no time. But it was good experience for me, and a reminder that I was still a "probie" at the very bottom of the totem pole. I got to man a push broom to help clean up the mess.

Responding from work, though, continued to be curious, at best. My coworkers were puzzled by the pager on my belt — "Did your boss give you that?" — and my sudden absences. In turn, I was always puzzled by the fact that no one else from work joined me on a fire truck. More than 1,000 people worked at Rodale then. Most of them lived in the borough or nearby. Our magazine titles included sports and fitness magazines, so many of our editors were world-class athletes, known for their great strength and endurance. Among them were a few Olympic hopefuls, and even a winner of the Boston Marathon (Amby Burfoot, 1968, with a time of 2:22:17). The Rodale community prided itself on community involvement. Yet I could count the number of volunteer emergency responders within the company on just one hand, including myself in the count.

Jeff Kuhns, in the print shop, was the only other Rodalean who ran with Emmaus. He was our Fire Police captain. Production supervisors Curt Hinkle and Dave Miller were fire officers in volunteer fire departments in nearby Richlandtown and Fountain Hill, respectively.

Four out of roughly 1,000! That is 0.4 percent. That may not seem like much, and it isn't. But, on the whole, Rodale had more volunteers than our national average. In 1984, the year I almost went through the floor, the population of the United States was 231.66 million. Of that number, roughly 1,103,300 were firefighters. Some eight out of 10 of them — an estimated 885,129 — were volunteers, according to the NVFC. That meant volunteer firefighters accounted for slightly *less* than 0.4 percent of our national population. So, strange as it might seem, Rodale wasn't doing too badly in the volunteer department, after all.

Still, as the Pennsylvania Dutch hereabouts say, it always "wondered me" why at least a few more of my coworkers didn't respond to fire calls. That was especially true of the staff of our *Men's Health* magazine. Why did I wonder? In a word: s-e-x. Each issue, *Men's Health* packed its pages with practical advice on how men can be more appealing to the opposite sex. As a result, *Men's Health* circulation in the United States steadily grew to 2 million. It became the largest and best-selling men's magazine in the country, and then the world. At last count, there were 39 editions of *Men's Health* in 46 countries, with global readership of about 24 million.

So, the old saying is true: "sex sells." Interestingly, *Men's Health* and other popular magazines all reported that no occupation is more appealing to the opposite sex than firefighters, both male and female. "Do Women Have a 'Fireman' Fantasy?" *Psychology Today* asked in the Sept. 21, 2011, issue. You bet they do, wrote Gad Saad, Ph.D., a professor of marketing at Concordia University. "Of all archetypes of a male hero, the firefighter ranks very highly on most women's lists," Saad said. "The fireman archetype is deeply entrenched in many women's psyches. Few women fantasize about accountants, office managers, and dental hygienists."

Want to get the phone numbers of all the hotties walking down the street? It's a piece of cake when you're wearing a firefighter's uniform, Saad said. No matter how handsome you might be, don't try it wearing civilian clothes. He was citing French research in which the man in a firefighter's uniform scored phone numbers almost three times more often than the man wearing civvies.

But the perks of being a firefighter get even better. "Firefighter" was the second happiest job, with a full 80 percent of firefighters saying they were "very satisfied" with their job, according to a 2011 report by the National Organization for Research at the University of Chicago. ("Clergy" came in first.)

Want respect? The 2007 Harris Poll showed firefighters at the very top of the charts, with 61 percent of adult Americans listing firefighting as the most prestigious of occupations. Scientists were second at 54 percent, and farmers ninth at 41 percent. The bottom of the barrel was covered by real estate agents/brokers (5 percent), actors (9 percent) and bankers (10 percent). Journalists tied with union leaders (13 percent) for eighth from last, just ahead of stockbrokers.

Question: "What's the difference between a cop and a firefighter?"

Answer: "Everyone loves a firefighter."

That's an old firehouse gag, but it's no joke. It's true. Laughter is a powerful medicine, and it lifted our spirits even in the middle of a national tragedy. On April 15, 2013, two terrorist bombs killed three and injured 264 near the finish line of the Boston Marathon. Six days later, with one bombing suspect dead and the other one in custody, the city began to heal. There were hugs for every cop on Boylston Street. School girls baked and iced big cookies with peace symbols and the initials "BPD." They gave one to every Boston police officer on the street as a heartfelt "Thank you!" from a grateful city. The "NBC Nightly News" with weekend anchor Lester Holt wrapped up that Sunday night with a burly Boston cop accepting a cookie, and saying, "I feel like a firefighter, I'm getting so much love!" And, over on the USA cable channel, in marathon reruns of "NCIS", "very" Special Agent Anthony D. DiNozzo Jr. wondered, "What is it with chicks and firefighters?"

Some people didn't even see volunteer firefighting as work, anymore. Instead, it was some bizarre brand of "leisure," sociologist Robert A. Stebbins, Ph.D., suggested in 1996. Granted, Stebbins classified volunteer firefighting as "serious leisure," but it was still leisure, right there along with recreational skydivers and gun collectors, and other "amateurs" (musicians, actors, baseball and football players, entertainment magicians, stand-up comics, archeologists, and astronomers), "hobbyists" (barbershop singers, cultural tourists, kayakers, snowboarders, mountain climbers, and other natural challenge enthusiasts), and "volunteers." (Never mind that firefighters have a higher incidence of post-traumatic stress than Vietnam veterans, according to Canadian research.) Academics aside, a lot of just plain ignorant couch potatoes in our society think that all firefighters get paid well for sitting around all day waiting for something to happen.

"The typical volunteer fire department resembles a club," according to an article by two sociologists, Kenneth B. Perkins of Longwood College in Virginia and John Benoit of Dalhousie University in Nova Scotia. Their paper was titled "Volunteer Fire-Fighting Activity in North America as Serious Leisure." They introduced their subject by saying, "We expect most readers will have little or no familiarity with this rather odd but most interesting form of volunteering." The paper was published in the January 1997 issue of the academic magazine *World Leisure and Recreation* (renamed *World Leisure Journal* in 2000), the official journal of the World Leisure Organization. "Mostly, the role of a volunteer firefighter is fun. Fun motivates the firefighter to do what most people see as dangerous; the community is protected from fire by those who are happy to provide protection without compensation." That's good, they wrote, because of the high and rising cost of fire trucks, firehouses and firefighting equipment. Fundraising activities, which they said often involved "beer drinking, horseplay and even some deviant behavior ... makes the volunteer fire department as a social club more attractive for the volunteers. This attraction, however, also encourages narrow recruitment and an insular culture, reinforcing the image of the volunteer fire department as a social club."

Sex and respect, untold happiness and job satisfaction, all in an environment of "serious leisure." What was up with those guys at *Men's Health*? Didn't they know a sweet deal when they saw one? Maybe it had something to do with the fact that they were health journalists. They spent an inordinate amount of time poring over medical and other scientific research on nutrition, fitness and health. Statistically, at least, they probably knew a lot more about the risks of firefighting than veteran firefighters did. The guys at *Men's Health* could probably rattle off all kinds of statistics, starting with the often-conflicting swirl of papers that say being a firefighter cuts your life short by as much as 10 years. Here's a sampling of some of the other troubling health news:

Heart Health — Firefighting is simply pure hell on your heart. "Firefighters at times operate at near maximum heart rate, 200 beats per minute, for periods in excess of 18 minutes," reported the Fire Department of New York (FDNY) after strapping heart rate monitors to firefighters. A Phoenix Fire Department fitness coach said, "Imagine the demand on a heart when it goes from sound sleep at a resting rate of 60 to full physical exertion of 180 to 200 beats per minute." That makes fire calls in the middle of the night especially dangerous. In any given year, heart attacks account for about half of all firefighter deaths.

Hearing Loss — The Klaxon horns, bells and other noisemakers that sound the alarm in firehouse sleep quarters can rob your hearing. So can the sirens, air horns and diesel engines on fire trucks. Then there are chain saws, gasoline-powered fans and other noisy equipment. Repeated or prolonged exposure to such loud noises causes a condition known as "tinnitus," a sometimes constant ringing of the ears. At its best, tinnitus is a nuisance.

At its worst, tinnitus drives some people to madness, and even suicide. Fortunately, the ringing in my ears is on the mild side.

Cancer Central — The more medical literature you read, the worse it gets. The University of Toronto reported "statistically significant excesses" of fatal brain tumors, other malignant neoplasms, and aortic aneurysms among firefighters in metropolitan Toronto. Compared to the civilian population, firefighters are two to three times more likely to develop brain cancer, liver cancer, colorectal cancer, and bladder cancer, scientists said.

Female firefighters, especially younger women, are more likely to develop breast cancer. Firefighters have elevated risks of stomach cancer, prostate cancer and skin cancer.

According to a legislative survey by Palm Beach County, Florida, Fire Rescue, "22 states, New York City, Canada and New Zealand have adopted legislation that presumes that if a firefighter contracts cancer, it is occupationally induced." On Aug. 29, 2011, Pennsylvania became one of those states with the passage of Act 46. The new law covers both career and volunteer firefighters. Benefits available under the law include retroactive and prospective salary and benefits, reimbursement for medical costs and workers' compensation benefits.

"Firefighters who have served more than four years will be entitled to a presumption that their cancer is job-related, similar to the process used when firefighters suffer from lung cancer, heart disease, or more recently, Hepatitis C," reported the Pennsylvania Firefighter Cancer Coalition. Act 46 protection continues for a legally mandated "600 weeks" after a person stops answering fire calls.

The website of the federal Centers for Disease Control and Prevention explained why. "Studies show that absorption of chemicals through the skin can occur without being noticed by the worker, and in some cases, may represent the most significant exposure pathway. Many commonly used chemicals in the workplace could potentially result in systemic toxicity if they penetrate through the skin (i.e. pesticides, organic solvents). These chemicals enter the bloodstream and cause health problems away from the site of entry.

"Historically, efforts to control workplace exposures to hazardous agents have focused on inhalation rather than skin exposure ... Standardized methods are currently lacking for measuring and assessing skin exposure."

Maybe all of that was why the guys at *Men's Health* stuck with jogging and other, more genteel physical activities where the biggest worries were a sprained ankle or shin splints. They had all of the time in the world to stretch and warm up before exercising. Sadly, that's just not the nature of fire calls.

Not even the ultimate convenience of having editorial offices right across the street from the firehouse could lure a single volunteer from the magazine. In fact, when *MH* Contributing Editor Joe Kita set out to research his 2002 Rodale book, "Accidental Courage: Finding Out I'm a Bit Brave After All," Joe said he never once considered trying his hand as a volunteer firefighter. Instead, he:

   * Went into solitary confinement to face his fear of loneliness.
   * Entered a demolition derby to face his fear of car accidents.
   * Did a stand-up comedy routine to face his fear of public speaking.
   * Spent a day as a high-rise window washer to face his fear of heights.
   * Let a knifethrower hurl knives at his head to face his fear of death.

Meaning no offense, Joe, but you could have saved yourself a whole lot of trouble just by running across the street to answer fire calls in Emmaus. It doesn't get any lonelier than in the total — midnight in a coal mine — darkness of a smoke-filled basement. Demolition derbies? They're all over our highways. And there are no tougher audiences than the constant comics and critics in a firehouse, or a classroom full of third graders during Fire Prevention Week. Afraid of heights? Check out the view from atop our 100-foot aerial ladder. Death never takes a holiday, and it's always watching over our shoulder on each and every fire call during just another day at the office.

That was especially true for me in the early 1990s when my Rodale office was on the second floor of the building that housed *Men's Health*. The building was directly across the street from the Central Station, so Chief Reiss gave me a key to the front door. Whenever there was a fire call, all I had to do was run down the stairs, bolt through a side door and dart across the street. But that key did a lot more than just open the front door of the firehouse. Whenever I turned that key, it also unlocked Pandora's box, and we never knew what kind of evil had just been unleashed on our town.

CHAPTER FIVE

Smoke Showing

The fire call this afternoon comes in as an "apartment building fire." Since my Rodale office is right across the street from the firehouse and I have a key to the front door, I'm already geared up in the jump seat of our attack truck when other firefighters come running in from the parking lot.

"Smoke showing!" says Firefighter Randy Wieder as he scrambles into the other jump seat on Engine 713. Seconds later, we have a driver and an officer in the front seats. The attack truck is rolling, red lights flashing, sirens wailing. Randy has his air pack on by the time we reach the center of town. Good timing. The burning apartment building is now only three blocks away.

As the truck pulls even with the side door of the building, we see wisps of black smoke puffing out from under the eaves.

"Somebody's inside," says Lt. Eric Loch. He's talking with the police on the scene by radio from the front seat. Randy and I pull the hose from the side of the truck nearest the building. The driver throws the pump into gear. Water surges through the line as we lug the squirming hose up the stairs to the apartment door.

"Ready?" I yell, my voice muffled by my face mask.

"Ready!" Randy replies. The wary look in his eyes isn't quite so convincing. Randy is one of our younger firefighters; he has never done this outside of our Tuesday-night fire practice. But firefighting really is the ultimate team sport. We all have our jobs, and we all have to do them, and well, or things go to hell in a hurry. Much as everyone always wants to be on the nozzle, we have to share. That means teaching our newer members how to hit a fire, head-on. I let Randy take the lead — and the nozzle. I've got his back.

"OK," I say. "Stay low. Search as we go. Hit the fire. Find the victim."

Heavy smoke billows out over our heads as we crawl in on our hands and knees. Lt. Loch holds the door open a crack. He keeps feeding us hose as we move deeper into the burning apartment.

We're lucky. It isn't as bad as it looks from the outside. Near the ceiling, smoke is so thick you can't see a thing. At waist level, it's only a heavy haze. Where we are on the floor, it's almost clear. The south-facing windows let in enough light so we can actually see where we're going, for a change.

There is no fire in the living room on the right, and nothing in the dining area to our left.

"Nobody here," says Randy.

"Keep going."

We start down the hallway and turn toward the kitchen on the right. Bright red and yellow flames shoot up the cupboards by the sink and lick out across the ceiling. They come from a small pot on the counter. It's an electric deep fryer. Directly over the fryer, heavy black smoke is coming to a rolling boil, furiously pumping out into the rest of the apartment.

Suddenly, I want to throw up. The last time I was in a house fire caused by a deep fryer, four members of one family lay dead on the smoldering second floor. I was tip-toeing over bodies, trying not to step in a hole and fall through the burned-out floor. One of the bodies was a 2-year-old girl. But that was years ago. I shake off the nausea.

"Hit it! Hit it!" I yell.

Randy faces the fire. He tucks his feet under his butt, straightens his back and opens the nozzle all the way. I strain against the hose to relieve the back pressure.

"Hit the counter ... narrow fog ... up the wall ... whip it around ... that's it! You got it!"

The fire is out, but we can't relax. The apartment's full of smoke. Someone's still inside. But where?

We leave the hose on the floor in the kitchen. On our hands and knees, we head down the hallway in search of the victim.

"Turning left into closet."

"Checking bathroom on right. Nobody in tub."

"Nothing under the bed. Checking piles of laundry."

"Clear in the back bedroom. Nothing here."

"You all right?"

"Yeah. You?"

"OK."

"Keep going. Gotta be here ... somewhere."

Finally, we reach the last bedroom on the right at the end of the hallway. Randy crawls left alongside the double bed. I turn right along the foot of the bed toward the windows. Both of us are searching under and over things with our hands. We could do a better job without all that smoke and heat. I stand up to open the windows.

That's when I see the victim. He's lying on the far side of the bed, stretched out just like a corpse at a funeral. He's out cold, as still as a corpse. My stomach starts doing flip-flops, again, because we're making enough noise to wake the dead.

"There he is," I yell. "On the bed. And he's a BIG one."

The man weighs every bit of 300 pounds. He isn't moving a muscle.

"You get his arms. I'll grab his feet." We start to ease the man off of the bed.

"Huh! HUNH?" the man mumbles. "Get ... away from me. Get your fuggin' hands offa me!"

It's the sweetest sound I ever hope to hear. Our victim's alive! Not just a faint flicker of life. This guy's a roaring bear, flailing his arms blindly to shoo us away.

"Lemme go," he bellows. "I can walk."

Fine with me. He's too big to carry, anyway.

With a bewildered look on his face, he lurches up to a sitting position on the bed, then begins looking around the smoky room. He doesn't have any idea what's going on, why his bedroom is full of smoke, or why two strangers in bulky yellow space suits and air packs are rousting him out of a sound sleep. Finally, he slides his legs over the edge of the bed. He wobbles down the smoke-filled hallway. We steady him on each side.

Outside in the fresh air and sunshine, the medics take charge of our victim. Randy and I strip off our helmets, air packs and bunker coats. We're soaked with sweat. A light breeze hits our skin like ice water. It feels great. We feel great! A successful rescue is a welcome change from carrying someone out in a body bag.

Then we look at each other and lose it.

"You believe that guy?"

"What? What happened?" another firefighter asks.

"Get your fuggin' hands offa me!" we say, cracking up together.

The ambulance crew checks out our victim. He's A-OK. He's coughing a lot and is still pretty groggy, but it's nothing that fresh air, a few aspirin and some black coffee won't cure before long. Turns out our victim had a little liquid refreshment while fixing lunch. He got tired of waiting for the French fryer to warm up, so he went back to his bedroom to rest his eyes — for just a moment. It was almost the last moment of his life.

Back at the station, we repack hose, refill air bottles and put the truck back in service. I'm walking back to my cubicle when my boss' secretary asks, "How was your fire?"

So I tell her about the deep fryer and how we rescued Sleeping Beauty. "That's nice," she says, without looking up from her typing.

"Nice?" Nice doesn't even come close. It's absolutely wonderful! And, since I came into work extra early, I'm going to leave a little early to celebrate.

At our farm, I climb onto the old John Deere tractor and head into the East field with the six-foot mower in gear. The grass is high. Soon, I'm surrounded by a living cloud of barn swallows. With pointed black wings and split tails, they look like a squadron of minifighter jets in a dogfight with an invisible foe. They soar, swoop and dive within a few feet of my head, greedily gobbling up the bugs that flee ahead of my mower.

My heart soars with the swallows. It's just great to be alive, and even better to know that someone else is still alive because of what our fire team did today. I will enjoy it while I can because I know too well from experience that not all of our fire calls will have such a happy ending. Sometimes the fire wins. I hate those days. And you never know which way it's going to go.

PART 2

First, A Spectator

CHAPTER SIX

'Be Careful What You Wish For'

The first thing our 3-year-old son, Don, did when we moved to Pennsylvania from South Florida was run right out to the suburban sidewalk in front of our new ranch house and excitedly announce, "Hey, kids! I'm here!" Six doors up the street, a young mother scooped up her two small children, went inside and closed the door. Don burst into tears.

Whether you move across town or across the country, as we did in 1981, it's not always easy being the new kid on the block. Outside of the handful of people I worked with at my new job at Rodale Press, we didn't know anyone in our new hometown, the Borough of Emmaus, Pennsylvania. Once a happy-go-lucky general assignment newspaper reporter, I was now solidly "in management." My title was executive editor of *The New Farm* magazine. Suddenly, it was not that easy to be just one of the guys.

A few months after we arrived in Emmaus, my wife, Melanie, got a part-time job as a reporter for *The Morning Call* newspaper based in nearby Allentown. *The Call* was lucky to land her. A graduate of Ohio State's School of Journalism, she already had an impressive stack of news clippings and more than a decade of solid experience covering everything from night general assignment to the religion beat for major metropolitan dailies such as *The Columbus Dispatch, Ft. Lauderdale News* and, most recently, *The Miami Herald*. Even better, Mel had a real nose for news and a winning way with people, especially total strangers. The ability to speak freely with people you've never met before is a big key to success as a reporter. Her assignment was the East Penn School District, which included Emmaus, neighboring boroughs and surrounding townships in the Lehigh Valley, the third most populous and fastest-growing area of the state.

Her new editor was Randall Murray. When Randall became East Penn bureau chief in 1980, the job came with standing orders from the newspaper's top management to get involved in the local community.

The father of two young daughters when he took the job, Randall immediately started coaching girls' softball. He joined the Mercantile Club, a private social club that happened to have a popular restaurant and bar opposite Borough Hall by the railroad tracks in downtown Emmaus. Best of all, though, Randall was free to do something he'd always wanted to do — become a volunteer firefighter.

It was something he never regretted, even though it landed him in the hospital — twice. He slipped and fell down a flight of ice-covered stairs at a house fire, injuring his spine. At another blaze, he was overcome by smoke.

Randall was lucky, though, too. During a chimney fire one Christmastime, he started to step off of a second floor roof — right into thin air. At the last second, the fire chief grabbed Randall by the collar and yanked him back onto the roof. Despite all that, Randall said, "I'm glad I did it. I met some good folks."

Emmaus Firefighter Randall Murray ready for action about 1980.
EMMAUS HISTORICAL SOCIETY PHOTO

Most of the time, his wife, Dottie, didn't complain much. More than most Americans, she clearly recognized the importance of all first responders, especially volunteer firefighters. That's because Dottie was a registered nurse, a flight nurse on the medevac helicopter operating out of nearby Lehigh Valley Hospital Center.

Randall's firefighter sideline, and the fact that citizen volunteers protected our new hometown, came as a complete surprise to us. For all of our adult lives, the firefighters where we lived in Columbus, Ohio, and Pompano Beach, Florida, were full-time, paid professionals. And, like most Americans, we took them completely for granted. We never stopped to think that things might be different here in a small town.

We should have been thoroughly ashamed of ourselves.

It never occurred to Mel and me to ask about our local fire department, even though the house kitty-corner in back of our new home was a burned-out hulk when we arrived in town. Black scorch marks rose above the windows, which were covered with sheets of plywood and blue tarps. A dumpster full of charred debris sat by the curb. A *Morning Call* article by our new friend, Randall Murray, told the sad tale:

On Valentine's Day, about six weeks earlier, the house caught fire in the middle of the night. A 53-year-old man was home alone. He was sleeping in a second floor bedroom when fire broke out in a corner of the recreation room below. Flames crept through the walls and floor spaces, ravaging the den and kitchen and filling the house with thick smoke. Finally, the man woke up. He grabbed the bedside telephone and dialed "O" for the operator, instead of the local emergency number. This was in the days before the 911 emergency call system. It was 3:45 a.m. He was quickly overcome by smoke, and passed out while on the phone. By the time operators traced his call back to Emmaus, it was too late. It was the first fire death in Emmaus in 11 years.

"For a $10 to $15 investment, that man probably wouldn't have died. He didn't have a smoke alarm in the house," said one fire official.

Randall Murray was one of three dozen volunteer firefighters who responded to the fire call. "I remember that call. The smoke line was about two feet from the floor. If the man had crawled out, he probably would have made it," said Randall.

That we Americans take our firefighters for granted is both weird and scary, because the vast majority of the firefighters in the United States are our friends and neighbors. They are volunteers, dedicated men and woman who drop everything — put their daily lives on hold at a moment's notice — and rush to our aid at all hours of the day and night, no matter what the weather.

We depend on these citizen-firefighters as our first line of defense in everything from fires and auto accidents to natural disasters, hazardous materials incidents, medical emergencies, water rescues, and a wide variety of what we loosely term "public service" calls.

These volunteers save taxpayers many billions of dollars every year in reducing property damage and the cost of operating fire departments, which small communities with modest tax bases just can't afford. More important, they save countless lives.

In 1982, when we were still settling into Emmaus, there were roughly 900,000 such volunteer firefighters in the United States. They accounted for about 80 percent — four out of every five firefighters — in the whole country.

Just a decade before, in the early 1970s, our nation had more than 1 million volunteers. But, for of a wide variety of reasons — increasing demands on people's time, longer commutes, more two-income households, tougher training requirements, new labor laws, poor fire department leadership — we have fewer volunteers every year. And while the number of volunteer firefighters is declining, the average age of volunteers still on the job is increasing. So is the number of emergency calls. Every year, fewer and fewer — and older and older — volunteers do more and more — with less and less.

"We're always looking for volunteers," Randall said one day. "Why don't you come to fire practice some Tuesday night? See how you like it."

Great idea! What better way to quickly meet more people from throughout our new town than to join the volunteer fire department?

I also had another, some might say ulterior, motive for wanting to join the fire department. While the pay and hours were better than any newspaper I ever worked for, life at Rodale was, in a word, boring. That's because for nearly 15 years, almost my entire working life at the time, I had positively thrived on the chaos of a daily newspaper, first as a photographer, then as a beat reporter and finally, as an editor. Editing a national magazine was prestigious, even glamorous at times. But the deadlines were many weeks, often months away. I missed breaking news, the need to write it tight, right and tonight. I longed for just a bit more excitement in my life, forgetting all about the old adage, "Be careful what you wish for ..."

CHAPTER SEVEN

Safe Behind a Camera

Chaos had been my constant companion since age 15, when I started working at a daily newspaper in my native Ohio. Journalism was a curious calling for a high-school kid with mild dyslexia and probably some degree of attention deficit disorder. Maybe that's why I quickly and easily found a safe haven behind a camera instead of at a typewriter. All I had to worry about was proper lighting, composition, exposure and catching the most dramatic moment in action shots, not spelling or grammar.

That was a relief, because the dyslexia was real. For example, once when I got bored in the fifth grade, my teacher suggested I read one of the action-packed books in our classroom library. She recommended "Guadalcanal Diary." I took the book from a shelf in the back of our classroom, and just stood there looking at the cover. I thought my teacher was nuts. Why in the world would she think I would ever want to read a book about a "dairy" on an island in the middle of the Pacific Ocean? It just didn't make sense. I still haven't read the book.

Growing up, I said numbers in reverse order from most people. Instead of starting with the lower number and saying "three or four," I always said, "four or three." Made sense to me to begin with the higher number. My dad laughed about that one night at dinner, then we just let it go. But when I got to junior high, my teachers knew something was slightly off. In sixth grade, two classmates and I spent a couple of hours a week in a special remedial reading class, doing exercises to focus on comprehension, spelling and grammar. I wasn't dumb; I just got my letters and numbers a little mixed up at times. I wasn't lazy, either. I could get all As, but only in subjects that really interested me.

I took private clarinet lessons from a music professor at Ohio Wesleyan University. In the seventh grade I played a complicated solo piece ("Evening" by Carl Frangkiser) on the alto clarinet at the Ohio Music Education Association statewide competition. The judge, Omar P. Blackman, later the longtime director of the All-Ohio State Fair Band, gave me the highest rating — 10 out of 10 possible As. "Excellent all-around playing. Very musical performance. Unusual for a seventh grader," he wrote on my scoring sheet. But junior high was often a struggle. Then came high school.

My freshman year, I took quickly and easily to photography as I completed Boy Scout merit badges in photography and journalism to earn my Eagle Scout rank. I was tall, skinny and shy. I wore both glasses and braces, and was not a jock, an honor student or one of the popular kids. But as soon as I started carrying a camera, it seemed everybody wanted to be my friend, or at least be in the picture.

Now I was a part of everything going on at Rutherford B. Hayes High School in Delaware, Ohio. I became the school's unofficial photographer. My photos started appearing in the school newspaper, in the yearbook and on the Youth Pages of *The Delaware Gazette*, my hometown daily.

The summer of my sophomore year, I started working at *The Gazette* as a staff photographer in charge of the darkroom, nearly all photo processing and engraving. The job put me and my camera along the runway in Atlantic City, New Jersey, at the 1966 Miss America Pageant the year Miss Ohio was from my hometown; on the sidelines at Ohio State University football games during Coach Woody Hayes' best years; on the presidential campaign trail with comedian Pat Paulsen; and in the front row at concerts by the likes of The Animals, with Eric Burden, and The Jimi Hendrix Experience. Heady stuff for a 16-year-old high-school kid. I felt like a combination of Annie Liebowitz, Ansel Adams and David Douglas Duncan.

It wasn't always fun and games, though. My junior year, *The Gazette* assigned me the job of covering the military funeral — of a friend. Ron Poole was a standout football and basketball player at Hayes. Two years ahead of me in school, Ron joined the Marine Corps after graduation. Then, on June 13, 1968, barely two months after he arrived in country, Lance Corporal Ronald Dean Poole was killed in action in Quang Nam Province, South Vietnam. He was just 20 years old. My cameras, which had captured Ron scores of times living life to the fullest as an athlete, refocused through salty tears on his flag-draped casket, a 21-gun salute, a bugler playing "Taps," and an American flag being folded at graveside.

My mentors and heroes were Art Ruth, chief photographer at *The Gazette*, and Sheldon Ross, a neighbor who later ran the photo department at *The Columbus Evening Dispatch* in the capitol city. Breaking news ruled. There were murders, drownings, and a lot of horrific traffic accidents. My parents' house was just west of the city of Delaware on U.S. Rt. 36 at a place Jan and Dean would call "Dead Man's Curve." The only other thing as common as car crashes was fires — house fires, car and truck fires, barn fires, field fires and mobile home fires. I learned quickly that no one was ever really safe from fire. Fire made no distinction between rich and poor, young and old, black and white, male and female. Everyone, everywhere was always at risk.

Art and Sheldon taught me all about photography, everything from composition and lighting to the fine points of film processing and printing. More important, they provided living examples of how to keep your head and your cool when everyone else around you is losing theirs in a crisis. That's because they were also volunteer firefighters, members of the Tri-Township Fire Department, which provided fire protection for my parents' house.

The day after graduation, I started work at *The Dispatch* as the summer photographer. I worked 4 p.m. to midnight, Monday through Friday and got $75 a week. That was great money at the time, even though I had an 80-mile round-trip commute from Delaware to downtown Columbus. I photographed Arthur Ashe playing tennis and Bob Hope and Jack Nicklaus playing golf, but breaking news topped the list. And fire was still king.

Two nights after my 18th birthday, while fellow Ohioan Neil Armstrong walked on the moon, a race riot broke out on the near East Side of Columbus. A 69-year-old white man shot and killed a 27-year-old black man in an argument over children playing in the old man's yard. Soon, someone firebombed the old man's dry cleaning shop. Minutes later, another fire erupted at 18th and Main. *The Dispatch* issued me the only "riot gear" on hand, a white motorcycle helmet. I covered the helmet with black duct tape after a few near-misses proved it to be the perfect target for M-80s and chunks of brick. My cameras and I followed D-Platoon, the "riot squad," into the rock-and bottle-throwing crowds on East Main Street. Shots rang out. A sniper killed a man at 18th and Main. The sky glowed a dull orange as molotov cocktails set off another 35 fires in the area by 1:30 a.m. It was a long night, but it helped me earn a raise, $5 more a week. It was the fabled "Summer of '69" that Bryan Adams sang about. But instead of being the high point of my life, it was just one step closer to picking up a fire hose.

CHAPTER EIGHT

No Matter Where You Work Tomorrow

"Can you write?" asked someone at *The Dispatch*. That was after my first and only year at Ohio University ended early and violently with antiwar protests, campus riots, clouds of tear gas, and the Ohio National Guard in gas masks lining the streets of Athens, Ohio, with fixed bayonets on their rifles. It was the spring of 1970. I was out of school and out of a job. The newspaper didn't need a summer photographer again. Instead, the Night City Desk needed a beginning reporter.

My writing experience during high school didn't amount to much, just a couple of fluff features, but I told the editor I would give it my best shot. *The Dispatch* took a chance and put me behind a typewriter. I was now a "general assignment" reporter, working 3 p.m. to 11 p.m. That meant I covered anything and everything Night City Editor Steve Bulkley threw at me. An old-school newspaperman, Bulkley was a merciless tyrant, and a stickler for detail. With a look or a few choice words, Bulkley routinely reduced interns to tears. He once drove a young female reporter into the Ladies Room and followed her inside, demanding a clarification of something she had written. "Forget everything they taught you up there at the Big Farm," Bulkley told new reporters, referring to the Ohio State University School of Journalism. "This is how we do it in the real world!"

Bulkley nit-picked everything: spelling, grammar, punctuation, *Dispatch* style and Associated Press style. Strunk & White's "The Elements of Style" had its place, as did the venerable "Chicago Manual of Style." But the "AP Stylebook and Libel Manual" became my new Bible. A self-taught grammar Nazi, Bulkley knew all of those books, inside out. He could diagram a sentence, naming the component parts of the language, how to use them properly, and why, as well as any college English professor. Bulkley loved a good story. "Never let the facts get in the way of the story," he warned. That did not mean you could be fast and loose with the facts. Every fact had to be completely accurate, right down to the very last detail. Bulkley was an advocate for the readers, who, he said, deserved to be entertained, as well as fully informed. That put him at odds with the copy desk. "Undercover nuns" he called the dayside copy editors. Bulkley swore the "nuns" operated by the "ACW Rule," which stood for "avoid colorful writing." He had a point. A reporter had ended a feature on a struggling self-help group in the ghetto with the colorful and upbeat quote, "We gonna make it, man!" Next day, the copy desk changed it to read, "We are going to make it!"

He was a stickler for details. "Was the shooting suspect released from jail on bond, or bail? There's a big difference," he said. "If you don't know which it was, ask the judge, dammit!" It wasn't enough to say someone was shot. "Where were they shot?" In the arm wouldn't do. "Which arm? Left or right? Upper or lower? What kind of gun?" Don't say a 'pistol!' Was it an automatic or a revolver? What caliber?"

Same applied to fire stories. "How many engine companies? How many alarms? How many firefighters? What was the cause? Got a damage estimate? They have insurance? Any injuries? What kind of injuries?" If there were burns, were they first, second or third degree? "What hospital? What's their condition? Did you get witnesses?"

"What? You don't know?" Bulkley screamed. "Find out! Or ... no matter where you work tomorrow!"

Bulkley was 49 when we first meet him on the night city desk. I was just 19. The rest of the night crew was barely in their 20s. "Steve's Kiddie Corps" is what the dayside called Melanie, Ron Ishoy, John Arnold, and me and photographers Tom Sines, Ken Chamberlain Jr. and Bob Fox. Bulkley had nicknames for most of us, too. Ishoy, naturally, was "Ronnie Reporter." Because of my long blond hair and drooping mustache, I was the "Blond Viking." Mel, who stood 5-foot-2 with eyes of blue, was the "Little Blonde." The name fit. She had shoulder-length hair, curves in all the right places and sensuous lips. At first, though, Bulkley called her "Little Miss Goody Two Shoes." She was the first female intern to work the night City Desk at *The Dispatch*, instead of joining "the rest of the women" in the Society section. But after a few days, all that changed. She finished a long and frustrating telephone interview by slamming down the phone and yelling, *"Son of a bitch!"* Bulkley stopped typing. So did the other guys on desk. They all grinned, then clapped. "Thank gawd," Bulkley said. "She's one of us!"

Together, we ruled the night. We owned the city. *The Dispatch* was an afternoon paper then. And, day in and day out, Steve's Kiddie Corps put out much of the best stuff in the paper.

Bulkley was the best teacher I ever had. For some reason, Bulkley had faith in me. And so he really picked on me and my copy. Bulkey was grooming me to take over the night police beat, a beat Bulkley had pounded for years and still loved. But the crusty city editor and others in top management needed more than Bulkley's gut to go on. They needed convincing with a solid set of news clippings that showed I knew a good story when I saw one, could develop reliable contacts and ferret out information that some people didn't want to share, while handling any kind of breaking news that was thrown at me.

Bulkley's plan worked. Four months later, our night cop reporter took off to bum around Europe, and I replaced him on the night police beat. "I'm doing you a big favor, kid," Bulkley said. "The other reporters don't realize it, but night cops is the very best beat on the paper. That's because the really big cop stories always make the front page. And whether people want to or not, nearly everyone reads cop news. Now, don't fuck it up! Or … no matter where you work tomorrow!"

CHAPTER NINE

Night Cops

My regular shift was from 6 p.m. to 2 a.m., Sunday through Thursday. I worked out of the "Press Room" on the first floor of the old Central Police Station at 120 W. Gay St. The press room was a real dump, much like a set out of the 1931 movie "Five Star Final" with Edward G. Robinson and Boris Karloff. It had some dusty filing cabinets full of yellowing news clippings and a month's worth of police reports, a few chairs, a grungy orange vinyl couch and two old oak desks branded with decades of cigarette burns. My desk sat next to the window. That was no bonus because I worked at night. The venetian blinds were never opened or cleaned. The desk at the oppose end of the long room belonged to the morning *Citizen-Journal*, my competition.

Three speaker boxes mounted to the wall above my typewriter monitored police and fire radios. Taped to the wall below was the Columbus Police "Ten Code." No matter what I was doing, some numbers immediately grabbed my attention:

10-3 — Officer in trouble.

10-18 — D.O.A.

10-20 — Drowning.

10-25 — Fire.

10-28 — Homicide.

10-43 — Shooting.

10-60 — Emergency, lights and siren.

On the opposite wall above the couch, yellowed tape secured two well-worn city maps. Unflattering cop cartoons from magazines and newspapers covered the bulletin board. It was a print newsman's paradise. Radio and TV reporters seldom poked their pretty noses inside.

My main responsibility was the City of Columbus. At police headquarters, I regularly checked arrest slates, went through the day's police reports, and made regular rounds of Accident Investigation, Clerk of Courts, and all of the bureaus: Records, Detective (Robbery, Burglary, Homicide), Vice, Narcotics and Juvenile.

By phone, I also covered all of the suburbs — Bexley, Whitehall, Grandview Heights, Upper Arlington, Gahanna, Hilliard, Dublin, Westerville, and Worthington — plus the sheriff's offices in nine surrounding counties and Ohio Highway Patrol headquarters. Using an old rotary dial telephone, I called all of those departments at least twice each night: first thing in the evening then an hour or so before the end of my shift. The local police, fire department and sheriff got calls every hour. Most departments shared the news of their community eagerly and freely. But a few, we knew from bitter experience, had standing orders not to give out the time of day. I called them anyway, just to let them know we still loved them. The few female dispatchers I spoke to regularly really did love me, or at least they loved my voice. It reminded them of the actor Sam Elliott, they said. That was how I came to have a very special friend in the Franklin County Sheriff's radio room. Her code name was "Ralph." She was my anonymous, mysterious "Deep Throat" contact. Ralph called me at work or at home, at all hours of the night, when hot news was breaking.

I hammered away on a clattering Underwood manual typewriter from the 1930s. "Hammering" the keys was vital, because I had three sheets of carbon paper sandwiched in between four sheets of copy paper. Various editors would then "cut and paste" paragraphs into an order more to their liking. They used long scissors and homemade paste they dipped out of old coffee cups with small paint brushes.

Fires broke out every day in Columbus, which had a population of more than 540,000 in 1970. Most blazes never made it into the newspaper. A handful rated a few paragraphs, but only if there was heavy damage or serious injuries. Every few months, though, a fire would be so big or bizarre that it took over the front page. In pictures and words, I covered most of those fires. The photo on the front cover of this book is from one. And each of the vignettes that follow moved me closer to the day when I strapped on an air pack and picked up a fire hose:

Six months after starting on night cops, I was filling in for another reporter who needed that Friday night off. It was 1:47 a.m., only minutes before the end of my shift. I was typing a quick note for the editor, who would come into the City Desk in barely four hours. There were a few things I had come across during the night that the day crew would have to follow up on. But then the fire radio crackled to life.

There was a report of a house fire on E. Stewart Avenue. It was a working-class neighborhood on the near South Side. Houses there were mostly wood frame, old and closely packed together. At this time of night, a worker there could be a bad one. I kept typing until I heard, "Working fire ... fully involved ... call an extra company ..."

My note stayed in the typewriter, unfinished. I grabbed my coat and sprinted for the press car parked out back, without looking up the location on the large city map on the press room wall. I pretty much knew where I was going. On night cops, you learned the city streets quickly, too quickly, sometimes.

As the first engines reached the scene, the whole rear of the two-story frame house was engulfed in flame. Fire was shooting from second floor windows at the front, Battalion Chief George Burke told me later. Intense heat peeled paint and melted aluminum siding on homes on either side. Some firefighters trained hoses on the neighboring houses to keep the fire from spreading. Others attacked the blazing house.

The street was full of fire trucks, ambulances and smoke when I pull up in the press car. Medics were loading someone onto a stretcher in the street. I grabbed my Nikon F off the front seat, plugged in the strobe, and started shooting. Think of the opening scenes of "Backdraft," the cameraman snapping pictures of young Brian McCaffrey clutching his father's still-smoking fire helmet after a natural gas explosion blew the boy's father into oblivion.

Minutes before, the 17-year-old on the stretcher had jumped out of a second floor window to escape the flames. His twisted right leg was now in a splint made of rolled up blankets. He was lucky. Four others didn't make it out of the house. A 43-year-old father, his wife, their adult son and the 2 1/2-year-old daughter of a cousin were all dead.

What was the cause of the fatal fire? The killer was a common electrical gadget. You probably have one in your very own kitchen and use it without ever giving a second thought to its deadly potential. It's a deep fryer. Investigators say the family's 18-year-old daughter was watching a late movie on TV downstairs when she got hungry. She loaded up the French fryer in the kitchen, then went back to the TV while the fries cooked. She dozed off — for just a few minutes.

That was all it took. The deep fryer boiled over. Flames shot up the kitchen wall and spread out across the ceiling, burning into the second floor where the others were sleeping.

When the girl bolted awake, the downstairs was full of smoke. She grabbed the fryer, threw it off the side porch into the yard and raced out of the house. About the same time, her cousin bailed out of a second floor front window. There was no hope — or help — for those still inside upstairs. Thirty firefighters battled for more than 15 minutes to bring the blaze under control.

After the initial knockdown, firefighters hunted down hot spots for more than 90 minutes. It was a brutal game of hide-and-seek. When they tore off pieces of asphalt siding and roof to get at smoldering timbers, flames shot up in another section of the house.

"That was hot up there," said the man in the dark topcoat and hat as he wiped sweat from his forehead. He looked like a homicide detective. But Lt. Kenneth Gilbert was a firefighter assigned to the Fire Prevention Bureau. His job was to investigate the fatal fire.

"Could you do me a favor?" the lieutenant asked.

"Sure."

I owed Gilbert. He was a huge help, freely answering all of my questions. He even posed for a picture with the deep fryer. How could I say no?

"I don't have a camera," he said.

Uh, oh, I knew what's coming.

"We need a record of the scene."

By "the scene," the lieutenant did not mean the photos already in my camera. As good as they might be, he wasn't interested in my shots of the outside of the house, his firefighters at work, or the injured boy on the stretcher. No, he wanted photos of "the scene," as in the scene of the deaths. That meant going into the still-smoldering house, up the charred stairs to the second floor, where the bodies still lay where they fell.

Reluctantly, I followed the lieutenant inside. We waded up the stairs through piles of wet, steaming plaster. Streams of water gushed from the walls and ceiling. I tried to dodge the waterfalls, but hot water full of black grit still found its way down the back of my neck.

From the head of the stairs, the devastation was incredible. Everything on the second floor that could possibly burn was burned. There was nothing left that resembled furniture, light fixtures or wall hangings. It was all steaming, soggy black rubble. Lath strips poked out of holes that firefighters had punched in walls and ceilings in their hunt for hot spots. Blinding, generator-powered spotlights backlit swirling steam and smoke, casting eerie silhouettes of firefighters with pike poles and axes.

The lieutenant was right. It was hot up here, something on the order of a self-cleaning oven that had only recently been turned down from "Clean" to about 250 F. It was wet. And it stunk.

"There are two bodies in here. One's over there," Lt. Gilbert said, motioning toward dark, shapeless piles. "And one's in front of you."

The body was only a few feet from me at the top of the stairs, within an arm's length of a window and possible escape. But there was no escaping this fire for him. The stairway had acted like a chimney. It fed flames directly into the second floor. The air was pure poison. The flames were too fast, too fierce.

I backed up to the stairway, slanted the wide-angle lens to take in as much of the room as possible, and fired off a couple of frames. The lieutenant and I picked our way through the rest of the upstairs that was still safe to walk in. I shot a few more photos, thanked Lt. Gilbert again for his help, and drove back to the press room in a deep funk. It was now past 5 a.m. I still had the fire story to write. In less than an hour, the day shift would arrive with endless questions that still lacked answers.

May 18, 1971 — All was well when security guard John Young checked the Doktor Pet Center in the Westland Shopping Center at 1:45 a.m. My shift ended at 2 a.m., but I was still typing away in the press room when Young passed the store again at 2:10 a.m. This time, he saw smoke pouring from the pet shop. When Franklin Twp. Fire Chief M.E. Olney arrived minutes later, smoke was billowing out of the roof. Flames were shooting up around the air conditioner on top of the pet store. Fifty firefighters from Franklin and Prairie township fire departments rushed to the scene with 14 pieces of fire apparatus, pumpers, aerial ladders, snorkels and rescue squads.

Firefighters battled the fire for about 90 minutes as flames or smoke spread to 17 stores. Falling debris hit Franklin Twp. Fire Lt. Jack Hughes on the head, knocking him unconscious. Medics gave oxygen to other firefight-

First responders and passersby search for signs of life among the 60 or so animals overcome by smoke in 1971 pet store fire.

COLUMBUS DISPATCH PHOTO BY GEORGE DEVAULT

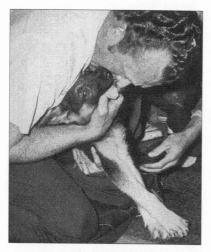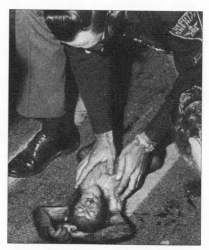

LEFT: **Autoworker Hank Linard gives mouth-to-mouth to a German shepherd puppy.**
RIGHT: **Franklin County Sheriff's Cpl. Jim Karnes gets a chimpanzee breathing again.**
COLUMBUS DISPATCH PHOTOS BY GEORGE DEVAULT

ers overcome by smoke. But the fire paled compared to the scene outside.

About 60 bodies, most of them puppies, littered the pavement when I pulled into the parking lot. Firefighters, sheriff's deputies and passersby searched through the bodies for survivors. They found only about 16 that showed signs of life. A chimpanzee got chest compressions from Franklin County Sheriff's Cpl. Jim Karnes. Then Deputy Jerry Steele slapped an oxygen mask on the chimp's face. Autoworker Hank Linard, who was on his way home from work, gave mouth-to-mouth resuscitation to a German shepherd puppy. The dog and the chimpanzee were fine, although the chimp had the hiccups. Some snakes, hamsters and guinea pigs also survived. No one gave them mouth-to-mouth.

On another night, the warehouse of a moving and storage company went up in flames. It was a huge fire. But the windowless warehouse walls hid most of the flames. Except for an orange glow, most of what you could see from the ground was a towering column of smoke. My pictures from the parking lot weren't going to amount to much.

Then I saw an aerial ladder extending over the back of the burning building, maybe 100 feet behind the flames. Firefighters weren't using the ladder at the moment. They were in reserve, waiting for orders.

"Hey," I said. "Do you guys mind if I climb up your ladder and shoot a few pictures? It's hard to see what's going on from the ground."

"You want to go up *our* ladder?" asked one of the firefighters.

"Sure, if it's OK."

"Be my guest."

Couldn't believe my luck. I stuffed a couple of different lenses in the side pockets of my sport coat, left my camera bag, flash and battery pack on the ground, and started up the 100-foot ladder. It was longer, and steeper, than it looked from the ground. A lot longer, and much steeper. The firefighters watched as I slowly worked my way upward. They were grinning. Why? What was so funny?

Near the top of the ladder, I locked one leg into the rungs and turned toward the fire. The view was spectacular. Balls of fire boiled up from inside the walls. I started clicking away, changing lenses, f/stops and shutter speeds to capture the heart of the fire. The boiling flames provided all the light I needed. Then everything went black. I couldn't see my hand in front of my face, let alone the fire. The wind had shifted, as the grinning firefighters knew it eventually would. I couldn't see. I couldn't breathe. But I knew I had some great pictures. So I unlocked my leg and began feeling my way down the long, steep ladder.

The firefighters were still grinning when I reached the ground.

"Get some good shots?" one of them asked.

"You bet!" I coughed. "Thanks, guys. Thanks a lot!" And I meant it. Climbing that ladder landed three of my photos on the front page the next day. It also cramped my thighs for days, and gave me renewed respect for firefighters.

Now and then, a serial firebug terrorized the city. Once, the firestarter just happened to work the same hours as I did. I covered all of his fires. He started small, torching garbage cans and dumpsters. But soon, he graduated to abandoned houses. The fires were all set at night. What if he started torching occupied homes where people were sleeping? His next blaze, in an old railroad warehouse, escalated to two alarms. Arson investigators redoubled their efforts. Soon, they arrested a suspect.

But the arson spree didn't stop with him behind bars. A few nights after his arrest, fire broke out in the Franklin County Jail. As the fire and police radios went crazy, the press room phone rang. It was "Ralph," my contact in the sheriff's radio room. "Inmates were trapped in their cells," she said.

The jail was only a few blocks from the press room in police headquarters. I pulled up outside just as ambulances started arriving. I followed the medics inside. Guards buzzed us onto the elevator. We rode up to the jail floor together.

The doors opened to chaos. Smoke filled the air. Many prisoners were already out of their cells. A prisoner lay on the floor. He was unconscious. Two other prisoners knelt beside him, trying to revive the man. They were barefoot, shirtless. A turnkey unlocked other cell doors, freeing more prisoners from their smoky cells. A handful of guards maintained order, as extra deputies rushed in from other parts of the building and the far corners of the county. Columbus police swarmed around the building. All of the cops feared the worst, of course. But this was no jailbreak. The only thing anyone was trying to escape tonight was smoke. It was everywhere.

The man on the floor was 19 years old, charged with auto theft. He was unlucky enough to be in the cell beside the accused firebug — who had just set his own bedding on fire. Medics treated 15 prisoners for smoke inhalation. The accused firebug got a seventh arson charge. I got some good pictures — and more smelly laundry.

Thankfully, bad fires didn't happen every day. That's why they were such big news when they did. Most nights around the cop shop were pretty routine. Some were just plain boring. On those nights, no matter how many phone calls I made and contacts I exhausted, I couldn't scare up more than a few paragraphs of fillers for the next day's paper. That was when I buried my nose in a book, with an ear on the police and fire radios, of course. I read science fiction, mostly. Crime novels, occasionally. Then along came a book that topped "Dune," "The Martian Chronicles" and "The Godfather," combined. It was "Report From Engine Co. 82." The author was Dennis Smith, a New York City firefighter who worked out of the busiest firehouse in the country at the time.

"This book seems to be about a particular group of firefighters working in the South Bronx, but the incidents described here tell the story of all firefighters working in this country," Smith began. "The problems in Boston, Cleveland, Chicago, Detroit, and Los Angeles are the same, only the names change."

The book was a page-turner. I couldn't put it down. Some 200 pages later, an exhausted Firefighter Smith sat on the stoop of a still-smoldering tenement building. Another firefighter cradled the blanket-wrapped body of a 2-year-old girl in his arms. The firefighters saved the girl's mother and sister an instant before the apartment exploded in flames, but there was just no way they could reach the baby in time.

"I look up at his eyes. They are almost fully closed, but I can see they are wet, and tearing," Smith wrote. "The corneas are red from heat and smoke, and light reflects from the watered surfaces, and they sparkle. I wish my wife, my mother, everyone who has ever asked me why I do what I do, could see the humanity, the sympathy, the sadness of these eyes, because in them is the reason I continue to be a firefighter."

Smith's book haunted me. I knew those eyes. I photographed them all the time. They might be blue, green or brown, framed in a white face, a black face, or a face of any color, sex or age, but they were all exactly the same. And I saw them at fires and auto accidents, everywhere, throughout the city, the suburbs, the townships and the boondocks.

I tried to interest the City Desk in a day-in-the-life series of stories about local firefighters. The editor yawned. "That's what they do. No big deal." That was easy for him to say. He'd never gone near a burning building in his life.

Bad fires always brought tears to my eyes, and it wasn't because of the smoke. Watching firefighters in action, I decided that firefighting was one of the few truly worthwhile callings in life. It was also something I thought I might like to do, if I ever got the chance.

CHAPTER TEN

Meant To Be a Firefighter

Looking back on it all, maybe I was meant to be a firefighter. Maybe Melanie was meant to be a firefighter's wife. Outside of all the fires we covered for newspapers over the years, both of us had a much closer association with fire than most people.

"Over an average lifetime, an individual's household will experience five fires," said the Consumer Product Safety Commission's 2004-2005 Residential Fire Survey. That figure included both small fires that went unreported and larger blazes that required the fire department.

The commission defined "fire" as "... any incident large or small that you have had in or around your home ... that resulted in unwanted flames or smoke, and could have caused damage to life or property if left unchecked."

Loosely defined, our collective "household" had personally experienced more than a lifetime's worth of fire — and we were barely out of our teens by then.

My first fire was when I was 14. My parents' garage filled up with black smoke. Summer sunlight streaming through a south-facing window shone through a bottle. It focused the sun's rays like a magnifying glass, igniting cloth and papers inside the garage. Mom noticed the garage windows were solid black when we returned from town. Our new house on the hill — "Woodchuck Hill," we kids called it — was mom's pride and joy. The house was a brick rancher with four bedrooms, two-and-a-half baths and a screened porch that dad never got around to screening. Mom paid for much of it with what was left, after taxes, from the $25,000 she won as the grand prize in Pillsbury's Best 10th Grand National Bake-Off in 1958. Her winning recipe, the ninth time she had entered the bake-off, was called "Spicy Apple Twists."

Mom went inside the house through the front door and quickly called the all-volunteer Tri-Township Fire Department. The response was immediate. Our neighbor, Mel Evans, was the first volunteer to arrive. It was the first time I had ever seen volunteers spring into action. Suddenly, people I'd known as farmers, friends and helpers all my life were transformed into superheroes who saved our new house.

A few years later, the same volunteers saved the day when a neighbor's field to the west of us caught fire on a windy day. Head-high flames raced through the fencerow behind our barn. They headed straight for my disabled '57 Chevy, which was up on blocks — with a full tank of gasoline.

Melanie experienced her first fire in 1968. It was near the end of her freshman year at Ohio State University. Before dawn on the morning of May 22, fire erupted on the 11th Floor of Lincoln Tower. Melanie was editor of the dorm newspaper at the time. The 26-story dorm was home to some 1,000 undergraduate students. State arson investigators later politely called the building design "unconventional." Students who lived in the dorm had another name for it — "firetrap." More than 70 percent of Lincoln Tower's residents had earlier signed a petition complaining that the tower was a fire hazard.

That's because each floor consisted of five suites that radiated, like the arms of a starfish, off of central elevator shafts in the center of the building. Each suite housed 10 to 12 students in rooms that contained two, three or four beds. Windows in the bedrooms were small, and sealed. Residents couldn't open the windows. To get out of their bedrooms and into the elevators or stairways, students first had to pass through common study rooms. It proved a fatal bottleneck.

An 18-year-old freshman from Ohio died of smoke inhalation. Fourteen others were injured, including the dead woman's 22-year-old roommate from Colorado. The roommate never regained consciousness. She died a week after the fire. This fire was no accident. It was set by an 18-year-old coed, who was later found innocent of any criminal act by reason of insanity and hospitalized. The firestarter was one of Melanie's reporters.

Fire was part of my college coursework, too. Throughout the winter of 1970, someone kept setting fire to the dumpster in the basement of my dorm at Ohio University. Then, one night, my dorm room filled with smoke. One of my roommates was studying late. He didn't want to disturb us, so he tucked his small reading lamp inside his pillow case on the lower bunk. Sometime in the middle of the night, he dozed off. The little lamp ignited his foam rubber pillow. We woke up to a room full of choking smoke. Someone threw the smoldering pillow out of a window onto the snow-covered patio. We doused the embers, then hid the evidence.

A few years later, Melanie and I were living in separate apartments in Columbus and working for *The Dispatch*. One evening, Melanie smelled smoke. She stepped into the foyer. There was a heavy haze of smoke in the air. It seemed to be coming from the furnace room at the bottom of the stairs. When she opened the door, she saw flames leaping up the wall. She slammed the door shut, ran back into her apartment and called the fire department. Then she scooped up Kim, her mostly Beagle rescue mutt, and rousted the residents of the three other apartments. The Reynoldsburg fire chief was the first firefighter on the scene. As an army of fire trucks rolled in with red lights flashing and sirens wailing, the chief easily doused the flames with a big fire extinguisher.

"Oh, I'm sorry for calling you," Melanie said. She felt bad about rousting out the entire fire department for a blaze that one man could put out so quickly and easily. "Don't apologize," the fire chief said. "If you hadn't called us when you did, this whole building would have gone up. I've told this guy (the landlord) about this before." The landlord was in serious trouble. Inside the furnace room was a lawn mower — and a big can of gasoline.

One day, in the middle of winter, fire paid me a visit at home. I was living in an apartment, probably once the servant's quarters, in the back of an old gothic mansion on East Main Street in Bexley, Ohio.

An enclosed side stairway led up to French doors that opened into a modest living room, an enclosed balcony and small kitchen on the second floor. A steep stairway by the kitchen went up to the third floor, a large bedroom with sloping sidewalls and a bath. It was cozy, quiet and private, perfect for a bachelor keeping odd hours.

Sometime in the early afternoon, I was waking up with my first pot of coffee when I smelled smoke — just a quick, faint whiff. By the time I took another breath, it was gone. I walked around the apartment to make sure nothing was smoldering in an ashtray.

A few hours later, I was upstairs in the bedroom. It was time to get ready for work. I needed a bath and a shave. I was looking forward to a nice, long soak in the extra-long antique bathtub. Then I smelled it again. Smoke, maybe wood smoke. But by the next breath, nothing. I doubled-checked the whole apartment, and even looked out into the side stairway. It was clear all the way down to the cavernous basement.

Finally, I was just stretching out in the tub when I heard knocking from downstairs. The knocking quickly turned to heavy, nonstop pounding. Then someone started screaming. I jumped out of the tub and, dripping wet, poked my head out of my third-floor bedroom window.

"Get out! Get out!" screamed a woman. "Your house is on fire!"

Orange flames danced out of the top of the first floor window beside the back door.

There was still no smoke or smell in my apartment, but I was getting out of there. Now! I threw on some clothes and ran downstairs, grabbing my coat, camera bag and reporter's notebook on the way out. There was no smoke in the stairway. I ran right out of the side door.

57

As I came around the corner of the building, firefighters in air packs were pulling hoses and attacking the fire. They had it knocked down in no time.

"Got a cause, Chief?" I asked the white hat directing the operation. "Any damage estimate?"

"How'd you get here so fast?" he asked.

"I live here."

After the chief finally gave the all-clear, I went back inside and called the office. Bulkley was not happy to hear I was going to be late for work.

"Where was this big deal fire, anyway?" he snarled.

"At my house!"

I was not happy, either. The heat was now off in the building, at least temporarily. It was January in Central Ohio. And my bath was cold.

A few months after Melanie and I got married in 1975, covering fires became something of a family affair for us. The telephone at home rang early one January morning. It was the City Desk. There was a bad fire at a fraternity house a few blocks from where we lived on East Lane Avenue, just east of the Ohio State University campus. The editor wanted us to get right over there and find out everything we could for the first edition.

It was the Alpha Chi Rho fraternity house on East 17th Street. Sometime around 2 a.m., pledges left to clean up the three-story brick house at the end of "Hell Week" lit a fire in the fireplace. It was the quickest way they could think of to dispose of the toilet paper that was spread a foot deep throughout the first floor. Sparks from the fireplace ignited the toilet paper. "Almost immediately," said Fire Chief Ray Devine, the entire first floor was engulfed in flames.

Across the street, someone at the Phi Gamma Delta house saw the flames and called the fire department. Two Delts rushed over with fire extinguishers, but it was too little too late.

"The whole first floor was on fire," said one of the Delts. "Flames were shooting out about six to eight feet from the windows, and we saw people jumping out the upstairs windows. One guy came out on fire — it was the worst I'd ever seen. I never felt so helpless. It really shakes you up. You never expect it so close to you."

Columbus firefighters finally brought the blaze under control about 4 a.m. Sub-zero temperatures froze regulators on their air packs and knocked out their radios. Two students were dead. Another, burned over 50 percent of his body, was in critical condition at the hospital. Eighteen students managed to escape the flames, at least six by jumping out of second-floor windows. Half a dozen firefighters suffered minor injuries.

Our joint byline on the front page that day was one of our last at *The Dispatch*. Although we were well established at the paper, when you're in your mid-20s, the grass is always greener somewhere else. So, while visiting a reporter friend in South Florida on vacation a few weeks later, we learned that the *Ft. Lauderdale News* was hiring. Little did we know that *The News* was always hiring. On a lark, we stopped by for interviews. We walked out with jobs. Back in Ohio, we loaded up a U-Haul truck, said "Good-bye Columbus," and headed south, changing both our latitudes and attitudes.

CHAPTER ELEVEN

Changes in Latitude

South Florida in 1976 was a newspaperman's paradise. Every other government official was corrupt or incompetent, or both, or so it seemed at times. Cocaine cowboys had running machine-gun battles in the streets. The soundtrack was a mix of Jimmy Buffett and the Coral Reefer Band, Bob Marley, Warren Zevon and Glenn "Smuggler's Blues" Fry. Daily news and views came from Edna Buchanan, Carl "Sick Puppy" Hiaasen and Dave Barry, all of "Naked Came the Manatee" fame. It was the raw material for "Miami Vice" and a dozen other cop shows.

There was always something juicy to write about. Assignments spanned the news spectrum, ranging from the very darkest depths of the underworld to boldly going where no man had gone before in space, the final frontier. One of my first front-page stories was about John "Handsome Johnny" Roselli, the mobster the CIA once hired to kill Cuban Prime Minister Fidel Castro. Roselli was also implicated in the assassination of President Kennedy. The big news was that Roselli's decomposing body was just found floating in a backwater of Biscayne Bay near Miami. The mobster had been strangled, shot and dismembered. Another day, "Star Trek" creator Gene Roddenberry showed "Star Trek" bloopers to some 8,000 Trekkies at the Hollywood Sportatorium. Lt. Uhura called Mr. Spock "Sugar," Dr. McCoy blew kisses at Capt. Kirk, and that stoic Vulcan, Spock, smiled, swore and wept. Roddenberry exacted sweet revenge on NBC executives, revealing that they originally wanted to dump Spock's character, "because nobody would believe that guy with pointy ears." In fact, NBC canned the first "Star Trek" pilot, he said, "because it was (deemed) too cerebral for you slobs out in the television audience." Network execs also didn't like a "totally logical" woman, instead of Spock, being second in command of the Starship Enterprise, because there was "no such thing as a logical woman." The Trekkies cheered wildly when Roddenberry announced that Paramount would soon start filming a full-length "Star Trek" movie. To remind the studio not to replace the original TV cast with Hollywood idols, many Trekkies wore T-shirts that said, "Paramount is a Klingon Conspiracy."

But behind the glitz of the Sunshine State's bustling "Gold Coast" lurked a villain more sinister than Klingons. Fire. Even houses made of cement block caught fire and burned. Cement roof tiles created extra hazards when roofs collapsed. Everything burned: migrant labor shacks in the Everglades, mansions and condos on the beach, and tract homes and mobile homes in between. Windows that were closed much of the year to contain air-conditioning and save energy also trapped heat and deadly smoke. Little-used heating systems were seldom checked or maintained. They sparked fires or quietly filled condos and cottages with deadly carbon monoxide.

All of the fire calls had a particularly bizarre South Florida twist. When an old DC-3 crashed and burned along I-95 at Oakland Park Boulevard, the thick black smoke was intoxicating. No wonder. The cargo hold was full of bales of marijuana. A woman in Hollywood cleaned beach tar off of her tennis shoes with gasoline. Then she tossed them into the dryer, and expressed complete innocence and surprise when the resulting explosion blew her out through the front door. Security bars on windows and deadbolt locks may have kept the bad guys out, but they also trapped people inside during fires. They made it doubly difficult for firefighters to reach trapped victims. Tiki torches and barbecue grills didn't mix well with endless alcohol, which was perhaps the most common contributing factor in South Florida fires. Every make of car burned, occasionally with a body in the trunk. In marinas and on the water, gasoline fumes filled engine compartments. Speedboats and yachts blew up and burned.

Hundreds of miles of navigable inland canals stretched from the Intracoastal Waterway to the Everglades. They were beautiful, and great for fishing, crabbing and boating. But they complicated the job of fire/rescue teams, who carried spring-loaded center punches to instantly take out the windows of submerged vehicles. And, in really dry years, the "river of grass," itself, burned, sometimes for days. Smoke filled the sky, closing airports and blocking out the sun in the Sunshine State.

But fires were just a small part of what I now wrote about. Tourism may have been big in South Florida, but farming was even bigger. It was the number one industry in the state. My focus was mainly the South Florida winter vegetable industry and its raging trade war with Mexico. Mexican imports drove prices so low that South Florida farmers left their tomatoes in the fields to rot. Faced with American hostages in Tehran and a worsening oil crisis, the Carter Administration sweet-talked South Florida growers into withdrawing their federal anti-dumping suit against oil-rich Mexico. Farming in Florida was under attack on all sides as housing developers bulldozed orange groves and vegetable fields to build tract homes, pesticides tainted our food, and rapidly growing cities started running short of water.

That's when I stumbled across a national conspiracy that sent my comfortable, predictable life as assistant city editor spinning off wildly in a totally unexpected direction. I was leafing through *Editor & Publisher*, the weekly magazine of the newspaper industry, when the headline on a full-page ad caught my eye: "Join our conspiracy."

The ad was from a guy I never heard of named Bob Rodale in a little town I never heard of called Emmaus, Pennsylvania. Whatever Bob was selling, he had my attention. Sensing a good story, I read on.

"A loaf of bread costs $7.66. Tomatoes, three large ones, $5.24," the ad continued.

"Is this merely the shopping list of a paranoid housewife trapped in a frantic nightmare? Not at all. Based on a recent report to the White House, those are some of the food prices you may be paying at the end of the century. But if you believe only inflation is to blame, think about this:

"Each day of the coming decades, there will be 5,000 new people to feed in the U.S. And the food they'll need will have to be grown on less and less land, because six million acres of agricultural land are being lost annually — half to developers, half to the ravages of erosion and irresponsible agricultural practices.

"Soon ... our food system will cease to be a major source of America's strength."

Whoa! Wait a minute. Whoever this Rodale guy was, he was really on to something, I thought. Writing about farming in South Florida, I saw exactly what he was talking about — every day. Growing winter vegetables in South Florida and trucking them north used too much fuel, I knew. But that wasn't the worst of it. In the early 1980s, produce prices were so low that even grocery chains in South Florida routinely trucked tomatoes and other winter vegetables in from Mexico through the border crossing in Nogales, Arizona.

Illegal pesticide residues were another worry. I accompanied a state produce inspector as he pulled samples of Mexican produce from the walk-in coolers of area groceries to test for pesticide residues. The tests came back positive for banned chemicals. But, by then, the food had already been sold and eaten by an unsuspecting public. Our food system was insane. Economically and biologically, our farmers were dying. Land prices were so high that they could only rent land until developers were ready to build more houses. Big farms were getting bigger and fewer, as they battled developers and new cities for land and water, and middlemen for market share.

"Observing this, some people think they detect a conspiracy to control production, distribution, and prices," Rodale's ad continued. *"We see, instead, too many people ignoring the danger signals. That's why, several months ago we proposed a "people's conspiracy" which we called The Cornucopia Project.*

"The response was quick and profoundly encouraging. Since then, more than 20,000 people have written to ask about The Cornucopia Project and its goals.

"There are no dues. No membership obligations. We're just looking for people who want to stop the waste of soil, food, and energy that is threatening America. If that's you, we have facts that can be important to you. Please write ..."

So I did. I knew a good feature story when it fell in my lap. I made copies of a few of my recent farming stories about disappearing Florida farmers and farmland. I dashed off a quick note to the mysterious Mr. Rodale: "Your Cornucopia Project sounds like a great feature story. Here's a taste of what's going on in South Florida. I'll give you a call next week. We can do a phone interview, and I'll do a feature on your project."

But before I could call Rodale, his people called me.

"Bob likes your writing voice," the caller said. "We're looking for an editor for our farming magazine. Are you interested?"

Geez, I don't know. Let's talk. Like many transplants from the North, Mel and I had been thinking about leaving South Florida almost since we got there. We tired quickly of endless concrete, condos, and Cadillacs. Even though it snowed in the Keys and the Bahamas our first winter in South Florida, we missed real winter and family in the North.

So, in late January, 1981, I flew from Ft. Lauderdale to Philadelphia and rented a car in the middle of the night. Philadelphia International was a zoo. The Eagles were getting ready to face the Oakland Raiders in Super Bowl XV (Raiders won, 27–10).

Mr. Rodale — "Just call me Bob, please" — turned out to be one of the most amazing men I ever met. He had a full beard and favored Earth shoes, but he was no crackpot. Far from it. Bob was the head of a large, successful family publishing business, Rodale Press, which was founded by his late father in the 1940s. Forty years later, Rodale was best known for pioneering magazines such as *Prevention, New Shelter, Organic Gardening, The New Farm,* and *Bicycling.* Rodale books focused on healthy living and eating, solar energy, bicycle commuting, women's health, breast-feeding, fitness, natural foods, and homesteading, among many other popular themes.

But Bob was much more than a savvy businessman. He was also an environmentalist, a visionary, and an activist. A former Olympic skeet shooter, Bob firmly believed in "leading the target," aiming just ahead of a clay pigeon before squeezing the trigger. That put him almost too far out front on many issues. *The New Farm* was a perfect example. Launched in 1979, when politicians and pesticide companies were urging farmers "get big or get out," and "farm fencerow to fencerow," *The New Farm*'s focus was organic farming. Regular writers included such champions of the family farm and the back-to-nature movement as Wendell Berry, author of "The Unsettling of America," and Gene "The Contrary Farmer" Logsdon, a former *Farm Journal* writer.

Bob was not afraid to put his money where his mouth was, which is why he operated the famous Rodale Research Center, a 300-acre experimental farm in Maxatawny, Pennsylvania, to scientifically prove and perfect practical ways to farm without chemicals. He also introduced the grain amaranth as a commercial crop and promoted composting, backyard fish farming, home-scale solar greenhouses, square-foot gardening, bicycle commuting, food self-sufficiency, organic gardening, and much more.

It gave me more than a possible new job to think about on the way home, which was by way of extra connections to Columbus, Ohio, so I could visit my maternal grandfather in the hospital. He was dying of liver cancer. Changing planes in Washington, D.C., the control tower at Washington National Airport was draped with a big yellow ribbon. The 52 American hostages were finally coming home after 444 days of captivity in Iran. Rodale's warnings about possible shortages of energy and food seemed even more urgent.

A few weeks later, Rodale offered to pay me with a lot more than the unlimited sunshine that South Florida newspapers prized so highly. In the spring of 1981, Melanie and I packed up our two young children and our dog, "Crazy Kim." We set out for the little town of Emmaus. We thought we were just going to a new job in a new town. We never imagined we were about to step into a ring of fire.

PART 3

Professional Volunteers

CHAPTER TWELVE

Auslander

How hard could it be to fit into a new town? After all, our last move was a breeze. Of course, I forgot that Emmaus was not South Florida, where practically everyone came from somewhere else. It soon became obvious that fitting in here wasn't going to be easy.

So, one dreary Tuesday night in March of 1982, I met Emmaus Firefighter Randall Murray, my wife's boss, at the firehouse at 7 p.m. for weekly fire practice. All of the firefighters were already in the large multipurpose room for a meeting as we walked in. Randall introduced me as a prospective new member. I was 30 at the time. That's old for a new recruit. Many of the volunteers my age had been firefighters since their teens when they joined the fire department as "junior" firefighters.

"Oi, cheese! Just what we need, another ladder!" boomed a heavily accented voice from the back row.

The wisenheimer was Deputy Chief Kenneth Young, or "Youngie," as he was known throughout the borough. All the firefighters cracked up. And I didn't blame them. I stood 6-foot-4, and towered over Randall, even when he stretched to 5-foot-7 to do his best to look just like Richard Gere. I didn't object. I'd been called worse. Randall, too. His nickname around the firehouse, I learned later, was "Chrome Dome." A thick skin and good sense of humor — the ability to dish it out, as well as take it — are essential to survival in any firehouse, especially for bald guys.

But the "Oi, cheese" threw me. Never heard that one before. So, I asked Randall about it later. That's local shorthand, he said, code for "Cheese and crackers. Got all muddy!" The phrase is a thinly veiled, but perfectly acceptable way of cursing, even in mixed and polite company. The catch was that "crackers" came out like "craggers." That's because this was the land of the "Pencil-bane-yah-Dutch," as the natives pronounce it, or the "Pennsilfaanish Deitsch," as the scholars correctly write it. It's the place where "chicken" is more commonly pronounced "chiggen," "pig" is "pick," and "bug" is "buck." "House" is "haus." "Once" is "vuntz." The correct local pronunciation of "January" is "Chan-yee-airy." My Dodge pickup is a "Dotch." And

"John" is "Chon," which made my green and gold tractor a "Chon Deere."

The Pennsylvania Dutch are a cultural jewel, a true national treasure. Although our pop culture doesn't celebrate them as much as the Italians, Irish or even Greeks, people of German descent are among the oldest and hardiest ingredients in America's melting pot culture.

These were not the picturesque horse-and-buggy Amish shown in tourist brochures for Lancaster County, Pennsylvania. They're the scions of German peasants and burghers who settled in cities of Allentown, Hershey, Lancaster, Reading, York and 20 surrounding Pennsylvania counties, starting in the 17th century.

Emmaus is deep in the heart of the Lehigh Valley, the factory-workin', beer-drinkin', polka-dancin' capital of Industrial America, home of Mack Trucks and the late, great Bethlehem Steel.

Natives call themselves, and each other, "Dutchmen," or "Dutchies." That is totally wrong, anthropologically, of course. There's absolutely no connection between these "Dutch" and the Dutch of the Netherlands. The real Dutch — the ones from Holland —settled far to the east. They were coastal flatlanders, who established towns like New Amsterdam, which became New York City after it was seized by the British. The Pennsylvania Dutch, on the other hand, were highlanders from the mountains, forests and fertile fields of the Rhineland's Palatinate in southwestern Germany.

Their use of "Dutch" is a corruption of "Deutsch," the German word for German. The proper term for the natives here is Pennsylvania German. But "Dutch," or even "Dietsch," was what they chose to go by.

Pennsylvania Dutch love a good joke, especially if it comes at the expense of another Dutchman. They're thrifty. Many, their relatives and friends swear, still have the first dollar they ever made. And they may be the original environmentalists. The Dutch never throw anything out, because, "Well, you chust never know when you might need it." They're handy, hardy, hardworking, fun-loving, private, traditional, and much more.

They love good food, providing it's the right kind of "comfort" food that includes lots of meat and potatoes. Through the Emmaus Newcomers Club, Melanie and I became good friends with Ron and Pam Heckman. Ron was no newcomer to the Lehigh Valley, though. The Frantz side of Ron's family went back to the mid-1700s in neighboring Berks County. The title of his family's hardcover cookbook was "Kum Esse (Come Eat)."

This was the land of scrapple or "panhas," as the Dutch call it. A place where heaping apple butter and cottage cheese on a slab of dark rye bread meant you were eating high on the hog. The Dutch here were "as different in ... spirit and character from the German-American culture of the big cities as the Cajuns are from the New Orleans French," food historian William

Woys Weaver wrote in "Sauerkraut Yankees, Pennsylvania Dutch Foods & Foodways" (Stackpole Books, 2002). "Sauerkraut Yankees" was the name given to Pennsylvania Dutch soldiers in the Civil War.

The Dutch shun debt. And, they don't like to be in your debt, even for a few dollars. If you want to make a Dutchman feel uncomfortable, do something nice for him that costs a couple of bucks.

Positive proof of that came the year that Melanie and I decided to do something different for our annual contribution to the fire department. Yes, volunteer firefighters themselves are often among the fire department's biggest financial supporters, buying more ham and cheese sandwiches and tickets to comedy nights, $5 drawings and other raffles than anyone. Crowds at pancake breakfasts, pork and sauerkraut dinners, and assorted other fundraising events are largely made up of volunteers, fellow firefighters from nearby fire departments, our families, friends and neighbors. We proudly put our money where our mouths are.

Instead of simply writing a check, we opted to feed the troops with an old-fashioned, homemade holiday buffet. That's because the usual procedure for the Tuesday-night fire practice closest to Christmas was to cancel "practice," and order a stack of pizzas with a variety of toppings. It's a nice thought. But steam from the hot pizzas quickly condensed in cold weather. By the second bite, it always tasted like we were eating soggy cardboard.

The buffet was Melanie's idea. "Holidays aren't special unless you make them special," Mel likes to say. So she cooks and decorates our home, for Valentine's Day, Easter, the Fourth of July, Halloween, Thanksgiving, and Christmas. Out comes her Grandma Wimmer's silver, Aunt Lucille's Williamsburg china, and Mom's Waterford crystal water goblets. We use the dining room, not the kitchen table. Family, friends and special occasions are terribly important to Melanie. That comes largely from her growing up as an only child, since her brother, John, was 16 years older and already out on his own for as long as Mel can remember. Mel always sends birthday and anniversary cards so that they arrive exactly on time. On the actual day of the big event, a phone call is mandatory. Even if she just ends up leaving a message, that's OK. It's the thought that counts. Her parents did well in naming her after the kindhearted Melanie Wilkes in "Gone with the Wind."

When my Miss Melly cooks, she goes all out. Her dishes come from countless cookbooks and folders full of handwritten and faded, butter-stained recipes that crowd the shelves around our kitchen table. Mel prepares everything from appetizers and salads to multiple desserts. It's genetic, I guess. She's descended from a long line of amazing German and Hungarian cooks. Some of her favorite dishes are beef stroganoff, Hungarian goulash, and chicken paprikash with lots of sour cream and paprika served over homemade spaetzels. Not only does Mel cook, but she bakes — bread or rolls, pies, cakes, cupcakes, and cookies — from scratch.

The menu for the fire department Christmas buffet started with chunks of cheese and trail bologna, with mustard on the side, and choice of crackers or rolls. Entrées included two big pans of chicken-almond casseroles, half a honey-glazed spiral-cut ham, and crockpot sausages, complete with peppers and onions. Side dishes ranged from a vegetable medley to fruit salad and cranberry chutney. And then there was dessert, starting with "kiffles," a traditional Hungarian cookie made with lots of cream cheese and butter, and apricot, cherry or poppy seed filling. Next was Hungarian crescent cookies made with sour cream, yeast and even more butter. Fillings ranged from apricot or prune to ground pecans. They were all dusted with powdered sugar. For those with more traditional tastes, there were also butter cookies, pecan tassies, fruitcake, cupcakes and pumpkin roll.

The "firehaus" buffet was a feast for the senses. The aroma was irresistible. Everyone was hungry. Everyone was drooling. But ... no one was eating. Why? We could't quite figure it out. To break the ice, I grabbed a plate, and started loading it up. "I'm not proud," I said. "I'll go first."

Slowly, other firefighters approached the table. Cautiously, they began adding items to their plates. I was on my second helping of everything when the longtime Pennsylvania Dutch fire chief sidled up to me, and started reaching for his wallet. "This cost you two some money," he mumbled. "Can I give you something for it?"

No, chief! Thanks, but this is our treat. Merry Christmas!

They don't quite know what to make of us. We aim to keep it that way.

The language continually "wonders me," as the Dutchies say. When the dinner platter is empty, for example, the food is not gone, it's "all." Babies aren't fussing, they're "gretzing." "Yah, well" or "mox nix" replaces "whatever." They "outen the lights" with the flip of a switch, and firefighters "make the fire ott." That's o-t-t, "ott!" Not out. And the catchall phrase that covers just about everything else, delivered in three guttural, but musical syllables, is "Whatthehell?" The word "say" pops up at the end of sentences as often as many Canadians use "eh," usually in combination with "now," as in, "Say, now! Didja know?"

When we arrived in Pennsylvania in 1981, some locals proudly wore T-shirts that said, "If You Ain't Dutch — You Ain't Much." They really meant it, too. The other side of the shirt sported a big picture of a groundhog raising its clenched fist to proclaim "Grundsow Power!" Every Feb. 2, the grundsow was king, not just in Punxsutawney, Pennsylvania, but also in some 18 "Grundsow Lodches" throughout southeastern Pennsylvania.

In each Lodche, hundreds of diehard Dutchmen gathered to eat, drink and speak nothing but Dutch (you're fined a nickel to a quarter for each English word spoken) throughout their annual Versammlung. The lodches date back to the 1930s.

Dutchmen even have what my Dutchie farmer friend Brian Moyer calls a "secret, verbal handshake" to see if someone is a true Dutchman and can actually speak Dutch.

"Kannst du micka funga?" cackled one of our new neighbors, 95-year-old Earl Shankweiler. (Can you catch flies?)

The appropriate response is, "Ja, wenn de hocka bleiben!" (Yes, when they sit still.)

The World War II generation was the last to grow up speaking Dutch fluently. Their children and grandchildren now take formal classes, study language tapes and buy Pennsylvania Dutch-English dictionaries to recapture their fading linguistic heritage.

The Dutch thought Melanie and I talked funny. Maybe we did. We still had a Central Ohio drawl. From years in South Florida, we're apt to ask "¿Que pasa?" instead of "Wie gates?" We might throw in a "y'all" or even an "all y'all!" "Say, now!" comes the reply. "Whatthehell is this, why?"

It's complicated. The Dutch dialect in southeastern Pennsylvania varied from county to county. Brian's Montgomery County Dutch was slightly out of synch with Earl's Lehigh County Dutch, which was a different language from what was spoken in Schuylkill County, up on the edge of the coal region. Even within counties, some words, phrases — and accents — varied from township to township. Some call it "bad German and worse English."

It all began in 1681 when King Charles II of England granted William Penn some 45,000 square miles in what is now Pennsylvania and Delaware to satisfy the crown's debt to Penn's father. But, unlike the rest of the New World, Pennsylvania never became a true British colony. "Germantown" was the name of a new borough founded in Philadelphia County in 1683. Germans flocked to Pennsylvania by the tens of thousands. As the coastal areas became more populated, immigrants pushed deeper inland.

The first settlers wandered into the Emmaus area around 1719. Many became "squatters" because there was a lot of wide open land, very few people and no government to boss folks around. After centuries of war, economic oppression and religious persecution in feudal Europe, such unlimited freedom must have made Pennsylvania seem truly like heaven on Earth. The flood of immigrants only increased. And in church records in the Palatinate back in Germany, priests repeatedly made the following sad notation about parishioners who left for greener pastures: "Ausgewandert nach der Insel Pennsylvanien (Emigrated to the Island of Pennsylvania)."

By 1725, it reached the point where James Logan, secretary to the late William Penn, complained to authorities "that there are so many as one hundred thousand acres of land, possessed by persons, who resolutely set down and improved it without any right to it." Just 10 years later, in 1735, the "King's Highway" became the first public road built into the area.

Pennsylvania Dutch accounted for about half of the population of Pennsylvania at the time of the American Revolution. They staunchly supported the war and the cause of independence. Most were Catholic or Lutheran, but it was the Moravian missionaries who established the settlements of Bethlehem, Nazareth and Emmaus, which finally received its biblical name in 1761. The name came from Luke 24:13-36, which tells of how Cleopas and another disciple met a resurrected Jesus of Nazareth while walking on the road to Emmaus. Centuries later, that story captivated a young Dutch painter named Rembrandt, who scandalized the art world by giving Christ a truly human face in the "Road to Emmaus," "Supper at Emmaus" and dozens of other paintings and sketches.

The Lehigh Valley was so solidly Pennsylvania Dutch that daily newspaper editorial cartoons were written "auf Deutsch," and good Italian names like "Iacocca" became "Yocco." Not surprising, since a good German name like "Iobst" — as in Iobst Travel and Emmaus Mayor Winfield Iobst — was pronounced "Yobst." Most Americans know Allentown-born Lee Iacocca as the former head of Ford and Chrysler. Lehigh Valley residents know — and revere — his family as founders of "Yocco's," the hot dog king. Emmaus took great pride in the fact that Yocco's, founded in 1922 by Theodore Iacocca, Lee's uncle, was headquartered in the borough. Emmaus had a Wendy's, a McDonald's and a Subway, but those who knew "gut essen" still went to Yocco's, Traub's Doggies and other mom and pop Dutchie eateries around town.

For more than 50 years, *The Morning Call*'s crusty cartoonist, William Richard "Bud" Tamblyn, did some of his best work auf Deustch. Perhaps his most celebrated cartoon was from September, 1945. After the end of World War II, former Japanese Prime Minister Hideki Tojo faced arrest as a war criminal. Tojo tried to commit suicide by shooting himself in the chest. But American military doctors and blood from Jack Archinal, a Pennsylvania Dutch soldier from Allentown, saved Tojo's life. Bud's cartoon showed a recovering Tojo in bed, draped with a Rising Sun flag. A servant politely inquired "How Hon. Sir feel this morning please?" Tojo replied, in Dutch: *"Tzimlich gude!"* [*Pretty good.*] The cartoon appeared in newspapers throughout the country.

For a century or so, Lehigh Valley industrial giants Mack Trucks and Bethlehem Steel put wheels under the economy and steel backbones in many of our architectural icons, everything from the battleship Maine, the Golden Gate Bridge, the Chrysler and Empire State buildings, Madison Square Garden and Alcatraz to Bonneville, Grand Coulee and Hoover dams.

But when we arrived in Emmaus, all of that was changing. The Rust Belt was dying. Information-intensive businesses such as Rodale Press, Air Products and Chemicals, Bell Labs and the booming health care and life sciences fields exemplified by Lehigh Valley Hospital Center were replacing heavy industry. White-collar jobs were reshaping the Rust Belt and the traditional blue-collar world of the Pennsylvania Dutch. In 1982, a year after we moved to Emmaus, Billy Joel came out with his hit song, "Allentown." All the factories did seem to be closing down.

How Dutchie was the Emmaus Fire Department? Last names on the active roster may provide a clue: Bauman, Drabick, Druckenmiller, Eisentraut, Engleman, Ernst, Fritch, Garloff, Gottschall, Haberstumpf, Helvig, Hillegass, Kerstetter, Kline, Kuhns, Lauer, Litzenberger, Miller, Mohr, Orach, Oswald, Pierog, Reiss, Schadler, Schaffer, Schmick, Seibert, Shafer, Stortz, Urland, Wisser, and Yoder. (There's an exception to every rule, of course. The exception at the Emmaus Fire Department was long-time Fire Police Captain Warren Godusky, a roofer by trade.)

Ja, so? Where did that leave me?

"*Ich bin ein auslander.*" A foreigner, an outsider. My grandfather wasn't native to the Lehigh Valley. I wasn't an Emmaus High School alum. I was "from away" — and always would be.

A name like "DeVault" just didn't quite fit. Never mind that there was a village named DeVault (Zip Code 19432) about 40 miles to the south, near Valley Forge. Never mind that I could trace the Glick side of my father's family all the way back to the late 1600s in the Palatinate. My sixth great grandparents, Johannes and Magdelena Herr Glick, arrived in Philadelphia in 1754. They settled in nearby Berks County and rest in peace there. Problem was, the rest of the Glicks didn't stay in one place long. They suffered from the German ailment known as "wanderlust." And, by about 1800, the children and grandchildren of Johannes and Magdelena were busy settling the wild Ohio Territory.

"We Pennsylvania Dutch, we don't take easily to newcomers," said my new barber, Barty Decker. Then he sounded a hopeful note. "We want to know what you're made of before we make up our minds. If we see that you're OK, and we take a liking to you, well then, you've got a friend for life."

CHAPTER THIRTEEN

You Bet Your Life

Would you go into a burning building with *that* person?

What person? Any person. Pick a person. It could be just about anybody because, for good or ill, that's exactly the way a volunteer fire department works. Whoever is handy — and can break away from whatever they're doing at a moment's notice — is who shows up at the firehouse when there's a fire call.

You never know who "that person" may be, especially on weekdays. In the middle of the night most everyone is home. It's a pretty safe bet the turnout will be halfway decent, that there will be enough well-trained and experienced firefighters to do the job. Weekdays are another story. You take what comes. Pickin's can be pretty slim.

So, think fast, would you go into a burning building with *that* person?

It's a question that trumped the obstacle of me being an "auslander," a total stranger ... "from away." Having others trust you with their lives is not something that happens every day. Yet that's exactly what's required in a volunteer fire department. You literally put your life in the hands of the person next to you in a burning building. And that makes the firehouse an even tougher place for a newcomer to win acceptance.

Emmaus Fire Chief Robert R. Reiss was always skeptical of new recruits, and for good reason. This isn't a job for everyone, because not just anyone can — or will — do what needs to be done, which might be anything. The job changes from minute to minute, depending on changing conditions. Whatever, whenever. That's the job.

Naturally, the fire chief had doubts about me. For starters, I'd never done anything like this before. Could I do the job? Just how active would I be? How much could he count on me to even show up for fire calls?

Could I climb ladders or work comfortably with a chain saw or an axe on a steep, rain-slick roof in the dark while wearing an air pack? Maybe, maybe not. Some people just don't do ladders. They're simply afraid of heights. No shame in that. But the chief had to know — ahead of time. The last thing he needed was to find out the hard way by having someone freeze half way up a tall ladder at a raging house fire.

Could I even wear an air pack? Maybe, maybe not. Not everybody can. The tight rubber mask that delivers life-giving air and blocks deadly smoke makes many people feel like it's really suffocating them.

Could I stand the sight of blood? Or worse? Then there was claustrophobia. How did I get along in confined and narrow spaces? Could the chief send me into a black, smoke-filled attic or basement crawl space without worrying that I'd freak out and have to be rescued? Was I afraid of the dark?

Just how much of me would he see around the firehouse? Would I be there for weekly practice every Tuesday evening? How about special training classes at night and on weekends? Would I show up at Saturday work details, help make hoagies or sell T-shirts to raise money for the fire department? The chief's worry list was endless.

It was also necessary and completely justified. I was a busy guy. I had a working wife and two young children. I lived and worked in town, close to the firehouse, but I also had a demanding, deadline-driven executive job that often required me to travel. When I had "free time," did I really want to spend it chasing fire alarms?

If I did work out, how long would I stick around? After all, the fire department was going to invest a lot of time and money in training and equipping me. What kind of return would it get on that investment? In a few years, would I use my training and experience from Emmaus as a steppingstone to land a full-time firefighting job somewhere else? Emmaus smokeaters easily landed firefighting jobs with the cities of Allentown and Easton in Pennsylvania; Roanoke, Virginia; elsewhere around the country; and in the military.

Chief Reiss also had seen too many people just plain fizzle out over the years.

When my tonebox went off in the middle of a winter night, would I rush right to the firehouse? Or would I go on instant "R&R" — reset and roll over? Would I pick and choose my calls, responding only to those that sound like they might really be something interesting?

Or would I be a shooting star? Shooting stars start out all gung ho. For vacation, they spend a week living at the State Fire Academy in Lewistown, Pennsylvania, enduring intensive training that rivals Marine boot camp. They fill their weekends with every local training course offered. Nights are spent on "sleep duty" at the firehouse. When friends and neighbors said they hadn't seen the star around for a while, "the wife" would snap, "That's because he's at the firehouse. He's *always* at the firehouse!"

Shooting stars quickly learn to drive at least one fire truck and run the pump. They move up the ladder, becoming an engineer, a lieutenant or even a captain. They run hundreds and hundreds of fire calls in just a few years. Then they burn out. And one day — poof! — they're gone.

Maybe I'd turn out to be a "whacker." What's a whacker? Only the lowest, most useless — and dangerous — form of life on Earth, at least as far as any fire chief was concerned. Whackers saw themselves as God's gift to the fire service. They talked incessantly about their vast firefighting experience and knowledge.

Problem was, whackers seldom actually fought many fires. They had more firefighting gear, radios and flashing lights in their personal vehicles than most fire engines carried. And the light bars on their cars often cost more than the cars. In the digital decade of the 2010s, every whacker carried a so-called smartphone. They used them to "text" their lovers from the jump seat of a fire truck while responding to fire calls, instead of properly gearing up. Then, at the first opportunity on the scene, they would shoot a "selfie" with the unfolding emergency in the background and post it right away on Facebook. One item not included in a whacker's tool chest was a helmetcam. Gripping video requires lots of action. Whackers seldom did anything worth recording for posterity at a fire scene. They may even make a big deal on social media out of attending the distant funerals of firefighters killed in the line of duty in other states.

Chief Reiss knew all of that, of course, which was why he worried constantly. But beyond that, he was not your usual fire chief. For starters, he didn't ask his firefighters to do anything that he hadn't done and didn't do regularly himself. Chief Reiss wore an air pack. He manned a hose line, took the heat and smoke, drove all of the fire trucks, and climbed ladders with the best of them. That set him apart from many chiefs, some of whom never put on bunker gear or left the comfort of their "command vehicle" at a fire scene.

Chief Reiss fit the classic definition of a good fire officer that David Halberstam described so well in his book, "FIREHOUSE" (Hyperion, 2002):

"The captain's character is elemental to the code of the firehouse, for he holds in his hands the men's very survival, regularly making decisions of life and death. By tradition the captain is the first in and the last out of any fire. It is one of the things, firefighters think, that differentiates them from the police. The higher up you rise among the cops, firemen believe, the less likely you are to expose yourself to harm; police officials tend to arrive on the scene after the heat of battle. But that is not true of firemen. When you become an officer in a firehouse, your burden and need to expose yourself to danger only increase. The officers lead the men into the fire and share their dangers. Thus leadership and title are not merely hierarchical with firemen, they are the basis of a sacred trust, and so officers are viewed through a brutal prism."

"*Brutal prism.*" Halberstam nailed it. There is no hiding your actions — or inactions — on the fireground. In the heat of battle, everything a fire officer says and does — or doesn't do — has effects and consequences that can often be quite severe. So firefighters, like soldiers in a firefight, constantly keep a close and critical eye on officers. Their lives depend on it.

The possible mortal sins of fire officers are endless: Indecision. Hesitation. Lack of resolve. Ignorance. Arrogance. Stupidity. Recklessness. Worst of all, at least to my mind, is seeming to not care about the safety of firefighters under their command.

You see it all on the fireground, the entire spectrum of that "brutal prism," from the very best to the absolute worst. Sometimes, it happens in the blink of an eye.

Case in point was a fire early one January. A greenhouse/nursery complex in a neighboring fire district went up in flames in the middle of the night. The place was full of plastics, fertilizers and pesticides. Flames were through the roof when the first pumper arrived in front of the building. The pump operator tried for a quick kill shot. He aimed his deck gun at the burning building, and emptied his water tank. He missed. The fire raged out of control.

I was on the second pumper. Three of us in air packs pulled two hose lines. We attacked from the side. We crawled in through what was left of the greenhouses: melting plastic on metal skeletons. A fourth firefighter followed us inside. He was one of our newest members. He was not wearing an air pack.

Soon, an officer came by. He called out to the new guy, and politely asked, "Would you like an air pack?"

"No. (Cough, cough.) I'm OK. (Cough, cough.) Thanks anyhow, Chief."

That officer was never one of my favorite people. But in that instant, I lost all respect for the man.

Less than a minute later, a junior officer happened by. He took one look inside, and screamed: "Hey! You with no air pack on! *Get the fuck out of there!*"

My hero.

Chief Reiss also happened to be a member of one of the most exclusive fraternities in the fire service. It is made up of firefighters who laid their lives on the line to save total strangers — and succeeded. Many people mistakenly think that firefighters make dramatic rescues every day. And why not? They do that all the time, and in just one hour, on TV. Same goes for cop shows and their blazing gun battles. Truth is, many cops serve their whole careers without ever firing a weapon anywhere but on the target range. Some never even unholster their weapons.

It's the same for firefighters and rescues. A firefighter can sweep the floor of the firehouse every day of a 30-year career and never be in a position to save a life, or make a "grab," as it's called in some departments. Saving a life depends on being in just the right place, at just the right time, and doing the right things, just right.

That fickle nature of fire calls was perfectly pointed out by *The New York Times* in a Sunday front-page feature about a probationary New York City Firefighter Jordan Sullivan ("Baptism by Fire," by N.R. Kleinfeld, June 20, 2014). "Probie" Sullivan had worked 96 days on Ladder 105 in Brooklyn without catching any serious fires. It reached the point where, other firefighters joked, if Sullivan was on duty, you knew it was going to be a quiet night, said *The Times*.

That all changed the night of March 16, 2014. A fifth-floor apartment was on fire. Children were inside. Two other firefighters with Sullivan inside the burning apartment had 24 years of service between them. In all that time, neither of them had made a single "grab," the newspaper reported. On his first real fire, after only 96 days as a New York City firefighter, Sullivan saved a baby that night. Another firefighter, from a rescue squad, also saved an 8-year-old girl. It was his first grab in nine years on the job.

Chief Reiss' initiation came on the morning of July 14, 1973. The scene was an old concrete bunker, a 14-foot-deep sewer pumping station near Keck's Bridge over the trout-filled Little Lehigh Creek, just outside of Emmaus. Three bodies lay motionless at the bottom of the pit. There was no breathable air inside, just deadly sewer gas. The only way into the pit was a 30-inch-square hatch in a concrete slab. The only way to the bottom was a rusty steel ladder that ran straight up and down. Two of the men, ages 17 and 20, had been dead for hours. But the third man, who had just gone into the pit to rescue them, might still be alive. He was unconscious, 250 pounds of dead weight.

Reiss was the first firefighter on the scene with an air pack. He climbed down into the pit. As strong as he was, Reiss couldn't bring the man up out of the pit all by himself.

Help soon arrived. Allentown Firefighter Michael Grim and Allentown Deputy Fire Chief Dale Werkheiser donned air packs. They joined Reiss in the pit. On the surface, Emmaus firefighters — Assistant Fire Chief John Shafer, Assistant Foreman Terry Oswald and Firefighters Gary Fritch and Kenneth Kemmerer — fed ropes down into the pit. Together, they muscled the unconscious man up through the tiny opening and into fresh air.

Could I ever do something like that? If faced with a life-or-death situation, what would I do? I honestly didn't know. No one can know until the time comes. And that's why Chief Reiss worried.

"Ach, don't be too hasty," white-haired Arthur Mohr cautioned Chief Reiss. Art was the chief's mentor. He was also something of a living legend in the fire service, not just in Pennsylvania, but around the country. During World War II, Art worked with both the Army and Navy. He visited airbases around the nation teaching emergency crews how to fight aircraft fires, first with water and then with foam. Art represented Mack Trucks, which began making fire trucks in 1910. He took the young fire chief under his wing, and helped Reiss turn the Emmaus Fire Department into one of the more progressive volunteer fire companies in the state and the nation. "The new guy will work out," Art assured the chief. "Wait and see."

That's all we could do, because only time would tell. My six months of basic training started for real with fire practice next Tuesday.

CHAPTER FOURTEEN

When Your Air Runs Out

The personal protective equipment that the Emmaus Fire Department issued to a wannabe firefighter in early 1982 wasn't exactly state of the art. And for good reason. Even back then it cost a few thousand dollars to fully outfit just one firefighter.

Emmaus did have good bunker gear. Lots of it. Some of the best that money could buy, as a matter of fact. But that only went to the frontline firefighters, the ones with the most training and experience. A warm body fresh off the street automatically got whatever hand-me-downs came close to fitting well enough. When you're a scrawny 6-foot-4 and all arms and legs, getting a decent fit was tough.

My faded yellow canvas raincoat was baggy and long. It came down to mid-thigh. Almost two of me could fit inside comfortably. Emmaus has a long and distinguished history of chesty firefighters, many with what we politely call thick middles. The department's gear clearly reflected that. The extra room inside the coat did have one unexpected advantage, though. It let me add a heavy sweater and other layers in really cold weather. If only the sleeves were longer. My shirt size is a 15.5-inch neck — with a 35-inch sleeve. When I reached for anything, too-short sleeves left a big gap between cuffs and the tops of my fire gloves.

My hip boots were black rubber, well-worn. The boots handled the length and width of my size-12 feet just fine. But like the arms of my bunker coat, they didn't handle a 36-inch inseam very well. The boots were just barely tall enough. They did keep water out, though, just as long as the tops stayed tucked under the hem of my long fire coat. That only happened when I stood up straight. But when I bent over or crawled on my hands and knees, big gaps opened up. The boots provided little protection from heat or cold, and zero padding for my bony knees when I was crawling across exposed attic rafters.

All of that would be extremely dangerous in a real fire, of course. But, for basic training with simulated smoke and no flames, the hand-me-down coat and boots were plenty good enough. They would do ... for now.

Still, there was one vital piece of equipment on which there could be absolutely no compromise. Ever. That was the air pack, our self-contained breathing apparatus, or SCBA, for short. It looks and operates much like a scuba outfit. SCUBA stands for "self-contained *underwater* breathing apparatus." Our air packs were designed for a different kind of swimming — through thick smoke, and in other conditions where there's not enough oxygen to support life.

Our air packs were made by Scott Aviation, which in the early 1940s pioneered on-board oxygen systems for American and British military pilots. The company introduced firefighting air packs in 1945. Scott quickly became the first name in air packs, a part of the language, like "Kleenex," which is what most Americans call the product we reach for every time we blow our noses.

At Emmaus, we reached for our Scotts whenever there was a fire call. It didn't matter what the call might be. If you were in a jump seat and heading out on a fire call, "You'd pack up!" Don't ask your officer if it's OK. It's a no-brainer. You're going to a fire, so dress for success. And safety. Yours and that of the people who may need your help.

Didn't matter if it was a flaming dumpster, a burning car or house, or a raging warehouse fire. "Pack up!" And be ready to attack the fire — or go inside a burning building for search and rescue — the moment you step off the fire truck.

If you didn't need an air pack when you got to the scene, you just took it off. It was good practice, a way to become more familiar and comfortable with your air pack and to inspect it frequently.

We had to be as comfortable, confident and capable with our air packs as elite military troops are with their favorite weapons. Our lives, and those of the people we're trying to rescue, depended on it. We had to become one with the air pack. That held true whether you were atop the 100-foot aerial ladder directing 1,000 gallons of water a minute into the upper floors of the old Hotel Macungie, worming your way through mountains of junk in a superheated attic, or searching a smoke-filled basement bedroom when your low-air alarm bell started ringing and you had only minutes to get out. The only way to do that was to wear the air pack constantly, faithfully and well.

That's why the first formal training class I had to take outside of weekly fire practice was on air packs. It was a Lehigh County Fire School, but it attracted firefighters from far and wide. Our classroom was the engine room at the Mack Southside station in Allentown. Our "lab" for the practical work was the "smokehouse" or training tower behind the firehouse. It was a two-day weekend class with both practical and written exams.

Passing grade was 70 percent, unless you were from Emmaus. Then you had to score a perfect 100. That's because our instructor was none other than "Youngie," Kenneth G. Young, the wisecracking, ball-busting assistant chief from Emmaus, where wearing air packs on fire calls had been mandatory since 1969. Youngie knew everything there was to know about air packs, or so he told us. We didn't doubt him for a moment.

The air pack we used at the time was the Scott IIa. A full air tank had 2,216 pounds of pressure per square inch. That's 45 cubic feet of filtered, compressed air in a steel tank that weighed 22 pounds. The air was bone dry. Breathing just one 30-minute bottle sucked a pint of moisture out of your body, Youngie warned us. So drink lots of water he said. It wards off dehydration, which slows reactions, clouds thinking and, under extreme emergency conditions, triggers seizures and worse.

There was a lot to learn about air packs. Not all of it was pleasant or reassuring for the person wearing the pack. Let's start with how long your air might last. Scott rated our air bottles at 30 minutes. But ...

"You'll get 10 to 15 minutes out of a bottle — max — when you're working hard in a fire," Youngie said.

Why? Lots of reasons, starting with your very own physical condition. If you're out of shape, overweight, your air won't last very long. Smokers use more air. How long your air will last also depends on how well you can control your emotions under severe stress, your training and experience, the mechanical condition of the air pack, the quality of the air inside the bottle, and whether your air tank is full. Going into a fire with a partially filled air bottle means you're not playing with a full deck.

Did you have a tight seal on your air mask? Youngie would soon find out. He cracked open an ammonia ampule and ran it around the edges of your mask. "Smell anything? No? Try this!" he said, jamming the ammonia into your breathing tube. He only did that to people he really liked.

What could keep your air mask from sealing smoke out and keeping good air in? Try just one day's growth of beard. If you had a beard or goatee, any facial hair other than a neatly trimmed mustache, you didn't wear an air pack. Even shaggy sideburns and long hair caused problems.

And then there were the five bumpy rubber straps of the head harness that held your face mask in place. There was a strap on either side of your chin and temples. A fifth strap was on the top of your head. Pull any strap too tight when you were gearing up in a hurry on your way to a fire call, and it distorted the edge of your mask. You didn't get a good seal. That meant you'd leak air, inhale smoke, and run out of air too soon. Loose straps were even worse, especially when they were already buried under your Nomex hood and your fire helmet. You couldn't do anything to tighten them without taking everything off, and the chief would be yelling for you to get inside the burning building for search and rescue — now!

So how did you know if you had a good seal when Youngie wasn't hanging around with ammonia or a cheap cigar? That's an easy one, and something Youngie drummed into our heads, again and again. After you put your mask on and tightened the straps, you placed the palm of one hand over the end of your breathing tube — and inhaled. If the mask collapsed onto

Emmaus firefighters like those pictured here first relied on the "Chemox" chemical rebreather. A 4-pound canister of potassium superoxide (KO2) was connected to one-way valves and air bags that acted like lungs. The wearer's moist breath caused the KO2 to release oxygen for up to about 45 minutes. KO2 is not necessarily the best thing to take into a fire. When exposed to enough water, it explodes.

EMMAUS HISTORICAL SOCIETY PHOTO

your face, you had a good seal. Then you put on the rest of your gear. If you couldn't suck the mask tight against your face, you did something wrong. Time to adjust your straps and try again. The last thing you wanted was to get deep inside a smoke-filed building and feel precious air gushing out the side of your mask. "So, slow down," Youngie said. "Make sure you do it right, the first time. The life you save may be your own."

What happened if you did run out of air inside a burning building? "That's an easy one," Youngie said. "Bend over ... and kiss your ass good-bye." He was kidding, of course. Sort of.

"There are several things you can do," he said. First was buddy breathing. We hooked a spare air hose into a special coupling on our partner's air pack. A black pouch on the side of each pack held a three-foot long hose for just such emergencies. Both firefighters could then breathe off one tank, provided there was enough air left to get you out of the building. The trick was to be able to successfully hook all of that up in a hurry, usually in the dark and under extreme combat conditions. Remember, you're in a burning building. It's full of smoke. You can't see what you're doing. You're wearing heavy leather gloves. Do you dare risk taking them off? Will you be able to find them again? Plus, you can't breathe. We couldn't practice this procedure often enough.

Suppose all air tanks are empty. "Try filter breathing," Youngie said. Disconnect your inhalation tube and stick one of your gloves over the end. Or, tuck the tube inside your bunker coat. Either way, you'll suck a lot of smoke. But it'll keep some of the worst pollutants out of your lungs, you hope. It may just keep you alive long enough to escape.

If your regulator failed or face mask fell apart, and there was any air left in your bottle, you could always lock your lips around the valve stem and try breathing directly off of the air bottle. "Careful! That's a high-pressure air bottle. Open the valve more than just a crack and you'll blow the wax right out of your ears," said Youngie. We took his word for it. No one volunteered to try bottle-breathing.

Under normal conditions, though, there was really no excuse for running out of air. All air packs had a low-air alarm. On our Scotts, an alarm bell started ringing when just 500 pounds of air pressure was left in your tank. That's less than one-quarter of a tank. When the alarm bell rang, your regulator automatically reduced air flow to three-quarters of normal delivery. Air pressure inside your mask dropped from 3 pounds to a skimpy 2.25 pounds. Breathing became noticeably more difficult. Under ideal conditions, you had nearly eight minutes of air left. In the real world, it meant you were four minutes, or less, from drawing your last breath. Time to get out! When the bell slowed, then finally stopped tolling, you hoped you were near a door or a window. You had 100 pounds of air left, enough for about one more minute.

The alarm bell was built into the pressure regulator. If you couldn't hear it, you could usually feel the vibration through your gear. You could also trigger the alarm yourself to call for help if you became trapped or disabled inside a fire.

Air-pack training didn't end with the weekend class. Besides weekly practice, there was the dreaded Breathing Rate Exercise Test that the chief tried to run at least once a year. It revealed how long we could make a bottle of air last. We'd be wearing full bunker gear and an air pack — about 60 extra pounds of gear — and breathing air out of the bottle, not just wearing the face mask, and leisurely breathing unlimited outside air. Scott said the air in the bottle should last for 30 minutes. Would it? Maybe, maybe not. That's what we were here to find out. So, gear up. Pack up.

Open the valve on your air tank all the way. Do you hear the low-air alarm bell "ding" when the air first comes on? That's the alarm mechanism cocking. OK, you're good to go. Just remember the chief's admonition, "This is not a race. You want to learn to pace yourself, see how long you can make your air last." Start the stopwatch. Let the test begin:

1. Climb a 10-foot vertical ladder, twice.
2. Carry a 50-pound weight 400 feet.
3. Walk 250 feet.
4. Stand at rest for two minutes. (Monitor checks time and tank pressure.)
5. Chop a log with a 14-pound sledge — 20 times.

(This is about the point where a rookie firefighter panicked one night at weekly practice. "Get it offa me! Get it offa me!" he screamed. It was like the air mask morphed into an alien predator that was suffocating him and eating his face. The first firefighter to reach him slipped a couple of fingers under the edge of his mask. Fresh air rushed in, and he breathed easier. Then we stripped off his helmet, hood, mask and pack, and opened up his bunker coat. He was done with air packs, for good.)

6. In the attic simulator, which is just tall enough to let a firefighter in full gear and an air pack pass through, crawl 20 feet down and 20 feet back on hands and bony knees across exposed rafters. It's totally dark inside and, depending on the whims of the training officer, sometimes full of artificial smoke. Claustrophobia, anyone?

7. Walk 250 feet.

8. Carry two sections of 1.5-inch hose or one section of 2.5-inch hose folded on the shoulder for 200 feet.

9. Lie on your side for two minutes. (Monitor checks, records vital signs.)

10. Run 600 feet. (Monitor records time, tank pressure.)

11. Lie on your side for two minutes.

12. Carry a mattress 50 feet to a barrel, go around the barrel and lug the mattress back to the starting point.

13. Cover a car with a tarp.

14. Drag one section of 2.5-inch hose 50 feet on your hands and knees.

15. Lie on your side for two minutes.

16. Climb a ladder twice, touching red flag at top each time.

17. Walk 400 feet.

If you have any air left after doing all that, keep walking until your tank is completely empty. Monitor writes down when the low-air alarm bell starts ringing, the time your air finally runs out, and your vital signs. Believe it or not, a few people do manage to stretch an air bottle out that far. We call them "Air Misers." They get a little green triangle on the sides of their helmets to mark the accomplishment. (I never got one, but I came close.)

So, how'd you do?

CHAPTER FIFTEEN

Slaying Dragons ... and "Dinosaurs"

Long-time Emmaus Fire Chief Bobby Reiss wasn't born in a firehouse. He just grew up in three of them. Then he spent nearly the rest of his long life in the one he built specifically to slay both dragons ... *and "dinosaurs."*

Firefighting runs in the Reiss genes. Bobby's grandfather, Jesse, was a volunteer firefighter, a charter member of Citizens' Fire Co. No. 2, founded in 1934. Bobby's father, Henry, was a volunteer firefighter. A pipefitter at Superior Combustion in Emmaus, Henry joined Emmaus Fire Co. No. 1 in 1937 when Bobby was just 3 years old. The kid didn't stand a chance. But, from an early age, he didn't buy the conventional wisdom that, "The proper way to do things is ... the way we've always done things." He looked, listened, and learned, then started thinking about better ways.

The Reiss family lived at 560 Jubilee Street, facing the railroad tracks. That was two blocks west of Borough Hall, the basement of which housed the Fire Company No. 1 — and the fire company's bar. The fire siren that alerted volunteers to a fire call was on the roof of Borough Hall. Telephones were still something of a luxury back then. Firefighters had no pagers or radios at home to alert them to fire calls. (Two-way radios, which cost the volunteers $10,000 in fundraising money, didn't go in the fire trucks until 1957. "Home alert receivers," 54 of them, didn't show up in the volunteers' homes until 1967, but only after the volunteers themselves raised another $10,000 to buy the radios.) The second of seven children, Bobby slept in his parents' attic. It was too cold there in winter, too hot in summer. But, year-round, the fire siren just two blocks away sounded like it was under the same roof with him. When the siren roared to life in the middle of the night, "It was boom, boom, boom. The old man ran downstairs and out of the house. My father used to run to the firehouse. He didn't have a car," Bobby said. The boy rushed to the windows. He scanned the horizon. If there was a glow in the sky, he slipped out of the house without his mother knowing and joined his grandfather, father and the rest of the volunteers at the scene of the fire.

Henry became fire chief in 1954. His handwritten fire log for 1954 didn't even cover a single sheet of spiral notebook paper. Emmaus had just 18 fire calls that year. But they were all real fires. The days of "smells and bells" — automatic alarms, washdowns at auto accidents or burnt toast — were decades in the future.

As a boy, Bobby was big for his age. His first love was firefighting. One of his most cherished possessions to this day is a crinkled black-and-white news photograph of a kid in a striped T-shirt. The kid was helping dozens of men stretch a supply hose two blocks along the railroad tracks to fight a devastating fire at the Pennybacker Foundry fire on July 23, 1944. Huge clouds of dark smoke billowed from the sprawling foundry building. The inferno looked like a scene from the attack on Pearl Harbor just 31 months earlier. The kid in the photo was Bobby Reiss, of course. He was 9 years old. But the photo came with a price. When the hose came uncoupled near where Bobby was standing, an old man chewed Bobby out in Pennsylvania Dutch, then kicked him in the seat of the pants. "It was my first fire call," said Bobby.

There was no television in those days. For entertainment, people gathered at the firehouse, which became the heart of the community's social life with its carnivals, Christmas parties and parades. Patriotic parades! Marching in formation was especially popular with all of the veterans recently re-

Nine-year-old Bobby Reiss (far right in striped shirt) helps haul fire hose
along the railroad tracks as the Pennybacker Foundry burns.
EMMAUS HISTORICAL SOCIETY PHOTO

Bedecked with flowers, Emmaus' brand new 65-foot Seagraves aerial ladder
is followed by a 1920 Ahrens Fox 1,000-gpm pumper, a 1928 Hahn service truck,
a 1928 Hahn 450-gpm pumper and a 1946 Cadillac ambulance
in the 1949 truck dedication parade.

EMMAUS HISTORICAL SOCIETY PHOTOS

turned home from World War II. Only about 7,500 people lived in Emmaus
in 1949. But, counting marchers and spectators, the parade to dedicate Emmaus' new fire truck, a 1949 Seagraves with a 65-foot aerial ladder, more
than doubled the borough's population for a day. The parade lasted for four
full hours. No wonder. The order of march included:

* 37 Fire company marching groups — with 1,900 marchers
* 15 Drum & bugle corps — with 850 marchers
* 20 Ladies auxiliaries — with 700 marchers
* 13 Senior bands — with 650 marchers
* 7 High school bands — with 400 marchers
* 2 String bands — with 110 marchers
* Nearly 100 gleaming fire trucks.

Every marcher in every unit was in full dress uniform. They were exactly one arm's length away from the next person in perfect military "dress
right dress" formation. Everyone was in step. "Flashy" is how Bobby described the marchers' outfits. Headgear included tall busby hats, plumed

Marching unit from Emmaus Fire Co. #1, just one of
three fire companies in Emmaus in 1949.
EMMAUS HISTORICAL SOCIETY PHOTO

shakos, cadet-style and other fancy hats. There were Nassau-style pith helmets, vanguard helmets, doughboy helmets and fire helmets. All the men
wore ties, long-sleeve shirts and white gloves. Women sported skirts, caps
and capes or snappy jackets. Shiny boots were not complete without gaiters
or white spats. Gold braid, brass buttons, and badges sparkled in the bright
May sun.

There was no record of how long the celebration lasted after the parade.
That was probably a good thing, considering that the custom at the time
was to buy a commemorative mug, then drink refills from the free-flowing
beer taps until you dropped.

That was not exactly what the town's founding fathers had in mind on
July 7, 1761, when the leaders of the Moravian *Gemein-Ort* (congregational
village) of Emmaus adopted 45 town regulations "for the physical and spiritual welfare of its inhabitants." As might be expected of a religious commune,
the main emphasis was on the spiritual. Rule 34, for example, specifically stat-
ed that "all gross heathenish Sins, to wit, Whoreing & Wenching, Gluttony &
Drunkenness, Cursing & Swearing, Lying & Cheating, Pilfering & Stealing,
Quarreling & Fighting shall not even be heard of in Emmaus, he that is guilty
of the like cannot be suffered to continue there." Rule 37 dealt directly with

Emmaus' Junior Fire Brigade, 48 strong.
EMMAUS HISTORICAL SOCIETY PHOTO

fire: "Every Man must be circumspect & careful in Regard to Fire & subject himself therein to such Rules as shall be establishe'd amongst us."

Despite such rules a full 110 years passed before history recorded any effort by Emmaus to get serious about firefighting. In 1871, the borough bought a hose cart. The cart had two shoulder-high wooden wagon wheels with long wooden spokes and steel rims. The spokes were painted bright red and trimmed with gold leaf designs. It had a brass bell, swinging brass lantern and two long, straight-bore brass nozzles. The cart carried a big reel of leather fire hose held together with brass rivets. Using metal handholds on the long wooden tongue, four men — not horses — pulled the cart to wherever it was needed. They connected to one of the handful of wooden fire hydrants around Emmaus, or quickly dug down into the ground and bored into a wooden water main. After the fire was out, they plugged the hole with a tapered wooden plug. The location of each plug was carefully marked in case it was needed again. And that's where we got the term "fire plug."

Emmaus' firefighters in 1871 were a dashing bunch. There were 15 of them in the only surviving photo of the first fire brigade. They wore fancy white shirts, cocky hats, and wide sashes around their middles. They looked like a platoon of Civil War Zouaves.

The historic hose cart became a cherished icon at Emmaus Fire Co. No. 1, which grew out of the 1871 fire team. No. 1 received its state charter on March 5, 1902. It was located at the very center of town. Population of Emmaus then was about 1,500. As the borough grew, it added another fire company about every quarter century. Citizens' Fire Co. No. 2 was incorporated on May 9, 1927, and used a Hahn pumper. No. 2's firehouse was on the far west side of the borough. By 1934, Emmaus had 514 volunteer firefighters. On Jan. 9, 1951, Emmaus Volunteer Fire Co. No. 3 became a reality with a firehouse on the far east side of Emmaus. The next year, No. 3's bar and "social quarters" opened for business. And business was brisk! That made three fire companies, and three social quarters with private bars in Emmaus. By 1960, No. 1 had about 1,000 members, No. 2 had 1,100 members, and No. 3 boasted 1,238 members. So the three fire companies had roughly 3,338 "members" — not firefighters — in a town with a population of less than 8,000. Many people belonged to two, or even all three, fire companies, at least socially. And why not? At No. 2, for example, on the day you paid your annual membership dues, your choice of schnapps or beer was free.

"First Pioneer Members of Emaus Fire Co. #1 — 1871," is the caption on this photo. For many years, "Emmaus" was spelled with just one "m," as it was written in old German script. The name was pronounced "E-moss." Pictured, from left to right, are Asst. Chief Bill Luckenbach, John Reinsmith, George Fisher, Edgar F. Romig, Wilson Kemmerer, Jake Schaffer, Howard Shipe, Edwin Rothrock, Isaac Giering, Henry Schuler, Eugene Miller, W.R. Miller, Edwin Gehman, Charles Zelner, and Fire Chief Joseph Finar. The borough's first firefighting equipment — a hand-pulled hose cart with wheels almost as tall as many of the firefighters — is visible at the far left.

PHOTO COURTESY OF EMMAUS FIRE DEPARTMENT

1871 hose cart, with only a little of its leather fire hose remaining .
EMMAUS HISTORICAL SOCIETY PHOTO

"No. 1 was the station for the old guys, where they'd go to play the card game 'Data,'" Bobby said. "No. 2 was known as Duffy's Tavern, because of its long, antique mahogany bar in the basement. For fundraising, they'd have carnivals, complete with Sally Starr (the popular TV cowgirl entertainer from Philadelphia)." When Bobby was a youngster and sent to fetch Henry home from "Duffy's Tavern," his father always gave the boy a nickel. Bobby would buy a pile of candy, then go upstairs to eat and play with the fire trucks until Henry finished his card game and beer. Afterward, Henry and a few other volunteers sometimes hoisted Bobby onto a fire truck and drove the truck a few miles over to Macungie — for a beer. "And I'd get my ass kicked when I got home," Bobby said. "No. 3 was the place you went to raise hell on a Saturday night. You watched the sun come up on Sunday morning."

After graduation from Emmaus High School in 1952, Bobby got a job in the borough's Public Works Department. He stayed there for 20 years, moving up from laborer to superintendent. In the process, he learned more about Emmaus' water mains, water pressure and fire hydrants than anyone alive.

Every Christmas, the firehouse needed a Christmas tree. Scouts combed the countryside. They marked the tree to be cut by hanging two bottles of whiskey from its branches. On one tree-cutting expedition, a firefighter went missing. No one could find him. But the whiskey was drunk and the tree was cut, and the crew headed back to the firehouse. When the tree rolled off of the truck, the missing firefighter rolled out of the tree.

"If you could survive after you fell off of the barstool, you could go on the fire call," Bobby said. "Half of the active members never held a hose. They joined because the Fireman's Relief Association paid a death benefit of $500 for a cost of $1 a year. It was a great deal. Guys were sometimes not in the best of shape at the fire. Others would go into the bar on practice night, and we'd never see them again that night." A few showed up at fires wearing fire helmets backwards and no other gear.

Fire coats, boots and helmets hung on the side of the fire truck. They were neatly organized, from small to large. "Of course, the little guys grabbed the big gear," Bobby said. "And, when you got to the fire, people asked, 'Did you bring a hose?'

"No! Did you bring a hose?"

Such conduct did not go unnoticed by the good citizens of Emmaus. When there was a fire call, Bobby said the typical reaction of what he calls the "sidewalk fire chiefs" was, "Oi, cheese! Here come the drungen firemen, again."

He didn't like that. Not one little bit. "I got tired of the goddamn drunks on the fire trucks," Bobby said. When he became fire chief in 1972, things started to change. He insisted on putting names on fire helmets, "so I knew who to order into a fire and who to put on the nozzle. Some guys just looked busy with a wrench or something, so they didn't have to go inside a fire."

Emmaus didn't lose any firefighters in the line of duty. But a fire police officer was fatally injured when he stepped back in front of a fire truck while directing traffic. His death galvanized many in the three departments. They became committed to improving safety and training and having the most professional volunteer organization possible.

And so, in 1973, the year after Bobby became chief, representatives of the three fire companies formed a committee. They started talking seriously about consolidating the three departments into a single central station. The members eventually voted on the question. The majority of firefighters approved. But Borough Council, in its infinite wisdom, said the citizens of Emmaus, including the thousands of social members, had to have their say, too. So the consolidation question went on the general election ballot in November, 1977.

On the Sunday before the election, firefighters went door-to-door throughout the borough. They passed out a 4-page informational flyer that explained how, with three fire companies, Emmaus had everything from expensive fire trucks to expensive firehouses in triplicate. A central station would save money, they said. A lot of money. It would also improve training and make it easier for the firefighters to train together on the same night of the week. It would provide better fire protection, since the central station

Under the watchful eye of his father, Henry, retiring Emmaus Fire Chief Robert Reiss
proudly pins his chief's badge on his son, James, in 2005.

PHOTO BY GEORGE DEVAULT

would be located in the geographic center of the borough, no more than
1.5 miles from any point in the borough. Response times would be quicker.

Yes, we'd lose "members," they conceded, but not "firefighters." More
than half of the "members" never held a fire hose in their lives. The question
immediately separated the "barflies" from the dragon slayers.

On election day, the consolidation faction also passed out brochures at
the polls. The question passed by 22 percent. The newly reborn Emmaus

Fire Department started off with a solid cohort of 80 bona fide firefighters. About 30 of them were young men, and a few were women, who started out as 18-year-old "juniors" in the 1970s. The group included Bobby's son, James, a future Emmaus fire chief, and Victoria "Tori" Schadler, who learned to drive all of the fire trucks, went on to become assistant fire chief, and worked for more than 35 years as the fire department's only paid, full-time employee. Other juniors later became officers in the Emmaus Fire Department, or they went on to be leaders in fire departments in surrounding communities. And so Emmaus became one of the first volunteer fire departments in Pennsylvania to consolidate, more than 30 years before Harrisburg started actively promoting the idea to eliminate duplication to improve training, service and public safety.

In the new Central Station at 100 N. Sixth St., alcohol was forbidden. The ban on beer and booze was the biggest break with tradition — and perhaps the most controversial part of the change.

"Gott damn!" scoffed a long-time fire chief from rural Lehigh County. "If I can't relax with a coupla beers after a fire call, then that's the day I quit the fire company."

Change, and the fire service's often steadfast resistance to change, was a frequent topic in all of our training classes. "Dinosaurs!" one of our favorite instructors liked to yell. "They're extinct, because all they know how to do is lay more dinosaur eggs."

Dinosaurs are a problem even in cities the size of Boston. "Bunch of dinosaurs" is how the Boston Fire Commissioner Roderick Fraser described his 13 deputy chiefs after they publicly complained to the mayor — and the news media — about Fire Chief Steve Abraira's handling of the terrorist bombings at the Boston Marathon on April 15, 2013. The chief's crime? He dared to institute a new policy that undid centuries of tradition that dictated the highest-ranking officer automatically assumed command whenever he arrived on the scene, even if officers who got there long before already had the situation well in hand. Commissioner Fraser later apologized for his name-calling, but he stood solidly behind his chief, and also his belief that the deputies were being unprofessional by resisting new policy. But it did no good. Controversy raged around Chief Abraira, Boston's first Latino chief and the first chief in the then 335-year history of the Boston Fire Department to come from outside of the department's own labor union. Less than two months after the bombings, Chief Abraira resigned.

Like most volunteer fire companies these days, the beer-loving Pennsylvania chief's department had Standard Operating Guidelines (SOGs), a written rule book that said if you've been drinking, don't respond to a fire call. That looked good on paper. But in practice, not many followed the

SOGs very closely. After all, they're only "guidelines," right? So, after most fire calls, that chief and many of his firefighters drank beer in the firehouse. They drank beer in the firehouse after weekly practice. They drank beer in the firehouse after monthly meetings. And when a fire call came in, they set down their beer cans, hopped on the trucks and roared off into the night. (Under a union contract negotiated in 2002, it was OK for firefighters in Reno, Nevada, to show up for work with a blood alcohol level of up to 0.08 or more than twice the legal driving limit for illegal drugs such as marijuana, cocaine, opiates and amphetamines, according to the *Reno Gazette-Journal*. In mid-2014, the firefighters' union offered to lower the blood alcohol limit to 0.04 and reduce the drug thresholds to match the federal limits for commercial driver's license standards, the newspaper said.)

Instructors at many fire classes openly pick on such chiefs. All officers are easy targets, of course. Cracking on the "white hats" in class guarantees a good laugh. Just like in the military, poking fun at officers, politicians and civilian bureaucrats helps instructors bond more quickly with students. Most students recognize the kernel of truth in what the instructor says: "We all know the election for chief isn't based on who's the best firefighter. It's a popularity contest, pure and simple. And it's usually won by the guy who buys the most beer." Never mind that the guy buying the beer may have all the social graces of a snapping turtle, and a personality to match.

And his actions, said Pennsylvania State Fire Commissioner Ed Mann, may also sometimes be based on "the nonsense that 20 years ago ... the fire chief down the road beat me in wrestling in high school, so now I'm going to buy a rescue truck because he has a rescue truck. But — wait a minute — the guy up the street is buying a ladder truck, which means he's going to try to take calls away from us, and we're closer, so we're going to buy a ladder truck."

In the typical Pennsylvania volunteer fire department, the rank-and-file members elect the fire chief, assistant chief and deputy chief every year. Sometimes the slate of officers completely changes or rotates every year or so. In other departments, being chief seems almost a product of divine right and lasts a lifetime. After the election, the three chief officers appoint captains, lieutenants, engineers and other positions. There are often no formal tests, oral, written or practical, for command positions. Political patronage, "a good old boys' club," some call it. Politics and cliques belong back in high school. They have about as much business in a fire department as an engine room pop machine ... stocked with beer.

But Emmaus' drastic breaks with tradition didn't stop there. And for good reason, starting with the fact that the usual way of doing many things was killing us. Literally.

In 2012, nine firefighters died in the line of duty in Pennsylvania. That tied with North Carolina for the most firefighter deaths in the country that year, according to the U.S. Fire Administration (USFA) in Emmitsburg, Maryland.

In the 30 years from 1981 to 2011, the USFA reported that Pennsylvania had the second highest number of firefighter deaths in the nation, a total of 291. New York had the dubious distinction of being first with 712 firefighter deaths, including the 343 New York City firefighters lost in the collapse of the World Trade Center. California was a distant third with 198 deaths.

Pennsylvania lost an average of almost 10 firefighters — every year — for 30 years. Four out of every five of those fallen firefighters (80.1 percent) were volunteers.

It was one of the reasons why, in the early 1980s, the Pennsylvania State Fire Commissioner's office joined the growing national movement toward voluntary firefighter certification. It was all about safety, the safety of both firefighters and the public we serve.

"The purpose of this program is to identify and recognize emergency service personnel whose accomplishments in training and education meets or exceed nationally recognized standards," said the commissioner's website. This was a level playing field. The same standards applied to firefighters everywhere, from career departments in New York City, Boston, Atlanta, Chicago, Detroit, Denver, Dallas, Phoenix, Los Angeles and San Francisco to the smallest volunteer departments in the Middle of Nowhere, USA.

Standards were set by the National Fire Protection Association. "A Firefighter I is a person who is minimally trained to function safely and effectively as a member of a firefighting team under direct supervision. A person meeting the requirements of Level I is by no means considered a 'complete' firefighter. This is not accomplished until the objectives of both Levels I and II have been satisfied. The Firefighter II may operate under general supervision and may be expected to lead a group of equally or lesser trained personnel through the performance of a specified task," said our training bible, "Essentials of Firefighting."

"Gott damn!" scoffed a long-time fire chief from rural Lehigh County. "If I gotta get a piece of paper that says I'm good to do what I've been doing for the last 40 years, then that's the day I quit the fire company."

Dinosaurs!

"We really are our own worst enemies in the fire service," Chief Reiss said. That became his mantra. He said it again, and again, and again, year after year, not just in private, but also at public hearings at the state and even the national level. "We're our own worst enemies ... because we just won't change. The way we've always done things is the way we have to keep on doing things. And we never tell people about all of the good things we do, the training we go through, the risks we take. When budgets are cut, when fundraising falls, when we lose good members and can't attract enough new ones, all we have to do to find the cause is look in the mirror. We've got nobody to blame but ourselves."

And so this hardheaded, second-generation Pennsylvania Dutch volunteer fire chief kept pushing his department and firefighters into the future. Emmaus soon became one of the first sites in the state offering certification testing. Over 20 years, the Emmaus Training Ground turned out more than 1,000 firefighters nationally certified at the grueling Firefighter I level. Emmaus was the first fire department in Pennsylvania to have at least 75 percent of its members certified as Firefighter I. That milestone merited a formal commendation from the state fire commissioner in a ceremony at the State Fire Academy in 1998.

There were some 77,000 volunteer firefighters in Pennsylvania by the time I got around to testing for Firefighter I. Turned out, I was not the only laggard. The program was 10 years old in Pennsylvania by then, but the number on my certificate was only 4,083. The numbers just went down from there. In 2000, I passed Firefighter II, and received certificate number 1,481. In 2007, I was certified at the advanced Fire Officer I and II levels. My certificate numbers were 985 — and 171, respectively.

Granted, it's not a perfect system. Few educational systems are. For starters, many people just don't have the time. In 2014, when 20-year-old Sam Springsteen, the son of musician Bruce Springsteen, passed Firefighter I at the Monmouth County Fire Academy in New Jersey, the amount of time required for Firefighter I coursework had risen to 188 hours. (Sam joined the Colts Neck Fire Department, which averages about 400 fire calls a year.) The course is usually spread out over about four months of night and weekend classes. You're not allowed to miss many sessions, especially those that demonstrate practical firefighting skills.

Some people just can't take tests very well. They may have a head full of knowledge, common sense and practical experience, but they do poorly on written tests. When one long-time Pennsylvania fire chief failed the Firefighter I test, members of his department razzed him mercilessly. Finally, he quit the fire service in disgust. For a few, failing Firefighter I brought on talk of suicide.

Then there are the physical demands of firefighter certification. Tests are tough, and rightfully so. Fighting fires is tough work. So is wrestling a 100-pound rescue dummy out a second floor window and down a ladder all by yourself, while wearing bunker gear and an air pack. It takes every ounce of strength you can scrape together. Not everybody can do it. And the older you get, the tougher it gets. I was 48 when I tested for Firefighter I. As I was fighting the dummy through the window, I couldn't help but wonder, "Why didn't I do this 10 years ago? Who's the real dummy here, anyway?"

Change in Emmaus didn't stop with certification. Bobby and his officers saw to it that Emmaus was an early adopter of advanced lifesaving technology and techniques. When the price was still up in the $15,000 to $20,000 range, Emmaus bought an infrared rescue camera (also known as a "thermal imager") that let firefighters see through smoke when searching for victims in a fire. It was also useful for finding hidden hotspots in burning buildings, people lost in the woods, and, so the rumor goes, sometimes spotting deer at night. We were among the first in the area to organize "rapid intervention teams (RIT)," specially trained and equipped firefighters who stand ready at emergencies to search for — and rescue — firefighters who get trapped or injured. But one new firefighting tool was so much fun it seemed almost like a big toy. We practically fought over who got to use it. That was the European-made IFEX gun, a long stainless steel tube with a pistol grip, a foregrip, and an air hose. When you pulled the trigger, it sounded and kicked like a 12-gauge shotgun. But, instead of buckshot, it fired plain old water. About one pint at a time, under high pressure from the compressed air in an air pack air bottle on the fire truck or on your back. Jam that baby under the hood of a car, pull the trigger two or three times, and the engine fire is o-u-t. Out! High pressure was the key. It blasted water broken up into such tiny droplets that it instantly sucked up huge amounts of heat, while still penetrating to the seat of the fire. It knocked down a whole room full of fire in no time, and kept firefighters from getting "zapped" by fires in live electrical equipment. I loved it!

On the administrative side, the focus was on something that continually confounded all of the experts. "Retention and recruitment," they call it. In plain English, that meant keeping the good people we have while also bringing in new members. It didn't always work. From 1980 to 1990, membership in the department dropped from nearly 140 to 48, while the number of fire calls more than doubled. Consolidation was mostly to blame for the drop in membership during that decade.

The problem was not confined to Emmaus, however. On July 24, 1996, *USA Today* reported that "Emmaus typifies a national trend in which the number of volunteer firefighters has dropped 5% since 1983, while the number of emergency calls has risen 48%." The headline on the story read, "Reason for alarm: The vanishing volunteer."

One of the first steps Chief Reiss took to keep volunteers was implementing a financial incentive called a "points system," a modest stipend that rewarded volunteers with a couple of bucks for each fire call, overnight "sleep duty" shift, fire practice or work detail they attended. My first year with the department, my points were enough for us to buy our first microwave oven. The oven quickly earned its keep reheating meals I missed because of fire calls. A new "length of service program" will provide a modest pension in our old age. For more than 22 years of service in Emmaus, mine will buy maybe one Happy Meal a month in my old age.

For greater safety, the chief instituted mandatory retirement at age 65, even though it took him and other old-timers off of the active roster long before they were ready to retire. Most fire departments in the state have no set retirement age. You can keep answering fire calls till you drop. And that's exactly what many volunteers do, well into their 60s, 70s, and 80s. Emmaus started a free but mandatory annual physical to help keep us healthy and save the borough big bucks on workers' compensation claims. Giving each firefighter an air mask, instead of sharing common masks that may or may not have been disinfected properly, saved us from continuous sinus infections, and probably worse.

The superheated gases inside a burning building create an atmosphere that experts call an "immediate danger to life and health." Everyone knows it will kill you in no time. But once the fire is out, firefighters can't wait to dump their air packs. Trouble with that is the smoldering building is still spewing out high levels of poisonous gases. The threat may no longer be "immediate," but decades later, it still proves disabling or deadly. And so the chief insisted that we continue to wear air packs while overhauling the building and searching for a cause.

Chief Reiss did not ignore our mental health, either. Long before it became common practice, he introduced psychological counseling — "critical incident stress debriefing," they call it — to help firefighters defuse the mental trauma routinely caused by horrific accidents and fatal fire calls.

Later, paid on-call shifts kept the firehouse staffed 24 hours a day, seven days a week. A crew for the attack truck was never more than a few minutes away on any fire call. That cut response times, and it increased safety for both the public and firefighters. Quarter-an-hour pay increases also rewarded each advance in training, certification and rank.

But there was a catch: The chief demanded a lot from us in return. We had to maintain minimum attendance, training and response standards. He "fired" volunteers who didn't. We had to keep up with training, especially annual refreshers on handling hazardous materials incidents, driving an emergency vehicle, working as part of a RIT team, flashover survival, and more. And so, Tuesday night became sacred for me. Just as many normal people religiously reserve certain nights for bowling, playing poker, bingo or going out drinking, Emmaus' volunteer firefighters scheduled Tuesday evenings for playing with fire.

The spectacular view inside of a flashover simulator.

CHAPTER SIXTEEN

"Playing" With Fire

I'm inside a giant woodstove. Fire's burning. Smoke's building. Temperature's rising. Where I sit on the floor, it's a relatively "comfortable" 150 degrees F, plus. A few inches above my head, the temperature is anywhere from 250 to 400 degrees. Five feet above the floor, it's about 600. At the ceiling, it's more than 900 degrees, hotter than the inside of a self-cleaning oven when it's cleaning — and automatically locked shut — to keep the curious from ending up on life support at the nearest hospital burn unit.

This particular woodstove weighs more than three tons. It's about 30 feet long, eight feet wide and eight feet high. The device is actually a corrugated steel (14-gauge) shipping container that's set up like a two-level woodstove with a combustion chamber, ash pit, air vents, damper, and flue. Seven other firefighters, a state-certified instructor and I are kneeling on the floor. We're wearing full bunker gear and air packs and are breathing air out of the air bottles on our backs. We try to stay low, kneeling with our butts on our heels. No one even thinks of standing.

A small fire of wood scraps and straw burns unchecked in a corner of the upper third of the structure, which is properly known as a "Swede flashover simulator." The device was developed in Sweden in the mid-1980s to help firefighters learn the warning signs of an impending flashover. A flashover occurs when the burning contents of a room reach ignition temperature and everything simultaneously explodes into flames. It happens quickly, often trapping firefighters in temperatures of 900 to 1,100 degrees. Few survive, which is exactly why we're baking ourselves in this crude oven. We need to know our enemy, recognize and memorize the telltale warning signs of an approaching flashover. We're literally playing with fire inside this huge metal box. "Twisting the dragon's tail," some say. Like Drew Barrymore in Stephen King's "Firestarter," we're well on our way to incinerating the world.

Flames lick the walls and ceiling, which are covered with full sheets of particleboard that give off cancer-causing formaldehyde (embalming fluid) and other poisonous gasses. The tan boards are turning black, starting to burn. We have two fire hoses. Both are full of water under pressure. But we're not doing anything to put the fire out. Just the opposite. We want to let it burn, reach its peak, almost. We want to see what few firefighters ever see — and live to tell the tale.

We let the fire build. Heat bears down on us, cutting through our heavy coats like they're T-shirts. Smoke changes color. The light show begins. Long, twisting ribbons of burning gases snake out into the air above our helmets. Yellow, orange, blue green: The changing colors are beautiful, hypnotic like the Northern Lights. We could watch these fire snakes all night. Instead, we take turns at the nozzle closest to the fire. The instructor's right beside us. The heat there is fierce, almost unbearable. Just before things get out of control, the firefighter on the nozzle fires a few bursts of water straight up into the air. They're like quick pricks with a sharp pencil. The shots are just a second or two each. But they have the same effect as Barrymore commanding her pyrokinetic fire demons to *"Back off! Back off!"*

The water instantly vaporizes. None comes back down on us. At least, it's not supposed to. If it does, we sprayed too much, and risk instantly cooking ourselves in a 1,000-degree steam bath. The short shots keep the worst heat where it belongs, at the ceiling, instead of "disrupting the thermal layers," as the instructor likes to say, and swirling the blistering heat right down on top of us.

Another firefighter rotates to the nozzle. Heat builds. Fire snakes dance. A couple more pencil pricks. *"Back off! Back off!"* The fire obeys. Everyone takes a turn at the nozzle. We call it a night, a good night. There were no burns, no melting helmets. The only thing steaming after we finally put the fire out is the nearest neighbor. He's hopping mad about all the smoke billowing around his house because the wind's blowing from the wrong direction, again.

The flashover simulator cost about $12,000 when it was added to the Emmaus Training Grounds on Klines Lane behind the Emmaus Waterworks in 1992. At the time, it was one of the first flashover simulators in the United States east of the Mississippi. The Pennsylvania State Fire Academy did not install a flashover simulator until June 2013.

The flashover simulator is just one item on a long list of additions to the Emmaus Training Grounds, which began humbly enough in 1968 with a four-story cement block training tower. Over the years, training fires got so hot they cracked the walls. Live burns on the grounds were suspended for years until an all-metal "smokehouse" that cost nearly half a million dollars made real fires possible again. There are basic and advanced air pack mazes, stations to teach and practice proper forcible entry techniques, hose advancement, raising and lowering ladders, water supply, fire suppression,

Dedication of "smokehouse" and training tower at the Emmaus
Fire Department's Training Grounds in 1968.

roof ventilation, vehicle rescue, confined-space rescue, firefighter survival,
and much more. The training grounds are both torture chamber and firefighter's fantasyland. They prove the undoing of many wannabe firefighters,
hone the skills of those who have the right stuff, and so save countless lives,
which is exactly their purpose.

(Full disclosure: "Flashover Survival" is a doctoral level course. It's not
for raw recruits. Same for "Firefighter Survival," which teaches us how to
scramble out of upper-story windows when there is a flashover or other

life-threatening emergency. Escape techniques include sliding down ropes and going down ladders headfirst. We're wearing full bunker gear and air packs, plus safety harness and lifelines, of course. "If you ever do this for real, you'll probably get hurt," instructors caution. "But you will be alive!" One can only hope.)

Nearly every Tuesday night, you can find the entire fire department at the training grounds for our regular weekly "fire practice." Special classes bring many of us back one or two more nights a week for many weeks in a row. Most 16-hour classes, such as basic vehicle rescue, incident safety officer, flashover survival, firefighter survival, emergency-vehicle operator, incident command systems, air pack basic training, hazardous materials awareness, basic wildlands firefighter, emergency response to terrorism: basic concepts, are perfect for two full days. Of course, those days are usually Saturday and Sunday. Weekends go by all too quickly. Here's a look at some of the other things we do at the training grounds:

Roof Simulator — Climbing a ladder onto any roof can be tricky, even in broad daylight, using both hands. Now, imagine trying it at night with wind driving rain or snow into your face. First, double check for electrical wires overhead, since metal ladders are excellent conductors. But no way can you get a firm grip on the ladder with both hands because you're carrying an axe and a big pry bar or maybe a heavy-duty chain saw.

Sounds like a surefire recipe for disaster, doesn't it? That's why we practice, and practice some more, in a place where a fall won't cause fractures or be fatal. At least, we hope it won't when mistakes are made, which they are. Our roof simulator is only two feet off of the ground. At its peak, the pitched roof is just 10 feet high. The slope is not too steep, but when you're carrying an armload of tools and wearing 60 extra pounds of gear, it's challenging enough.

The ladder is a "roof ladder." Spring-loaded hooks at one end secure it to the peak of the roof, so you don't have to worry about it sliding out from under you. Just make sure the roof is not burning out from under you.

How do you get a roof ladder up on the roof? Simple. In real life, you carry it up a extension ladder on one shoulder, while climbing the extension ladder to the roof of the first floor, or maybe even the second floor. It depends ... on the location of the fire ... the construction of the building, and a lot of other variables. Then, while standing on the extension ladder and using both arms, you muscle the roof ladder over the eave and push it up onto the roof until the hooks catch over the peak of the roof.

Once your roof ladder is securely in position, climb aboard. Just keep a firm grip on the roof ladder, and watch your step, as you ease off of the extension ladder and onto the roof ladder. Your work platform is now the roof ladder. Take your axe and "sound" or thump the roof in a few places to make sure it's still solid. Next, give the Halligan bar a mighty swing, and sink the spike head of the tool up to the hilt in the roof a couple of feet from the roof ladder. The Halligan, also known as the "hooligan tool," is the ultimate multipurpose emergency tool. The one-piece steel bar comes in lengths of from 24 inches to 42 inches. Depending on size, it may weigh from six to 10 pounds. At one end is a huge "claw" or fork that's perfect for prying open doors or popping car doors or hoods. The other end consists of an adze, and a long tapered pick end, or a spike. With the spike sunk firmly in the roof, the head of the Halligan becomes a secure foothold. With one foot on the roof ladder and the other foot on the Halligan, the drill is to then cut a hole in the roof with a chain saw or axe. Our goal is a hole at least two-foot square. Four feet square is better. That allows superheated gasses and smoke to escape from inside the burning building. For maximum benefit, you want to do this almost directly over the fire.

Why is ventilation important? Think of a bag of microwave popping corn. You're tired of having so many unpopped kernels in the bottom of the bag, so you nuke the corn just as long as possible without scorching. At the very last second, you yank the bag out of the microwave, and rip the top wide open, releasing a buttery cloud of white steam. If you wait just a few seconds too long, acrid smoke pours from the bag as the white puffs inside turn to black charcoal. You burn your fingers. But, hopefully, there's no red glow deep down inside the bag.

Whether you're cutting holes in the roof or smashing windows or doors for ventilation, good communication and coordination are essential. Before you open up anything, make darn sure that the hose teams inside have water and are ready to go. Any ventilation feeds fresh air to the fire. It turns a tame little pussycat of a fire into a fire-breathing dragon in seconds. The results can be deadly.

Air Pack Maze — A pair of 12-by-56-foot mobile homes (purchased for $25!) might not sound like much of a challenge, but they're the ruin of many would-be interior firefighters. That's because they're completely gutted, interconnected with a short "tunnel," and then rebuilt ... six different ways from the way you come in. Trailer No. 1 is the "basic maze." Trailer No. 2 is "advanced." Crawl through them both, and you'll come out the other end with an empty air bottle, drenched in sweat, and dragging your air pack behind so that your body can fit through the ever-tightening tunnel.

It's nothing at all like the air pack maze scene in the movie version of Nora Roberts' "Blue Smoke." No flames light your way. There's no light of any kind. Every crack and little hole that might allow even a pinprick of light inside has been carefully sealed. You're in total, suffocating darkness. (Nora is spot on with her description in the book.) That's why Hollywood will never be able to get a lot of firefighting right on film. The color of fire at this stage is inky black, which completely hides the faces of even the brightest movie stars.

Each trailer has two tiers of 3-foot-square tunnels that go up, down, and around. There are hanging wires that snag your gear. Do you have a pair of wire cutters somewhere in the cargo pockets of your bunker pants, just in case? There are movable trap doors, tilting boards, up ramps, down ramps and false passages that lead to ... absolutely nowhere. In real life, that sometimes happens with stairways when a house gets a major makeover. You're merrily humping hose up the stairs in the dark and smoke to reach the fire on the second floor before it gets into the cache of ammunition, when ... Wham!" ... your helmet slams into something solid. It's not a trapdoor, but a solid floor. Someone completely closed off the inside stairway to create a separate upstairs apartment. They just left the stairs intact to mess with you.

Don't worry, in our training maze, "panic doors" are strategically located here and there, in case you have to bail out. An instructor with a flashlight is always close by. There are lights inside, but instructors seldom turn them on. Wastes electricity. You *know* there is a way out. You keep reassuring yourself with that thought as you crawl through the blackness. But on a real fire call, there might not be an exit. That's why we do this in practice, over and over again. Keeping your cool when it looks like there's no escape may someday save lives, starting with your own.

Sprinkler Station — Many commercial buildings and even some homes now have sprinkler systems. They're a fantastic tool to slow or stop the spread of fire early on. But once they're activated and start spraying water all over the place, they also cause a lot of damage. Besides turning off the water main, the best way to shut off a sprinkler head is to jam two wooden wedges into the small opening that's spraying water in all directions. You do that from a stepladder set up directly underneath the sprinkler head. The water's under pressure. It's not just a limp trickle. Both arms are fully extended, straight up. Water sprays in your face. No matter how you try to avoid it, water runs into the sleeves of your bunker coat, and then down your arms.

Work fast, fumblefingers, before the cold, cold water runs down the whole length of your body inside your bunker gear and fills your boots.

Forcible Entry — Rule No. 1: Before you smash any locks, glass or door frames, try opening the door. It may already be unlocked.

You'll look pretty stupid and cause a lot of unnecessary property damage by destroying doors or windows that are unlocked, instructors caution. It's a big "Oops!"

Rule No. 2: Remember Rule No. 1.

Smashing windows is simple enough. Stand to one side and whack the glass with the flat side of an axe head or a Halligan bar. Then use whatever tool you have to clear the shards of glass from the window frame to allow a safer entry. Gloves and eye protection are mandatory.

Doors are a little trickier. They come with all kinds of different frames and locks. On most residential doors, one firefighter works a Halligan bar into the door frame near the lock. Then another firefighter whacks it with an axe or a sledgehammer. That pops the lock or splinters the frame, or both.

But nothing can prepare you for what you may find inside. Case in point is an early-morning fire call when the dispatcher warns responding crews that the nearest fire hydrant is "disabled." Actually, it's been deliberately trashed, smashed by a tractor-trailer truck. That semi now blocks the only road leading to the burning building. The pumper can't get close to the fire. Our 150-foot preconnect hose doesn't quite reach the front door, so we quickly add an extra section of hose.

As soon as the door flies open, we know we're in trouble. Our flashlights reveal a seemingly endless, perfectly straight line of two-liter plastic pop bottles along one wall. They're full of a yellowish liquid that looks suspiciously like gasoline. Spot fires burn here, there, everywhere. There's no single point of origin, no neat burn pattern. This was no accident. Someone obviously sloshed gasoline all over the place, then lit a match. Even with the extra section of hose, we can barely reach the far wall inside the building.

The whole place is a dark, spooky maze. Looks like the lower level of the killer's house in "Silence of the Lambs."

We're deep in the dark inside, spraying water on a small fire at the head of the stairs when my walkie-talkie crackles to life.

"Attention, all interior crews ... use extreme caution," warns the dispatcher. "Police advise the man who set the fire is still inside. He's got a gun!"

And we don't. All we have is a fire hose. Our axe and Halligan bar are back at the doorway. The big room is full of firefighters now.

"Everybody out!" I yell through my air mask.

Firefighters look at me like I'm nuts. "Whaddaya mean, out? We just got here!"Assistant Chief John Shafer and I start herding bewildered firefighters toward the door. John has the nozzle. If need be, it will make a good club. I grab an empty half-gallon wine bottle sitting nearby, and listen for the click of the hammer cocking on a Colt Python. If Jame "Buffalo Bill" Gumb, the psychopathic killer from "Lambs," jumps out of the darkness at us, we're going to go down swinging. Where's Jodie Foster when we need her and her Smith & Wesson .357?

Once we're out of the building, two Emmaus police officers don air packs. One is former Emmaus fire lieutenant Todd Garloff, a good man to have on your side in a firefight. Cautiously, the cops go upstairs with flashlights and drawn weapons. They find the arsonist in bed, a gun still clutched in his dead hand.

We're lucky. We get to go home that morning. A few months later, on March 8, 2000, firefighters responding to an eerily similar fire call in Memphis don't go home. As they arrived on the scene, the gunman who set his house on fire charged out of the garage with a gun blazing. He killed two Memphis firefighters and a sheriff's deputy.

"We don't expect this," Memphis Fire Chief H.J. Pickett told *The New York Times*. "We're here to fight fires. You want to say it's part of the job, but it's not."

Part of the job or not, attacks on firefighters have become more common over the years. On Christmas Eve, 2012, volunteers from the West Webster, New York, Fire Department responded to a report of a car fire. As they climbed off of the first fire truck at the scene, a gunman waiting in the dark ambushed them with an assault rifle. Two firefighters died. Two others were seriously wounded. Just four months later, in suburban Atlanta, Georgia, a gunman lured Gwinnett County firefighters into his home by faking a heart attack. He held four firefighters hostage at gunpoint for four hours. Finally, police stormed the house. The gunman was killed and a police officer was wounded in an exchange of gunfire. The firefighters received only minor injuries.

Around the country, the attacks have continued. By late 2013, the Federal Emergency Management Agency recommended that fire departments seriously consider adding body armor — bulletproof vests — to standard firefighting gear.

After six months of basic training and then answering enough fire calls, I finally got measured for brand-new gear. It was beautiful, custom-fit for my lanky limbs, 36-inch inseam and arms, and 34-inch waist. There was thick padding on the knees. Heavy leather patches also protected knees, shoulders, elbows, cuffs and cargo pockets. There were deep pockets on the chest for radios, and bright reflective strips on ankles, wrists and waist.

The gear also came with some very special labels. They were not prestigious designer labels from Armani or Gucci, but warning labels that were sewn into both my new bunker coat and pants. The lettering was all in bold

LEFT: New bunker gear doesn't stay that way for long.
RIGHT: "Jethro," whom we bought from fellow firefighters Curt and
Doreen Hinkle, curls up on bunker gear after a fire call.
PHOTOS BY RUTH DEVAULT

red type. Much of it was in capital letters. Clearly, the labels were written by lawyers, not the manufacturer's marketing department:

DANGER
DO NOT USE THIS GARMENT IF YOU HAVE NOT READ AND UNDERSTOOD THE ENTIRE FEMSA (Fire and Emergency Manufacturers and Services Association) OFFICIAL USER INFORMATION GUIDE AND ALL LABELS FOR STRUCTURAL FIRE FIGHTING PROTECTIVE GARMENT!

* Fire fighting is an ULTRAHAZARDOUS, UNAVOIDABLY DANGEROUS activity. Neither this garment nor any other will protect you from all burns, injuries, diseases, conditions or hazards. No protective garment can replace proper training and constant practice in fire fighting tactics and safety. Consistent with OSHA regulations, this garment is offered for fire departments (paid or volunteer) or other employers to evaluate and decide for themselves whether or not it provides an acceptable level of protection for their emergency operations. You may be KILLED, BURNED, INJURED OR SUFFER DISEASE OR ILLNESS with NO WARNING and NO SIGN of damage to this garment.

115

* You will increase your risk of DEATH, BURNS, INJURY, DISEASE OR ILLNESS if you do not strictly comply with the entire FEMSA OFFI-CIAL USER INFORMATION GUIDE and LABELS.

* Wearing this or any protective garment may increase your risk of heat stress which may cause heart attack, stroke, dehydration, or other conditions resulting in DEATH, INJURY or ILLNESS.

* You may NOT feel heat under this garment before suffering a BURN... .

DO NOT REMOVE THIS LABEL.

There was just one tiny problem with my beautiful, clean and new bunker gear. It didn't stay beautiful, clean and new for very long. As soon as it arrived, we had another fire call.

PART 4

Baptism by Fire

CHAPTER SEVENTEEN

How Was Your Fire, Honey?

Dec. 7, 1984 — It's a normal, quiet Friday morning in downtown Emmaus. Temperature is in the high 20s. Sky is clear, pale blue. Sun is shining brightly. Around the Triangle in the center of town — the standing joke is the founding fathers were too cheap to build a town square — the part-time special policeman is leisurely halting a trickle of traffic on Chestnut Street to let a few package-laden Christmas shoppers across the street. There's not much wind and no snow on the ground. Inside the landmark John Gould Store, the clerks are stocking the shelves with another shipment of Christmas cards, gift wrap and other holiday necessities. Across Main Street in Richard's Market, Richard is busy slicing meat and getting all of the fixings ready for the lunchtime crowd that will soon come charging in for his famous sandwiches. Tellers in both banks are filling their cash drawers, preparing for the weekly flood of paychecks that will soon need to be cashed to grease the gears of commerce. At Wentz Hardware they're setting out the latest in snow blowers, snow shovels and ice scrapers. The 60-foot pine tree in the center of the Triangle has just been decorated from top to bottom with big red bows. Its hundreds of lights will officially be turned on at a special ceremony on Sunday evening. Borough workers are hauling in the last of the traffic barricades for the big event while a radio repairman tests the borough's two-way radios. The holiday countdown is on. Only 18 shopping days left until Christmas. It's not quite 10 o'clock in the morning, but up and down Main Street, the downtown merchants are getting ready. Another Friday is building toward an evening rush hour, Main Street will be choked with traffic in both directions, sidewalks overflowing and cash registers jingling madly. There is peace on Earth, goodwill ...

Then the emergency telephone at the Emmaus Communications Center clatters to life in the basement of Borough Hall. The dispatcher on duty is Grace Fritch. She's the mother of Emmaus Firefighter Gary Fritch and a Mom of sorts to many other firefighters, also an institution in her own right in Emmaus. The ringing phone automatically switches on a tape recorder: *Ring ... ring ...*

Caller # 1: (Sounds of sobbing, choking, gasping.)

Dispatcher: *Emmaus Comm Center.*

Bell Telephone operator: *She said, "Help, help, help! FIRE!" My party left the phone. I don't know where she is.*

Dispatcher: *Operator, get your supervisor — and trace the call.*

Operator to supervisor: *This lady came on screaming, "Fire, fire, fire!" I connected her with the fire department. I don't know where she is now. The fire company is on the line and wants you to trace the call.*

Supervisor: *Did you ring her back? What's the number?*

Operator: *Yeah ... She has the receiver off. Hold on ... Just a minute, ma'am ... OK, we're trying to trace this call. Just a minute, ma'am. You can hear something crackling ... Ma'am? Can you hear something crackling?*

Dispatcher: *Yeah.*

Operator: *She must have left the house then.*

Dispatcher: *I don't blame her.*

Operator: *I hope she did.*

Hello? Ma'am? I can hear somebody in the background. Ma'am! Where are you located? Hell-oh!

Dispatcher: *Give us a street!*

Operator: *She's not ... Ma'am! You can hear it.*

Dispatcher: *I hear her. And I hear something going on.*

Operator: *Yeah, you can hear, you can hear something crackling.*

Dispatcher: *Your supervisor is checking this out, right?*

Operator: *Yes, two of them are. Hello? Ma'am, where are you located?* (Sound of TV or radio in background, more crackling, rustling, other noises.) *She hung up.*

Dispatcher: *No, she didn't hang up.*

Operator: *Unless the line went dead.* (More garble, blaring audio in background, crackling noise.) *I wonder. Should we contact the police?*

Dispatcher: *This is the police department. We handle fire, ambulance and police.*

Emmaus Ambulance on radio: *32 to 33* [dispatcher's call number].

Dispatcher: *Yeah. 32.*

Ambulance: *32 is 10-7* [out of service], *quarters.*

Dispatcher: *10-4* [acknowledged], *32. 09:50 hours.*

Ring ... ring ...

Dispatcher: *Wait, hold on a second. Uh, Betty can you get that?*

Second Dispatcher: *Emmaus Comm Center.*

Caller #2: *Hi, um, there is a fire at 656 Fernwood Street in Emmaus. Our driver just called in, and he said the house is ablaze.*

Operator: *Now she hung up on us. Ma'am?*
Dispatcher: *What is it? 656 Fernwood Street. All right, I got it.*

The dispatcher throws the switch that activates a high-low alarm tone on all Emmaus Fire Department radios and personal pagers. "Beep!" screams the pager on my belt.

"*Emmaus Fire Department, respond dwelling fire, 656 Fernwood Street. Emmaus Fire Department, respond dwelling fire, 656 Fernwood Street. 09:50 hours.*"

I'm at work. And I'm in the middle of something urgent, so I don't run for the door right away.

Fire Chief Robert Reiss: *31 to 33.*
Dispatcher: *31.*
Fire Chief: *What do you have?*

Ring ... ring ...
Dispatcher: *Emmaus Comm Center.*
Caller #3: (An elderly woman. Her voice is frail, trembling.) *There is a fire at 656 Fernwood ...*
Dispatcher: *Is there anybody in the house?*
Elderly woman: *I don't know.*
Dispatcher: *OK. OK, thank you. Bye-bye.*
Elderly woman: *There must be. Yes! The car is there.*
Fire Chief: *Is there anyone in the house? Can you find out?*
Dispatcher: *This call came in through the operator. There is possibly somebody inside the house.*
Fire Chief: *10-4.*
Engine 34: *34 to 33.*
Dispatcher: *Unit calling 33?*
Engine 34: *34 is 10-8* [responding], *fire call.*
Dispatcher: *10-4. 09:53 hours.*
Policeman on the scene: *Oh, man! Let's go, fellas. It's really burning — bad!*
Dispatcher: *33 to 31. Be advised, per police, it IS a worker!*
Fire Chief: *Is everybody out of there?*
Policeman on the scene: *Let's go! There are supposed to be two people in this thing! It's really burning — bad!*

Engine 35: *35 to 33. 10-8.*
Dispatcher: *10-4, 35. 09:55 hours.*
Asst. Chief: *Portable 2 to 31.*

Fire Chief: *31.*

Portable 2: *Supposed to be two people trapped up in the back.*

Fire Chief: *31 to 34.*

Engine 34: *34.*

Fire Chief: *You'll have to get that ladder off. Portable 2, come in.*

Portable 2: *Go ahead, Chief.*

Fire Chief: *Are they on the second floor?*

Portable 2: *Yes, they are, Chief.*

Fire Chief: *I didn't catch you. Are they on the second floor?*

Portable 2: *Yes, they are, Chief. The people are on the second floor.*

Fire Chief: *34, you're going to have to get that ladder off, right off the bat. Get those people out!*

Unidentified unit: *... whole front of the house!*

Fire Chief: *Sound a second alarm!*

Dispatcher: *10-4. 09:56 hours.*

Emmaus Fire Department, respond second alarm, dwelling fire, 656 Fernwood Street. Emmaus Fire Department, respond second alarm, 656 Fernwood Street. It IS a worker. 09:57 hours.

Whatever I'm doing at work, it can wait. I hop in my pickup and shoot down the alley, but I get stuck at the traffic light at Third and Main Streets. When the light changes I'm off like a shot. I turn left in front of opposing traffic and gun it up Main Street. Luckily, my shifter doesn't lock up when I jam it into second. It's smooth sailing all five blocks to the firehouse.

Central Station: *Central Station to 31.*

Dispatcher: *Emmaus Ambulance, a driver is needed for a second ambulance for a dwelling fire at 656 Fernwood Street. 09:58 hours.*

Engine 35: *35 to Portable 2.*

Portable 2: *35, come to the scene. 35, give us your people!*

Central Station: *Central Station to 34.*

Engine 34: *This is 34. Go ahead Central Station.*

Central Station: *34, do you want 37* [a pumper] *or 36* [aerial ladder] *to roll?*

Engine 34: *Standby a minute ...*

Ring ... ring ...

Dispatcher: *Emmaus Comm Center.*

Caller #5: *Hi. This is Gretchen from Red Hill* [Savings & Loan]. *Can I have an escort to the bank, please?*

Dispatcher: *Uh, you're going to have to hold on for awhile. We have a dwelling fire. Can you call back later?*

Engine 34: *34 to Central Station.*
Central Station: *Central 'by.*
Engine 34: *Respond with 36.*
Central Station: *36 will be responding with three.*

Ladder 36 with three. That's me. We have a driver and an officer in the front seat. The lone firefighter, I'm in the jump seat on the passenger's side, behind the officer. The opposite jump seat is empty. There is no time to wait for anyone else. Minutes matter on this call. Maybe even seconds. They may mean the difference between life and death, if it's not already too late. The fire has an incredible head start, from the sound of it on the radio. If we had known the address when the call first came in, it might not be such a problem. But it sounds like the fire was so far advanced when the woman called that heat and smoke knocked her out while she was on the phone. That delay may cost her her life. As I struggle into the shoulder straps of my air pack, I just pray she got out in time — and no one else is inside. God help them if they are because, by now, we may not be able to.

Ring ... ring ...
    Dispatcher: *Emmaus Comm Center.*
    Caller #7: *Hi. This is Nancy Shot at WSAN* [a local radio station]. *We have a report of a fire ... Do you have any injuries?*
    Dispatcher: *We have no idea.*
    Radio reporter: *Is it two-alarm?*
    Dispatcher: *Who's calling?*
    Radio reporter: *WSAN.*
    Dispatcher: *I'm sorry. You're going to have to call back later.* (Click.)
    Ladder 36: *Ladder 36 to base 33. 36 is 10-8, fire call.*
    Dispatcher: *10-4, 36. 10:04 hours.*
    Actually, we've been 10-8 for about two minutes. We're already more than halfway to the fire. The radio is so jammed with calls from everyone at the scene that our officer can't get a word in edgewise. We're flying down Harrison Street in our 1972 American LaFrance ladder truck with the 100-foot aerial ladder. Whoever is driving is pouring it on. We must be doing at least 50 miles an hour in a 25 zone. Good thing the cops aren't sitting at the bottom of the hill by Meadow Pool with their radar gun, as usual. They must all be at the fire.

We'll be at the fire in a minute, too. Red lights flashing and sirens wailing, the officer hangs on the air horn as we cross four-lane Lehigh Street. We have the green light, but that doesn't always mean much at this intersection. Can't be too careful.

With that in mind, I quickly check over all of my gear: Rescue strap, pocket flashlight, air pack, good seal on my air mask, helmet ear flaps down over my Nomex hood, chin strap tight and coat collar up, buckled and snapped. Good. Now, let's just get there and get to work.

Waiting is the worst part. We're only seconds away, but my mind races with questions. From the chatter on the radio, we know it is a worker, and a bad one. We know there may be at least one person trapped inside. Are there more? How many? Where? What room? What will the fire conditions be like? Is it anyone I know? Our good friends the Bentleys live on Fernwood Street. Billy Bentley is in my son's class at elementary school. What's their house number? Please, don't let it be the Bentleys.

Enough! I have to control my breathing, slow it down to conserve air once I turn on my air tank. Suddenly, the driver jams on the air brakes. We're at the fire.

Engine 36: *36 to 31. Where do you want us?*

Fire Chief: *Air packs! Front of the building! Immediately!*

The chief's in my face as I step off of the truck. I've never seen him so wound up. No wonder. We haven't found the caller yet. She may still be inside her burning house. It's an older, two-story frame building on a corner lot. The house has been added onto again and again in the back. Flames have been knocked back from the front door and part of the first floor by the first hose crew. It was no easy battle. You can tell from all the scorch marks around the front door that the first hose team really took a beating. The rest of the house is a raging, smoke-filled inferno. A towering column of heavy, dark smoke blocks out the sun.

"There is a body inside that door," the chief yells. "Find it!"

The closest firefighter with an air pack is Lt. Jim Reiss, the chief's son. We team up, stop for a moment, kneeling on the front porch to check our air packs. Then we crouch down below the smoke and crawl in through the front door on our hands and knees. Heat and smoke hit us like a club. My face mask has a good seal, but with the first few breaths I can already taste the bitter smoke in my mouth as we swim into a thick soup of heat and smoke. I feel the poison seeping through my clothes and into my skin. (The human body is like a sponge. I'll taste and smell the smoke in my hair and fingernails for days. It happens at every worker.) Darkness closes over us. The fire swallows us whole. I can't see. I feel like I'm smothering. For just a moment, I want to rip off my face mask, jump up and run outside. But if I do, I know that I won't even make it to the front door.

So we push on, deeper and deeper into heart of the inferno. We don't have a choice. We don't have a hose line, either. Except for our bunker gear and air packs, we are completely defenseless against the fire. This is strictly an emergency search-and-rescue mission. Hit and run, a lightning charge, a quick but thorough search and a hasty retreat — hopefully, with a living victim. We're moving fast, breathing hard and constantly yelling back and forth inside our face masks so that we know where the other person is, what he's doing and how much flame, heat and smoke we're dealing with. It's so hot inside the burning house, and conditions are so unstable, that the chief fears we might get instantly incinerated by a flashover. That possibility is not far from our minds, either. But Jim and I take some small comfort from the fact that everything that could possibly burn inside the house is already in flames. If there was going to be a flashover, it's already happened and engulfed the people who live there.

We start our search to the right in the front room. Maybe we turn that way because the smoke is not quite as thick or dark as in the other direction. There's just a tiny bit more light coming in through the windows in the next room. It's not much more light, but maybe just enough to attract a confused and panicky fire victim. Another rescue team comes in behind us. They turn left into the darkest room.

Jim and I are crawling over, through and around great piles of burning debris: furniture, clothing, newspapers and magazines. There are piles of stuff all over the place. Flames are everywhere, on everything. Bright red, orange and yellow fingers of flame dance freely over chairs, a coffee table and an ironing board. Where's the iron? Is that the culprit that unleashed this fire? Our insulated coats, pants and heavy leather gloves are not fire-proof, but they will protect us from the worst of the flames and glowing coals, just as long as we keep moving. We're not about to sit still.

Working more by feel than sight, we search corners, under and around furniture. We're hoping that everyone is already out of the house. But we're also praying that if someone is still inside, we find them quickly. If we're lucky, we can get them outside to fresh air and bottled oxygen in time so that they'll live. But we find no one. We see only hungry flames licking higher and higher as the fire roars back to life. Suddenly, our air pack alarms start ringing, first mine and then Jim's. Those incessant, angry bells mean we have only a few minutes of air left. It's time to get out. The other team is still searching the darker side of the first floor. Good luck, guys!

The fire chief and other officers call for more hoses, more pressure, more firefighters, as the whole house erupts in flame again. *"Going full tilt!"* the radio crackles. Then someone calls the ambulance crew to bring a stretcher to the east side of the house. The other search crew found what we were looking for.

Police Unit 104: *Call the coroner and tell him to come out here.*
Dispatcher: *10-4. 10:19 hours.*

Ring ... ring ...

Caller # 12: *Yeah, do you know if they have that fire at 656 Fernwood under control yet?*

Dispatcher: *No.*

Caller: *They don't?*

Dispatcher: *No.*

Caller: *Oh, God!*

"Oh, God!" is right. This fire's a long way from being under control. And one of the rescue teams just found the second victim upstairs. We're moving a ladder to the front porch roof and climbing with coils of rope and a Stokes basket, a body-shaped stretcher made of welded metal and wire with foot-high sides.

Dispatcher: *Coroner notified. 10:21 hours.*

Ring ... ring ...

Caller #13: *Hey, what's the problem?*

Dispatcher: *I got a fire. I don't have time to talk.*

Ring ... ring ...

Caller #14: *Yeah, good morning. This is Domino's Pizza. Would it be possible for you to let us know when they come back in with the trucks because we'd like to send some pizzas to the firehouse for them?*

Dispatcher: *What's your phone number?*

Fire Chief: *Contact the Red Cross and see if you can get some coffee out here for these guys.*

Dispatcher: *10-4. 10:40 hours.*

I sure could use a cup of hot black coffee. Three fingers of whiskey would be even better. Maybe tonight. But even the Red Cross coffee is going to have to wait. I'm climbing an aluminum extension ladder on the side of the house, carrying a coil of heavy rope and an extra air bottle. Our guys are muscling the second victim out of a second floor window. It's no easy job. He's a tall, big man who was overcome by smoke long before we got to him.

Now his body lies faceup on a small porch roof outside a bedroom window. Asst. Chief Ed Orach, his air mask hanging from the front of his once-white bunker coat, looks directly at me across the fallen man. Ed has tears in his reddened eyes, but they're not caused by the thick smoke. Ed's one of the firefighters who found the body. The man's wispy gray hair is tousled from sleep. It looks like he just got out of bed. He's wearing white flannel pajamas with blue stripes. "Somebody ... get a blanket ... now," Ed shouts.

The blanket arrives. We cover the man and strap him into the Stokes basket. With a heavy rope attached to the basket, other firefighters ease the basket down another ladder while I climb up onto the main roof. Angry, dirty brown smoke boils from the peak of the roof. An air pack alarm starts ringing on a firefighter manning a hose on the roof. Exhausted, he hands me the nozzle and scoots along the roof on his butt to the nearest ladder. From there, it's down to the ground for a much-needed breather, a cup of Red Cross coffee and a fresh air bottle. I turn on my second air bottle and join the attack.

Half a dozen firefighters line the peak of the roof. They are armed with axes or pry bars. Shingle by shingle, board by splintering board, they open the roof so I can hit the fire inside with the hose. Forget the Red Cross coffee. All I want to do now is get even with this fire that smothers old men in their sleep.

Ring ... ring ...

Caller #15: *Good morning. Nancy Shot, WSAN News, again. Any more information on the fire?*

Dispatcher: *Uh, we're still in a state of emergency here. Could you call later?*

Ring ... ring ...

Caller #16: (Elderly woman.) *Uh, where was the fire this morning? I didn't want to go out and look. I saw the trucks go by ...*

Dispatcher: *Who is calling, please?*

Elderly woman: *Well, you wouldn't know me. Was it bad? Is it over?*

Yes, it's bad. And, no, it's not over. Firefighters on the roof are still ripping off shingles, splintering boards and choking on smoke. They're a motley crew. They come from fire departments all over the area and wear bunker gear and helmets in all different styles and colors. The dirty yellow gear is from Emmaus. The brown and red gear is from Western Salisbury Township. We may not know each other by name, but our training has been similar, and at the moment our sole purpose is identical. Side by side, as though we have worked together for years, we pursue the fire. When heavy smoke blocks out the sun, the men without air packs back off. Those of us in packs press our advantage and attack, attack, attack. Back and forth, back and forth, the seesaw battle rages on.

Portable 2: *Go ahead, Chief.*

Fire Chief: *On the partition where you're at, has anybody gotten up through the ceiling, or has that all burned out?*

Portable 2: *We've got a hole in the end of the building now, Chief. We're trying to get one big board out of the way so we can really work.*

Fire Chief: *All right, just be careful because that roof is old.*

Ring ... ring ...

Caller #18: *Hi. It's Gretchen again from Red Hill. Are they available yet? Or ...*

Dispatcher: *They're still tied up. We've got a third alarm.*

The radio crackles with questions, answers — and orders. Bring the video camera, blank tapes and batteries. Did you get an ETA on the coroner? Where is Dr. Barnes? We need another ambulance driver. Get a borough truck to bring some road salt up to the scene. Water running off from the fire is turning the roads into a skating rink. Three firefighters have smoke inhalation.

Fire Chief: *Notify the state fire marshal.*

Dispatcher: 10-4. 10:59 hours.

Ring ... ring ...

Caller #19: *Yes, uh, good morning. Brian Burns, WAEB Radio... I'm calling to ask you about a fire that I guess broke out around 10 o'clock.*

Dispatcher: *Don't have anything we can give you right now. If you can call back later. I'm sorry to cut you off. It's really busy ...*

Portable 11: *Notify AOH* (Allentown Osteopathic Hospital) *on the hotline that we're going to be bringing at least three.*

Ring ... ring ...

Caller #21: *Hello. Nancy Shot, WSAN, again ...*

Ring ... ring ...

Caller #22: *Ron ... The Globe-Times ... fire this morning somewhere in the borough?*

Ring ... ring ...

Caller #23: *Hi.* Globe-Times *calling. We just need ...*

Ring ... ring ...

Caller #25: *Yeah, this is Ron ... The Globe-Times. I'm trying to get a location on Fernwood Street where that fire was ...*

Dispatcher: *33 to Portable 11. AOH notified. 11:22 hours.*

Ring ... ring ...

Caller #27: *Hi, Steve Samuelson from* The Globe-Times *...*

Emmaus Ambulance: *321 10-8, hospital. 11:26 hours.*

"Take a break," the chief says. "But keep an eye on the front of the house in case anything flares up." I'm kneeling in the wet, half-frozen front yard with a charged 2-inch hose across my knees. My air pack face mask hangs at the ready from a clip on my bunker coat. Another fresh air bottle is on my back. The pale sun is shining, but it doesn't provide any warmth. A few snowflakes whip by as the wind knifes into my wet gear. It's getting a lot colder. My frozen fingers are wrapped around a paper cup full of steaming Red Cross coffee. Finally!

Then I feel a gentle hand on my right shoulder. I turn and look up into the face of a petite blonde bombshell in a trench coat and designer sunglasses. She has a reporter's notebook in her right hand and a pencil at the ready in her left hand. A professional 35 mm camera hangs casually from one shoulder. I've seen her before from a distance at fire scenes. She's an ace news reporter for *The Morning Call*, the daily Allentown newspaper. She moved up here from *The Miami Herald* a few years ago. Created quite a stir. She lives in Emmaus, so we see a lot of her around town. Figures that she's the only reporter with the brains and ambition enough to come right out to the scene to answer all of her questions. Someone trained her extremely well on how to cover breaking police news, right down to the lead pencil she carries. Ballpoint pens are useless in the cold and wet.

What a woman! I suddenly picture myself safe at home, in bed between the flannel sheets — with her.

"Hi honey," she coos, smiling. Then her eyes narrow, critically, as she gauges the thick soot on my helmet, the black crud spattered all over my soaking wet bunker gear and all of the dirt on my cheeks. A look of genuine concern creeps across her pretty face.

"How are ... *you?*" she asks. Funny question for a reporter to ask right off the bat at the scene of a three-alarm fire with two fatalities and at least three injuries. Whatever happened to what, when, where, who, how and why?

"I'm cold, wet, hungry and I stink. We have two dead civilians. Three of our guys are on the way to the hospital with smoke inhalation, and I have a ton of crap to do back at the office. How is your day going?" I ask.

"Whole lot better than yours, from the sound of it," she says.

Just then an Emmaus cop runs into the yard. "Lady, don't bother the firemen!"

The little blonde turns, gives the hulking cop "the look," and stops him in his tracks with three icy, well-aimed words: "He's *my* husband!"

CHAPTER EIGHTEEN

Fire from the Sky

Flying conditions are ideal: At 1 p.m. in Allentown, Pennsylvania, there are scattered clouds at 3,000 feet, with an estimated overcast ceiling of 8,000 feet. Visibility, for 20 miles in all directions, is unlimited. The temperature is a pleasant 73, with a dew point of 69. Wind is "calm." There are no gusts.

It's a perfect day for flying and, although it's only early afternoon, that's exactly what Peter C. Miller has been doing on and off for the past four hours. He's the pilot of a plane carrying skydivers aloft for a balloon festival. He's been doing this for two-and-a-half days. Now, it's the last afternoon of the 1989 balloon fest. He's almost done with his job.

On the ground, area residents are taking full advantage of the balmy weather, which is unusually good for July 30, when high heat and humidity normally turn the Lehigh Valley into a giant sauna. Burgers, steaks and hot dogs sizzle on backyard barbecue grills. Friends and families are visiting each other, drinking cold beer, relaxing and just enjoying the good old summertime. Traffic on the five-lane section of Lehigh Street that links Allentown with suburban Emmaus is heavy in both directions. It surges in and out of the many shopping centers and stores that line both sides of the highway. Do-it-yourselfers are stocking up on building supplies at Wickes Lumber. Next door, homeowners are buying plants and gardening supplies at Dan Schantz Greenhouse. Crowds are enjoying a leisurely lunch at Finley's Restaurant or something a bit quicker at Taco Bell and Burger King. The huge parking lot at the South Mall is full of cars as people wheel shopping carts in and out of Jamesway, Weis' supermarket and the dozens of other stores there. This is also Allentown's "Auto Mile." At the many new- and used-car dealerships along Lehigh Street, scores more are kicking tires, shaking their heads at the price stickers, and trying to figure out how much of a trade-in they can get for their old clunkers.

At the Queen City Airport, one mile to the northeast, hundreds of spectators are gathered for the third and final day of the Lehigh Valley Balloon Festival. Huge, brightly colored hot-air balloons are not the only attraction, however. There are also the skydivers, daring men and women who leap out of a small airplane nearly a mile above the earth. Pulling expertly on the lines of their parachutes, they swoop and circle, sometimes trailing colored smoke and bright banners, and land with pinpoint precision at the airport, to the wild cheers of the crowd.

Miller is the man who makes all of that cheering possible. He's the pilot of the jump plane. His call sign is N2639G, but the control tower at Allentown-Bethlehem-Easton International Airport (ABE) calls him "3-9-Golf" on the radio, for short. Redheaded and bearded, the cigar-smoking Miller lives to fly.

Although certified to teach industrial arts in public schools, he teaches flying, instead. At age 46, Miller has a total of 11,442.5 hours of flight time, more flight time than some captains of 747s. He's a licensed Airline Transport pilot, the highest of the Federal Aviation Administration's four ratings. He's certified to fly both single-engine and multiengine aircraft, helicopters and even gliders. A flight instructor, Miller has both land and sea ratings. His pilot's license isn't big enough to hold all of his different certifications, so he has three licenses.

Miller also has his own flying business, The Ugly Airplane Co., named after a bank repossession he bought that friends say is the ugliest airplane in the world. At one time, the company owned eight planes and flew shuttle flights to Philadelphia International Airport. Miller provides flights for skydivers and even tows banners at air shows in Pennsylvania, his native New Jersey, New York and Delaware.

Queen City Airport, elevation 399 feet, is what's commonly known as a "non-control airport." That means there is no control tower. There are an estimated 17,500 towerless airports throughout the country. There is no radar at Queen City. Pilots use the Unicom radio frequency, which is something like a Citizen's Band radio of the sky, to advise other pilots in the area of their presence. If someone is near the radio in the Queen City office, a pilot might also be able to learn if either runway is being used. Mostly, though, it's the responsibility of each pilot to see and be seen.

Queen City is a busy little airport. Miller's is one of 96 private planes housed there. Every year, there are about 50,000 takeoffs and landings on Queen City's two asphalt runways. Runway 14/32 is 3,389 feet long and 80 feet wide. Runway 17/25 is 3,940 feet long and also 80 feet wide. Planes coming in for a landing on Runway 25 swoop so low across Lehigh Street that it looks like they're going to come down on Denny's Restaurant or Blockbuster Video.

Miller is always cautious, friends say. He never takes chances. In fact, just yesterday he had scrubbed a jump because the hot-air balloons unexpectedly lifted off before he reached the right altitude with his jumpers. The jumpers begged him to keep going, to let them make the jump. But he said it wasn't safe. And instead of risking a landing at Queen City with all of the balloons, he flew the jumpers to the Quakertown airport some 10 miles to the south.

Miller is flying a Cessna 182, which is considered an ideal skydiving plane because of its high wing and gutsy 230-horsepower engine. He has 561 hours of flight time on that particular plane. All weekend, he has been in regular radio contact with the ABE control tower, which is located a little more than five miles to the northeast on the other side of Allentown. Using his transponder and an assigned code number, he has also been a regular fixture on the radar screen at ABE.

Also in the sky this Sunday afternoon is a Beechcraft A36 Bonanza. At the controls is Dr. Abdul Kahn, a 43-year-old heart surgeon and licensed private pilot. The Beech is designed to carry six passengers comfortably. It's full to capacity. Dr. Kahn is sitting in the left front pilot's seat. In the right pilot's seat is Stephen Remo, 42, a Continental Airlines pilot. Like Miller, Remo holds an Airline Transport rating and is a flight instructor, both on single- and multiengine aircraft. He's also a flight engineer. Behind Remo sits his wife, Kathleen, 37, a registered dietitian and former student pilot. She's holding Alicia, the couple's 2-year-old daughter on her lap. In the right hand seat at the back of the plane is Dr. Mohammed A. Malik, 45, a trauma surgeon, a licensed private pilot, and the proud father of four sons. His 12-year-old son, Raymond, is in the seat beside his father. Raymond is learning to fly.

It is a joyous occasion for the group. They are celebrating the arrival of a new airplane. Kahn, Malik and another partner just bought the sleek Beechcraft two days earlier. It's a beautiful airplane with retractable, tricycle landing gear, a 285-horsepower fuel-injected engine, and only 1,280 hours of flight time. They are on a short familiarization flight, so that Kahn can build up flight time on the new plane to meet insurance requirements. They have been in the air for about one hour. Kahn is not using a transponder, nor is he in radio contact with the ABE tower. Two witnesses later report hearing the Beechcraft briefly on the Unicom frequency as it approaches Queen City. Neither Miller nor Kahn has filed a flight plan. They are not required to.

Everything is perfectly normal, according to a control-tower tape of Miller's conversation with ABE Radar Arrival Control:

1:24:26 p.m. Cessna: Allentown, 3-9-Golf's airborne up to forty-five hundred.

1:24:29 p.m. Radar: 3-9-Golf, radar contact. Report prior to jump.

1:24:33 p.m. Cessna: (Transmission "unintelligible," believed to be acknowledgment.)

1:27:51 p.m. Radar: 3-9-Golf, maintain four thousand on your climb for traffic.

1:27:54 p.m. Cessna: 3-9-Golf.

1:30:10 p.m. Radar: 3-9-Golf, traffic no longer a factor. Climb to requested altitude. Report prior to jump.

1:30:15 p.m. Cessna: Thank you.

1:30:57 p.m. Cessna: Allentown, ah, 3-9-Golf. We're about one minute prior.

1:31:00 p.m. Radar: 3-9-Golf, roger.

1:32:40 p.m. Cessna: 3-9-Golf, jumpers away.

1:32:43 p.m. Radar: 3-9-Golf, roger.

1:33:16 p.m. Radar: 3-9-Golf, frequency change (from ABE to Unicom) approved.

1:33:18 p.m. Cessna: Bye.

Miller puts the Cessna into a gradual right-hand descent. He is heading for runway 17/25 at Queen City Airport. When Miller turns, the Cessna's wing dips about 20 degrees. That suddenly creates a "blind spot" below and to the right. At the same time, from another direction and a lower altitude, Dr. Kahn is already on a downwind approach, lining up for a landing. His destination is also runway 17/25.

From more than five miles away, the air traffic controllers at ABE can't possibly see what is happening. Miller disappears from ABE's radar screen at 1:34:10 p.m. at an altitude of 1,600 feet, as is normal for a descending aircraft preparing to land. Kahn is not using a transponder, so his plane never appears on the radar. He is not in radio contact with the tower. Controllers don't even know he exists. But scores of people on the ground certainly do. The planes are only about 1,200 feet above their heads, the length of four football fields. Some spectators have been watching for skydivers to appear. Others are drawn by the noise of the engines. Then everyone, little children, mothers and fathers, even passing motorists, can't tear their eyes away as the two planes grow ever closer.

Surely, some onlookers think, fighting a rising tide of suspense, one or both of the planes will suddenly veer away. They are much too close, already. But neither plane changes direction. The planes keep heading right toward each other. Each is traveling at about 100 miles per hour. The distance between them is disappearing rapidly. Then they pass the point of no return, and there is no doubt about what will happen next.

"It sounded like a car accident," 33-year-old Stephen Silfies later tells investigators from the National Transportation Safety Board (NTSB). The Mack Trucks worker has been watching the skydivers from his parents' backyard a few blocks to the south on Greenleaf Street in Emmaus. The final NTSB crash report totals 297 pages.

Debbie Moyer, a 24-year-old homemaker from Allentown, is walking to her car outside of Hess' Department Store in the South Mall when she sees the two planes bearing down on each other.

"There was a loud bang like a car crash," she tells the NTSB. "I screamed to my husband: 'Oh my God! The planes hit! They're coming down. Get out of the way!'

"It all happened so fast [a matter of seconds]. Pieces flew everywhere as the plane (Cessna) came twirling straight down like a whirling top. I thought it was going to land on Jamesway.

"The other plane (Beechcraft) went swaying down over Lehigh Street into the rear of a car dealer parking lot. They both immediately exploded as they hit the ground.

"Immediately after the crash (at the Jamesway site), my husband ran over to see if there was anything he could do. There was nothing anyone could do. The plane (Cessna) was in complete flames. The police arrived about a minute later.

"As I watched the plane and the person in it burn, I felt so helpless and sick to my stomach, we left the scene."

Flight instructor Raymond W. Franke Jr., 21, is taxiing out from the Queen City terminal, preparing to take off, when he hears the pilot of the Beechcraft on the Unicom radio frequency. Franke later tells the NTSB he doesn't remember what the pilot said, but assumes he was announcing that the Beechcraft was entering the landing pattern.

"I continued to the run-up area and did my run-up and announced on Unicom that I was departing 25 at Queen City," Franke tells investigators.

"At that time, the jump plane announced 'jump plane entering downwind at Queen City.' Waiting to see where he was at I looked off to the left and saw the jump plane in a steep descending turn to the right and the A36 already established on downwind and the jump plane just continued his bank and descent, and descended into the right side of the A36. At this point the wing of the jump plane struck the A36 and separated. When they hit it caused an explosion. When the jump plane hit it fell just about straight down. The A36 was hit in the fuselage and right wing and roof area (trailing edge). It rolled off to the right and spun in. Both aircraft were in flames on the way down."

NTSB interviews continue: Allentown Police Officer David Lee Shoemaker is driving out of Emmaus on Lehigh Street. He's off duty. His wife Brenda and two teenage daughters are in the car with him.

"As we passed in front of Kelly Buick my wife saw what she thought was a model airplane falling. I looked up and realized it was a small plane, not a model. As we watched, we saw the plane come down like a pancake and the left wing came off. The sky was full of what looked like black snow and pieces of metal.

"I pulled into the center of Lehigh Street in front of Finley's Restaurant and stopped. The street was full of running people, cars and pieces of plane falling out of the sky. I could see flames at Jamesway and flames behind Knopf Pontiac. I used my portable radio to call the Allentown Communications Center and reported the incident and called for as much help as I could get. It was obvious there were no survivors."

Shoemaker begins taking names of witnesses and securing the scene as best he can. The 40-year-old officer tells federal investigators he is determined not to let anyone tamper with airplane debris or any other evidence that might be vital in determining the cause of the crash.

At 1:34:28 p.m., the screaming electronic signal from an aircraft Emergency Locator Transmitter (ELT) fills the control tower at ABE airport. The ELT is activated by Miller's Cessna slamming into the pavement of the South Mall parking lot — just 75 feet west of the busy Jamesway store.

At about the same time, the FAA supervisor on duty steps out of the elevator at the top of the ABE control tower. He glances out of a window. Toward the southwest, two columns of thick black smoke billow skyward.

A control tower phone rings. It's the Airport Fire Department. A firefighter asks whether the tower has just lost two planes. No one in the tower knows anything about any crash. Why are you asking? The firefighter says he's monitoring the county fire radio, as usual. Lehigh County Communications Center is dispatching every available unit in the Emmaus area — police, fire, rescue and ambulance — to a possible midair collision near the South Mall.

Melanie and I are working in the garden. It's our usual summer Sunday afternoon. We're cleaning up the remnants of spring-planted crops, getting things ready for fall crops. We're working up a sweat. I'm pulling the last of some overripe daikon radishes. Mel heads into the house to get us some iced tea. That's when the pager on my belt goes off.

"*Attention, Emmaus Fire Department,*" the dispatcher begins. The tone of her voice immediately worries me. I know instinctively that this is not going to be an automatic alarm or a wash-down at an auto accident. Something really awful is happening.

I straighten up from the radishes and start walking toward the garage where my bunker gear is hanging. "*Possible plane crash,*" the dispatcher continues. I start running. Mel is just coming out the back door. She has a tall glass of iced tea in each hand. A quizzical look flashes across her face when she sees me running.

"Fire call," I yell as I dash past her and disappear into the garage. She nods knowingly. It figures. Whenever we're completely wrapped up in our own little world, have the whole day perfectly planned, we always get a fire call.

As I struggle into my bunker pants, my pager goes off again. *"Midair collision ... two private planes ... Hess' South Mall,"* the dispatcher continues. There's naked fear in her voice now. I'm shaking, too. A plane crash? At a shopping mall? On a Sunday afternoon? God help us!

Mel walks around the end of the garage, still carrying the iced tea, as I bolt through the door. "Midair collision ... South Mall," I say, climbing into my pickup. "They're calling out everyone."

"Did it hit the mall?" she asks.

"I don't know. Sounds bad. Gotta go."

"Be careful!"

"Always. Love you. Bye."

I race up Main Road. Downshifting into second, I barely stop at the intersection as I turn down the road to Emmaus. At the crest of the hill, I look to the right through Leibert's Gap. There, at the base of South Mountain on the other side of town, two towering columns of black smoke rise hundreds of feet into the air. They merge in a hazy black shroud over the valley.

Central Station is deserted when I wheel into the parking lot. All of the trucks are gone. The huge overhead garage doors stand wide open. Shoes, boots and sandals litter the floor. Gear hooks on the walls are empty. A cloud of diesel exhaust still hangs in the air. The entire fire company just left in a big hurry.

Radios on the engine room wall blare nonstop chaos. Everyone is talking over everyone else. All frequencies are jammed. Fire police are setting up roadblocks on Lehigh Street. Pumpers are arriving at the scene. Others are just leaving distant stations. Ambulances and paramedics are en route. Officers on the scene are calling for more hose lines, more water, more pressure, more personnel. Pumper drivers try to acknowledge the commands. Police call for more ambulances, more firefighters, federal investigators, the coroner. Wailing, yelping sirens and yelling fill the background of each transmission. No use calling incident command for instructions. All of the trucks are already out, anyway. I close the firehouse garage doors, grab the rest of my gear and head for the scene.

A row of orange cones blocks the highway as I turn onto Lehigh Street. Fire Police Officer Janice Engleman waves me away with her flashlight. Then she recognizes my truck, sees my bunker gear. She pulls a cone out of the way and waves me through with a worried smile. She replaces the cone and turns back toward the smoke hanging over the road ahead.

There's no traffic. The usually busy Lehigh Street is deserted until I top the small rise by Finley's Restaurant. There, cars are parked helter-skelter everywhere. Crowds of people mill about. That's as far as I can go. I pull in front of Dominos Pizza and park, cut my lights and head across the street toward the nearest column of smoke. Landing gear and other airplane parts lie scattered in the roadway and the grass. Smoke still rises from a smoldering pile of rubble near Jamesway. It's the Cessna, which came down nearly inverted, nosedown.

The worst of the fire is knocked down. A hose crew is advancing on the hot spots. Police are already taking measurements, interviewing witnesses, tagging debris. Medics stand off to one side. Nothing they can do for the man in the mangled plane. Then I see a white helmet beside the pumper. It's Assistant Chief John Shafer.

"What do you need, John?" I ask.

"Nothing, right now. We're OK here, thanks. But I think the chief could use some help across the street. That's the worst of it."

He's not kidding. As bad as it is, the smoldering wreckage of the Cessna is nothing compared to what's left of the Beechcraft and its occupants. If I knew then what I was getting myself into hustling across Lehigh Street, I would have climbed back in my pickup and gone straight home.

The Beechcraft crashed near the back of a large parking lot full of new cars behind Knopf Pontiac. The plane has a fuel capacity of 74 gallons. No one knows how much was left at the time of the crash. Whatever was left blew up on impact. NTSB investigators say the Beechcraft hit the ground "in a nearly upright, wings level condition at a steep, nosedown angle and at a high rate of speed. A large fire erupted immediately. Examination of the wreckage indicates a very high-energy impact. The center and forward sections of the fuselage and the inboard sections of both wings were consumed by fire. The impact created a sizable crater through the asphalt and into the earth underneath." The plane fell in a driveway between double rows of shiny new cars. The fireball from the explosion completely destroyed the nearest car and heavily damaged the rear of another. Two other cars sustained minor heat damage.

An Emmaus pumper is parked in the narrow lane between the rows of new cars. Our big rescue truck is not far behind. Several hose lines snake across the pavement between the new cars to the wreckage. Two crews of firefighters wearing air packs are busy knocking down the hot spots in the plane and the cars. Initially, firefighters attack the blaze with a thick spray of protein-rich foam that suffocates the fire by cutting off its air supply. Now, fluffy chunks of white foam float here and there on the pooling water. I help move the hoselines and unpack salvage tools. Then, Emmaus Fire Chief Robert Reiss tells us to knock it off and gather around in front of the pumper.

The fire's out, he says. There's no one to rescue. The medics can only stand by and watch. There are no survivors. With that realization, our mission suddenly changes dramatically. We are now all under the command of Lehigh County Coroner Wayne E. Snyder. The coroner stands only 5-foot-5, but he is a tower of calm, professional efficiency. Methodically working his large hands into white, latex surgical gloves, the coroner carefully explains what we have to do next. It's very simple, really. The six occupants of the Beechcraft are still in the wreckage. Someone has to separate the people from the plane. This will be a long, slow, messy process. Everything has to be moved carefully, one piece at a time, so that the coroner and NTSB investigators c an properly organize and catalog the remains to unlock the mystery of the crash.

One crew will be needed to police the large area around the crash site, looking for any stray pieces of the plane or its occupants. There will be a lot of each. Another team will sift through the wreckage. This is going to take a lot of hands, a lot of elbow grease and a lot of nerve. The coroner wants volunteers, and volunteers only, especially for the team that will work inside the wreckage. The coroner will direct that team, personally. This is not going to be pretty. In fact, it's going to be damned awful, he warns us. What he is about to ask us to do is the kind of work that turns stomachs and spawns nightmares. So if your stomach is not made of cast iron and the sight of blood bothers you, do us all a favor and excuse yourself now. It's nothing to be ashamed of, he adds. Some people can handle it; some can't.

Good advice. But none of us really knows what to expect. That includes our veteran rescue squad members. We've handled some nasty scenes in the past, but none of us has ever tackled anything quite like this before. Glancing warily over our shoulders at the wreckage, we all say we'll do what we can. The coroner says he can't ask for any more than that.

We each struggle into a pair of cold, clammy latex gloves. Wearing our fire boots, bunker pants, T-shirts and helmets, we carefully wade into the wreck. The Beechcraft is balled up into a big clump of mangled metal and flesh. With body bags ringing the scene, we start at the outside edge of the wreckage and slowly work our way toward the middle. It's slow going. The coroner carefully notes the location and condition of everything we find and sees that the right pieces go in the right bags. Police, NTSB investigators and other officials hover all around, making notes, taking measurements and snapping photographs.

I'm only dimly aware of the other firefighters policing the edges of the crash scene. They look under parked cars and comb through crown vetch on the embankment of the parking lot retaining wall. Gingerly, they pick up something here, something else there. Everything disappears into plastic bags.

"Here, take this," the coroner snaps.

Without looking up from where I am working, I trustingly reach toward him. My right hand closes around something long, warm and soft. It's an arm. I don't know whose arm. I don't want to know. It doesn't matter.

"Where does this go?" I ask.

"In that bag, behind you."

"This one?"

"No! The one to the right."

Shoes that are still occupied are scattered here and there in the debris.

"Got an L.A. Gear here," says one firefighter.

"I got a Nike," says another firefighter.

"In the bag with the other Nike, over there," prompts the coroner.

Snyder was elected coroner less than two years ago. He replaced a man who had held the post for 23 years. The coroner's job was part-time. It paid $20,900 a year when Snyder took office. A big part of his campaign focused on upgrading the coroner's office and pay so that unattended or suspicious deaths could be properly investigated 24 hours a day, seven days a week. He's made only modest progress toward reaching his campaign goals. The job is still part-time. Snyder doesn't have much help. But at least the coroner's pay is up to $25,000 a year now.

The coroner is not in the best of moods when he arrives at the scene. As we peel back layer after layer of the wreck and the tragic scale of the disaster becomes more obvious from the growing number of body bags in use, his mood blackens. Squatting on his haunches, the coroner is wrestling with a bulky object loosened from one side of the main wreckage. He finds a pocket in a pair of men's trousers. It's a hip pocket. There's a wallet inside. The coroner rifles through its contents until he finds some identification.

Suddenly, he starts talking in a loud voice. He's almost shouting. I can't quite catch everything he says, since he is turned more toward Chief Reiss, who is working right beside him. But it's something to the effect that no amount of money — especially not a lousy, stinking $25,000 a year — is enough for picking up pieces of his friends! The wallet, the pants and the rest belong to someone the coroner knows, Dr. Malik, a close colleague and friend who once treated Snyder's daughter. Dr. Malik headed an emergency room trauma unit at Lehigh Valley Hospital Center. He and Snyder worked closely together investigating many violent deaths.

I don't know how Snyder does it, how he keeps control as well as he does, how he keeps going. I don't think I could. No caring human being should have to do what he's doing. Most of us would simply go to pieces. The coroner keeps a tight, professional grip on his emotions. He doesn't have a choice. There's no one else to take over. We still have a lot of work to do.

Seemingly everything and everyone in the plane has been piled on top of the engine that is buried in a foot-deep crater in the asphalt. The pile includes several intact seats. The seats are still occupied, with seat belts fastened. We unbuckle the seat belt, but still can't free its occupant. Something else is holding him.

"Lift," the coroner commands. "Push forward. Hold it, right there."

With both hands, one under each armpit, I hold the victim erect. I lift upward slightly, while the coroner and the chief manipulate the wreckage underneath.

It seems to take an eternity. As they work, my 12-year-old son fills my thoughts. That's weird, I muse. Why think of Don at a time like this? Then it hits me. The person I'm holding is about the same height as my son. His build is about the same. Even his weight is about the same. His teeth are fitted with braces, just like my son's.

I know it isn't my son, of course. Don is safely at home. But that doesn't stop tears from filling my eyes. The chief and the coroner are taking forever with what they're working on. Finally, I break my stare and look away. I take a long, deep breath and let it out very slowly in what probably sounds a lot like a long, sorrowful moan. One of our newer firefighters looks over at me with questioning eyes.

"Kinda gets to ya, huh?" he mumbles.

I just shake my head, tighten my grip. My arms ache. I can't hold that position much longer. How can I even begin to explain to the other firefighter that, at that moment, I am no longer a firefighter but a father, and my heart is breaking for the lifeless child I hold in my arms. I don't know his name or anything about him, where he lived or where he went to school. I just know that whoever this boy's father is, he'll never hold his son close to him again. This young life is gone forever, snuffed out in the blink of an eye.

I wonder: Did the people on the plane know what was happening? Did they suffer?

"No! Absolutely not," the coroner declares. It all happened too fast. They never knew what hit them. Looping down from the right, the Cessna rams the Beechcraft broadside at about the middle of the passenger compartment. Its wings are at about a 20-degree angle, which means the pilot of the Cessna is "blind" to anything below him. The Beechcraft, in turn, is "blind" to anything coming from above on the right and slightly to the rear, federal investigators, confirm. With each plane traveling about 100 miles per hour, the initial midair impact is tremendous. It's all over in an instant.

Closing my eyes, I say a silent prayer for all of them, but especially for the boy and for his father, whoever he is, wherever he is. The gloved hands of a total stranger can never replace the strong, loving arms of a father's hug, I know. But if this were my son, I know I would at least want him treated with respect and compassion in my absence.

Then, suddenly, he's free. We gently empty the seat. Another body bag is zipped shut. We move on to the next victim. At least we start to. That's when we notice the ghouls.

A growing crowd of onlookers lines the chain link fence across the back of the car lot. People stand in single file along the narrow top of an overgrown embankment above the railroad tracks and the gully behind them. It's a tough location to reach. They really have to work to get there. A couple of people are clicking snapshots with cheap point-and-shoot cameras. One is grinding away with a video camera.

Ghouls! What kind of people would go so far out of their way to look at this?

The crowd contains men and boys, women and young girls. There are even small children. The crowd keeps growing. People are running up the narrow path along the railroad tracks to have a closer look. We can't believe it.

"Hey!" yells a firefighter. "We have to be here. You don't. Go home!"

No one budges. More people clamber up the embankment from the tracks below.

"What the hell are you looking at?" another firefighter yells. No one answers. A young man with a beard hoists a 2-year-old child onto his shoulders for a better view. Without the high fence surrounding the car lot, these people would be hanging over our shoulders.

"Get outta here!" yells a rescue squadman. "There's nothing to see."

A newly arrived spectator presses another video camera against the fence and hits the "record" button. A tiny red light glows on the front of the camera. A TV news helicopter from Philadelphia circles overhead.

It's too much. A handful of us charge the fence, screaming. "Get the fuck outta here! What's the matter with you people? Scram!"

The crowd doesn't move. Spectators just look right through us, their blank stares transfixed by the carnage in the car lot.

The medics stop our charge after only a few steps with an armload of soft white sheets from an ambulance. They hang the sheets on the fence to block the view. The gawkers just move beyond the sheets to keep staring, taking pictures and pointing.

Finally, a uniformed Allentown police officer storms up the path. He orders everyone out of the area. The gawkers don't want to leave. Like us, the cop has absolutely no patience for these people. He's about to get physical when the last of the gawkers finally saunter away, staring back over their shoulders for one last, lurid look.

And we return to our gruesome work. Hours later, the coroner says we've done all we can possibly do. We hose off our tools and boots, pack up the trucks and head back to the station as the ambulance crews and crash investigators take over the scene. I have never been so glad to get out of anyplace in my life.

Back at the station, we have hours more work ahead of us. Hoses have to be washed. Air packs must be cleaned, air bottles refilled. Tools and bunker gear need to be cleaned and disinfected. Trucks have to be washed. It's all standard operating procedure. Everything has to be cleaned, serviced or repaired and returned to its proper place, put "back in service" as soon as possible so we're ready for the next fire call. Being busy is a blessing. It takes our minds off of what we've been doing all afternoon.

Walking back into the engine room with an armload of gear, I remember the attendance sheet. After every fire call, we have to sign in. Beside the signature line are spaces for the number of the truck you rode, a brief description of your duties during the call and a place to mark whether you wore an air pack. Firefighters with white or yellow helmets usually just write "Officer" or "Driver" beside their names to describe their duties. Most of us with the red helmets of line firefighters simply write "Rescue." I sign my name. Then, without really thinking about it, I write "Rescue" in the duties blank. Glancing up at the signature above mine, I can't help but notice how a friend described his duties differently: "Pick up body parts." "Jeez," I think. "Sure glad I wasn't doing that." Sometimes, the mind's natural defense mechanisms can be truly merciful. My friend was policing the perimeter of the crash site. After that, we don't see much of him around the station. Finally, he just drops out of the department and disappears from our company altogether.

The sign-in sheet is in its usual place on the desk under the wall-mounted radios beside the double doors of the engine room. Sitting on the desk are four boxes of pizza that the guys at Domino's Pizza just delivered with their compliments. I'm starving. We haven't had anything to eat or drink all afternoon. The station is full of tired, hungry people, but only one box is open. Only a few slices are missing from the first pizza. As soon as I lift the lid of the box, my stomach tells me why. I drop the lid and walk away, empty-handed. As much as I love pizza, it's going to be a long time before I want pizza again. Come to think of it, it might be a long time before I want to eat anything again. My usual hearty appetite has completely disappeared.

Mel knows I will be hungry whenever I get home, so she goes out of her way all afternoon to prepare one of her famous super suppers. She peels, boils and whips up a big batch of fluffy mashed potatoes. There are peas and carrots and tossed salad, all fresh from the garden. The center of it all is a small pork roast, complete with a little sauerkraut, which greets my nose the moment I step into the house.

Mel wants to know all about the crash, of course. I pour each of us a big glass of red wine and tell her what I can, as much as decency allows, anyway. She understands. After all, Mel's an old newspaper reporter. She's been to her share of fatal accidents and fires.

It's almost time for the local evening news. We switch on WFMZ-TV. They don't say much we don't already know: Two small planes collided in midair near South Mall. Seven people, including two children, are dead. There's a short interview with the coroner, then footage of the remains of the Cessna and the Beechcraft.

"That's where you were working?" Mel asks.

"Uh-huh."

"Oh, Lord!"

Dinner's ready. I take a second glass of wine before I can bring myself to sit down at the table. I pick politely at the meat, devour the mashed potatoes and excuse myself.

Later, I go upstairs. Our 12-year-old son, Don, is in his room. He's sitting on his bed, reading. I sit down beside him. We start talking. He asks about the plane crash. I tell him what I can, say that a little boy about his age died. Then our eyes meet. I throw my arms around him. My eyes burn. Tears run down my cheeks. I can't let go. I squeeze him, harder and harder. Suddenly, he starts squirming, struggling to get away. I squeeze him so hard I scare my son. I scare myself. Melanie is watching all of this from the bedroom doorway. Tears fill her eyes. I kiss Don on top of his blond head, hug my wife and go outside to work in the garden until well after dark. My whole family must think I've lost my mind. Maybe I have.

Sleep comes slowly that night. It's shallow, fitful. Whenever I close my eyes, all I can see is the crash site, fancy running shoes, the stubborn seat — and more.

CHAPTER NINETEEN

Stress? What Stress?

Two days later, everyone who worked the crash gathered at Central Station for a special meeting called by the chief. Attendance was not mandatory, but it was strongly recommended. More than 50 of us crowded into the multipurpose room, filling it to capacity.

We were introduced to a counselor, a psychologist. He was specially trained in something called Critical Incident Stress Debriefing (CISD). He explained that CISD was a relatively new, highly effective procedure to help emergency service personnel relieve and deal with some of the psychological stresses that linger after a major disaster.

The year was 1989. It was early in the dawn of the definition, diagnosis and treatment of a controversial new psychological condition known as post-traumatic stress disorder (PTSD). Barely a decade had passed since psychologist Charles R. Figley, Ph.D., then a professor at Purdue University and a former Marine, introduced the idea of PTSD in a book titled "Stress Disorders Among Vietnam Veterans: Theory, Research, and Treatment." PTSD manifests itself in myriad forms, ranging from insomnia and nightmares to substance abuse and even suicide. Talking about the stresses of the job, rather than bottling them up inside of you and toughing it out, as tradition demanded, was another one of Chief Reiss' cutting edge innovations.

"How many here have had trouble sleeping since the incident?" the psychologist asked. "Any nightmares? Trouble eating? Depression?"

Hands went up around the room after each question. A lot of hands.

"Good! That's perfectly normal. Shows you're human," he said.

Then he asked us to introduce ourselves. One by one, we went around the room, saying who we are and what we did at the crash site. We were also supposed to say how we felt about what we saw and did. Our crew from the car lot pretty much said the same thing:

"George DeVault, Emmaus firefighter. Saw the smoke driving to the station ... was part of the rescue crew ... removed the victims from the car lot."

Man after man, the answers were the same: Terse, tense, guarded, almost combative. There were no details, no emotion, no tears. We didn't —

couldn't — open up. We wouldn't — couldn't — let go of the departed. We were still guarding them from the ghouls at the fence.

It was just the opposite for the medics. They couldn't hold back. One was in tears almost as soon as she started speaking. It was no wonder, I guess. "No survivors" was an extremely difficult, almost impossible concept to grasp for people in the habit of saving lives every day. Accept defeat? Never! No matter how bad the situation, there was usually someone, even just one person, who had at least a fighting chance at life. With the proper combination of tools, training and techniques, the medics routinely brought people back from the edge of the grave.

Not this time. There really were no survivors. Everyone in both planes was dead. And there was not a thing all of the medics put together could do to change that. Simply put, they were not needed. They were powerless, totally impotent. And few things are worse than being totally helpless in an emergency.

What still bothered a lot of people was the spectators, especially those clicking souvenir snapshots or making home movies of the mayhem. Some gawkers just never shut up: "Ooh, look at this! Gawd, look at that!"

Right away, the psychologist began blaming the news media. "That's not surprising," he said. "KYW, every five minutes would broadcast the headline, 'Seven people die in midair collision on Lehigh Street.' That draws people like a magnet."

I wanted to clobber the guy. He knew that's what KYW Newsradio does with everything. Tune to 1060 AM, and it's, "All news. All the time. Give us 22 minutes. We'll give you the world." Many people, especially those along Lehigh Street and around Jamesway in the South Mall parking lot, were a part of the disaster. They were shopping, driving by, quietly going about their daily lives when they came within a few hundred feet of getting maimed or killed. They didn't need the radio to tell them about the crash. They saw it, heard it, felt it.

And just what was Mr. Know-It-All doing in this meeting, anyhow? He wasn't at the scene. He didn't see the bodies. He didn't cradle a dead 12-year-old in his arms. He didn't fight back tears because the child reminded you so much of your own son. He didn't have any right to be here. He was no better than the ghouls hanging on the fence with their damn cameras, I thought.

My hands clenched into fists. I wanted to knock that smug, professorial look off of his silly face. His pontificating was profane, a sacrilege.

But I didn't say a thing, even though that's what we were supposed to do. Getting it off our chests was what this meeting was all about. We were supposed to yell and scream, rant and rave, or cry, if we felt like it. But no one really let loose.

Guess I should have spoken up. That became obvious a few weeks later when Melanie and I had to fly to Detroit. I didn't particularly want to fly, but it was business. We had to get there and back as quickly as possible. Through *The New Farm* magazine, I had recently ghostwritten and published what quickly became a classic farming book, "Booker T. Whatley's Handbook on How to Make $100,000 Farming 25 Acres." One of Dr. Whatley's biggest fans was Tom Monaghan, founder of Domino's Pizza and then owner of the Detroit Tigers. Monaghan had hired Dr. Whatley to set up a Whatley-style farm on Domino's corporate campus in Ann Arbor. I had a meeting with Domino's top management to talk about sponsoring a new magazine just for highly diversified farmers producing high-value crops for direct sale to local consumers.

Everything was fine until I stepped inside the plane and looked down the long aisle between the endless rows of seats. Then I froze. And the seats became smoldering funeral pyres. The flight crew and other passengers were dismembered corpses.

"Are you OK?" Mel asked from behind me. She sounded worried. Everyone else was impatient. They wanted to get into their seats, but I was blocking the road.

"Yeah," I said, taking a deep breath. "I am now." Everything returned to normal. The new magazine never materialized, but our flights to and from Michigan were flawless. And I never experienced anything like that again, despite acquiring half a million frequent flyer miles over the next 20 years while "commuting" to Rodale's publishing operation in Moscow, Russia. (I "transferred to the Russian front" not long after Bob Rodale and four others were killed in an auto accident in Moscow on Sept. 20, 1990. Rodale had founded one of the earliest Soviet-American joint ventures. He was preparing to launch *"Novii Fermer-New Farmer,"* a magazine for the expected flood of new — independent — farmers in the Soviet Union, when a bus went left of center and hit his van head-on near the Moscow airport. Again there were no survivors.)

Even while safe and secure in a big, blue leather seat in Delta's Business Class section with white table linen, real silverware and endless red wine (I had a "Starving Artist" upgrade coupon on a $495 round-trip ticket!), I still felt slightly out of synch with everyone else on the 19-hour JFK to Moscow round-trip. To this day, the only way to get me into a pair of running shoes or a certain brand of chinos is at gunpoint.

There is a growing body of scientific evidence that says I am not alone. Far from it. Research from around the world — Canada, Germany, the United Kingdom, Kuwait, Japan, Taiwan, Australia and Israel — shows that firefighters everywhere are often as shell-shocked as many combat veterans.

Canadian psychologist Wayne Corneil, Ph.D., reported that Canadian firefighters (17.3 percent) in his studies suffer PTSD slightly more often than Vietnam-era veterans (15.2 percent), while U.S. firefighters (22.2 percent) are afflicted more often than wounded Vietnam combat vets (20 percent). By contrast, Corneil says, only about 1 percent of the general population suffers PTSD. In the United States, the PTSD rate among crime victims is just 3.5 percent.

Such findings are not routinely reported on the nightly news or even in *The New York Times*. They appear mainly in obscure scientific publications such as the *Monitor of the American Psychological Association, Psychosomatic Medicine* or the *Journal of Traumatic Stress*.

Corneil said the firefighters in his study averaged 3.91 "severe emergencies" a year. Those included, among other things, fatal auto accidents and fires, shootings, stabbings, suicides, and industrial accidents that often involved amputation or beheading. Over the years, the effects piled up.

Corneil studied career firefighters in urban departments. They worked assigned shifts, then punched out and went home where they really were "off duty." Volunteer firefighters, on the other hand, are almost never off duty. Like military troops deployed in a foreign combat zone, we are on call 24/7. The big difference is we're not on the frontlines halfway around the world. We're at home. We're in our own beds, with our own families and friends, in familiar places where we should always feel completely safe, relaxed and secure. But we don't. We can never really let our guard down because, day or night, our pagers may go off any second.

Volunteer firefighters don't leave the scenes of death and disaster on battlefields thousands of miles away. We see them every day, driving to and from work or just running errands. Our families see them, too. Melanie surprised me when talking about trees and powerlines brought down by Superstorm Sandy. She didn't say they're at Shimerville and Mill Roads.

"They're at that corner. You know ... where the drunk driver crashed through the hedge and hit that poor woman as she stepped out of her house." Yes, I know. I remember. Broken pelvis. I can still see her grimace, hear her cry out in pain as we eased her onto a backboard.

If Corneil's average of 3.91 "severe emergencies" a year doesn't seem like much, do the math. Round 3.91 up to four, then multiply by 30. After 30 years as a volunteer firefighter in a small town, battlefield landmarks that bring back sights and sounds best forgotten lurk around almost every corner.

And, try though we might, neither Mel nor I can pass a certain hillside pond without looking. We see it every time we take South Fifth Street to or from town. It's the place where, for a moment, Mel knew I died in a water rescue during Hurricane Floyd.

CHAPTER TWENTY

Attack of the Man-Eating Pond

It's the phone call everyone dreads: "George, this is Brian with Emmaus Ambulance. We're transporting your wife to Lehigh Valley Hospital. She was just involved in an auto accident."

No! His words hit me like a heavy fire boot planted squarely in the crotch. I can't believe this is really happening, but it is.

She's OK, he assures me. No blood, no broken bones. Just badly shaken, clearly suffering a concussion.

It's what he doesn't say that worries me. Is it mild, moderate or ... massive?

"Undetermined."

He just says come to the ER. Stat!

Mel was stopped, third in line, waiting to turn left at the light on South 10th Street beside Pizza Hut, when ... wham! A woman in a minivan rammed her from behind.

"I was only going 5 miles an hour. And ... I wasn't on my cellphone," the other driver protested to police. Right. That's why both of her airbags deployed and the rear of Mel's Mercury Cougar crumpled like a beer can.

Mel was wearing her seat belt. Thank God. That helped, a lot. But she still took a good hit. Mel blacked out, she believes now because she can't remember much. She got out of the car for a moment, probably to check the damage, she thinks. She's not sure.

Next thing Mel knew, she was back in the Cougar, sitting in the driver's seat. When she opened her eyes, a paramedic was in her face.

"Hi. What's your name?"

"Uh, Melanie. Who're you? What happened?"

"You had a little accident. Are you OK? Is there someone I should call?"

"My husband. My neck hurts. I don't feel so good."

She remembers telling him to get her license from her purse. And feeling "fuzzy."

"OK. We called your husband. We're going to take you to the hospital now. He'll meet you there."

The ambulance crew was a buncha blabbermouths. They just wouldn't shut up. They kept talking — asking all kinds of dumb questions — as they slid Mel onto a full-length backboard, strapped her down, and applied head restraints made of orange foam blocks and Velcro. The endless questions are standard procedure to keep accident victims from slipping into unconsciousness and shock. Then the medics lifted her onto a gurney, snapped another set of straps that work like seat belts, and wheeled her into the back of the ambulance.

The questions kept coming. "I think I just want to go to sleep now," she said, again and again.

"No!" the medics protested, doing their job. And, again, they started with what Mel remembers as "all those annoying questions."

I met her in the ER. It was obvious she took a hard hit to the head. But by evening, after several tests, the doctors finally said it was OK for her to go home. That was easy for them to say. They weren't driving. Nothing much was left in her stomach, but she still tried to throw up three times on the short drive home.

Mel had strict orders to stay in bed — and rest!

It was tough to keep her down, though, especially with all of the work that had to be done around our farm. We were running a CSA (community supported agriculture) or vegetable "subscription service," as we liked to call it, for 100 area families.

The next day was Thursday, pickup and delivery day. The veggies must go through!

It was also Sept. 16, 1999. And Hurricane Floyd was lashing the East Coast with high winds and torrential winds. The rain gauge on the greenhouse already held 4 inches, yet the storm showed no signs of letting up. If anything, it was getting worse.

Some friends were helping Mel pack up the last of the vegetables at our farm. They worried about her, especially since she needed to run inside to throw up every so often. As our son, Don, loaded the last six bags of veggies into the front of my pickup, both my Emmaus and Vera Cruz pagers went off. Ordinarily, I might be a little selective about answering a fire call when making a vegetable run. But this was no automatic alarm set off by high winds. It was a rescue call, a "water rescue" on top of South Mountain. A man was being sucked into a 20-foot deep drain pipe, the dispatcher said. As Don unloaded my pickup, I ran inside and climbed into the extra set of bunker gear I kept in the laundry room closet. I plugged in the blue light on my pickup and shot down the driveway.

I was a captain with the Emmaus Fire Department at the time, and also a firefighter with Vera Cruz. I had "standing orders" from Emmaus Chief

Robert Reiss to report directly to the scene of any emergency between my house and the firehouse. With a two-way radio in my pickup, I was the chief's eyes and ears in the rugged country south of the firehouse. This call was only halfway to the firehouse, so I headed for the scene.

Rain's coming down sideways. The roads are awful. Main Road East by Phil's Automotive looks like a lake. One hundred yards later, the road is completely covered by angry brown water where Leibert Creek always floods the highway. It's a raging river. Water is so high I have serious second thoughts about driving through the flood, but there is no quick way around it. I hug the crown of the highway where the water is shallowest and say a little prayer.

All the way, I'm trying to figure out where — and what — this emergency call might actually be. There simply aren't any big bodies of water around here, just a few little ponds and creeks. Of course, a hurricane can change the geography in low-lying areas in a hurry. But on top of South Mountain? Blinded by rain, someone probably just ran off of the road into that little drainage basin by Gunther Heussman's farm, I figure.

Nope. Lots of muddy water flows across the road and into the basin, but there's no car in the drink. Also, there are no flashing emergency lights yet. Chief Reiss radios that he's already on the scene, wherever the scene turns out to be. So, windshield wipers on high, I keep driving, straining to see through the wind-driven rain.

Cresting South Mountain, I start down the other side toward Emmaus. I still don't see anything. Then I spot the chief's car way down in a yard below a big gray house on the left side of road. I wheel into the circular drive, cut the lights and engine, and start down the hill toward the chief's car.

Life-and-death struggles automatically hit the "record" button, burning permanent images into the hard drive of our brains. I can still see everything that happened next in high-definition and technicolor. I can replay it as a continuous video loop, shift into slo-mo, or cut to a series of still photos. Being an old newspaper photographer, I favor still photos with the whirring motordrive and clicking mirror of my old Nikon F.

Whir-Click — Wide-angle panorama of a half-acre pond perched on a sweeping hillside overlooking the Lehigh Valley. A woman runs along the grassy east bank. She's sobbing, screaming hysterically. "Help! Help! He needs help!" The woman's soaking wet. Pelting rain plasters dark hair to her head and face. Chief Reiss and a uniformed Emmaus cop stand on the far bank. About 40 feet out into the water are two men, their heads barely above the water. One man has gray hair. He looks like he's in his 60s. The other man is in his 30s. He's wearing a rain slicker with the hood up. They're struggling, obviously in serious trouble.

The older man is treading water, bobbing up and down, which he's been doing for about 15 minutes. He has to be really cold and tired by now. After all, it's mid-September, definitely not summer swimming weather. He's trying to keep the younger man from flopping face-first into the water and drowning. The younger man is stuck solidly in one spot. Something mysterious and menacing, unseen beneath the dark water, locks his legs in a death grip. It's a drain pipe. He's literally being sucked down the drain.

Whir-Click — Close-up of the cop's black shoes. They're shiny, mirror-like. I can almost see my reflection on his toes. The crease in his gray wool uniform pants is razor-sharp. He's barely moving, trying to keep muddy water in the grass from squishing up on his spit-polished shoes. The cop has a huge coil of rope.

Whir-Click — There is only one thing to do. "I'm going in," I say to the chief. He doesn't argue. It seems like a snap decision, but it's not. A hundred thoughts race through my mind first. It's risky, but it's a carefully calculated risk. This is a pond, I reason, not a raging river. This is not swift water. There's no current, no rapids, no rocks to knock me out. It's a water rescue, true. But the victim is immobile. He's stuck in a pipe. I'm not trying to rescue a drowning man, who could easily kill me in a desperate attempt to save himself. And I grew up swimming in our family's farm pond.

Whir-Click — Close-up of cops' hands. I give him my pagers and strip off my bunker gear. I hand the chief my glasses and watch, grab one end of the rope and wade into the water, fully clothed. I'm wearing blue jeans, thick wool socks and a blue Emmaus Fire Dept. job shirt with denim elbow patches and collar. I should be wearing a life jacket, maybe a wet suit and a helmet, and have a lifeline attached to me. I don't. We don't have half of that equipment. I should also have a certificate that says I am trained to do this. I don't. Closest I can come is the Lifesaving merit badge I earned as a teenager in Boy Scouts. That's tough. If need be, I'll beg forgiveness later. This is life-and-death.

The mud is cold and thick. It stinks. The pond is deep, about 20 feet at the center. The side drops off rapidly. Two steps and I can't touch bottom anymore. The water is black, cold as the ocean in Maine in the summer. Takes my breath away. Rain's pouring down. Water in the pond is rising.

Whir-Click — I'm out in the water, swimming. Breaststroke, my eyes just above the surface of the water, I keep the two men in my sight at all times. The man in the pipe is not going anywhere, I know. But the gray-haired man might. He's swimming freely and is the biggest danger to me. If he cramps up or starts going down, he could easily take me with him. He may be an ally, but he's also my enemy. I'll keep the drain pipe between him and me. If he can't touch me, he can't drown me. The other man's much less of a threat, but I still must be careful. Who knows what could happen? They're dying out there.

Whir-Click — Zoom in on two frightened faces. There's no cheery chitchat — "Hi, I'm George. I'll be your rescue swimmer today" — like on TV. This is combat engineering. Do, or die.

The men are happy to see me, especially the gray-haired man. He's getting tired of trying to keep himself afloat, while holding the younger man upright. The other man doesn't know or much care about anything, except that he's in great pain. His right leg is being beaten to a pulp by the incredible force of water gushing into the 10-inch wide drain pipe that holds him prisoner. He's fighting fatigue, panic and pain, lots of pain. Shock and hypothermia can't be far away. There's no time to lose.

What to do? We constantly train to rescue people from crushed cars, trucks and buses, from confined spaces such as manholes, storm sewers and huge steel tanks, or construction trenches that collapse, burying workers alive. But this? Who'd a thunk it?

Whir-Click — Think back to the ABCs of first aid — airway, breathing, circulation. The man in the pipe can't breathe. The drawstring on his rain jacket hood is strangling him. I untie the string, pull the hood back off his head, knocking off his glasses. They disappear into the water. He doesn't care. Neither do I. I'm still trying to figure out how we're ever going to get him, and the rest of us, out of here alive. Why did I ever swim out into this pond? Seemed like a good idea at the time. Now, I'm not so sure. What should I do next?

Now that he can breathe, I have to get a rope around him. But how? Where? What knot should I use? There's only one knot that you can trust with a life. Guaranteed not to slip or come undone. The bowline, one of the first knots you learn in Boy Scouts.

I get behind the man in the pipe, grab the drain pipe with my knees. The whirlpool starts sucking the bottom of my sweatshirt into the pipe. I scoot back, loosely lock onto the pipe with my feet, instead of my knees. Then I pass the rope around his chest and form a loop in the rope. My hands are a foot under water. I can't see what I'm doing. I snug the rope up under his armpits so he won't slip out when they pull on the rope from shore. I finish the knot by feel, remembering a knot lesson from Scouts:

"The rabbit comes up out of the hole ... goes around the tree ... and back down in the hole." I add a couple of safety half-hitches for insurance.

"Pull!" I yell to the guys on shore.

"Stop!" the man screams. "You're cutting me in half."

He flails his arms, pushing me down into the water as he fights to remain upright.

Whir-Click — Fade to black. I'm looking up through murky water. "This is not a good place to be," I remember thinking. I don't want to die. I especially don't want to drown. I can't think of a much worse way to die.

I plant my feet on the pipe and push off to escape his reach. This has to be the craziest thing I've ever done in my life.

Whir-Click — Surfacing, I gasp for air, then look to the east bank. It's lined now with firefighters and other first responders. I see a white helmet. It's Vera Cruz Assistant Chief Jason Tapler. He has a walkie-talkie mic in each hand. His mouth is wide open. I read his lips. Three words that say it all hang in the air.

This is getting pretty old by now. Seems like I've been in the water for hours. The water's cold and dark. It's almost black, just like the stormy sky. Wind's howling. Rain's still coming down sideways. It's a hurricane, and I'm getting dunked in an ice-cold pond by a total stranger, who may not have a snowball's chance in hell of ever getting out of here alive. Am I going to die with him? My wife's gonna to kill me.

Whir-Click — Suddenly, something touches me from behind, then lifts me up a few inches. It's a pair of big hands. They belong to Emmaus Firefighter Keith Frankenfield. He's wearing a safety harness linked to a safety line that stretches back to the shore. He hands me a 5-inch-wide ladder belt with a big carabiner. It's what we use to keep from falling off of the 100-foot aerial ladder. I cinch the ladder belt tight around the trapped man's chest, wind the rope through the carabiner and pop his left foot out of the pipe.

Whir-Click — The man's face goes ghostly white. I lay two fingers on his throat.

"No pulse! I don't have a pulse. Pull, pull, pull!" I scream.

The rope snaps tight. Four firefighters on the shore pull with all their might. The pipe and all four of us in the water shift slightly toward shore. Then ... *POP!*

There's a sickening sucking sound, and the man's free. The guys on the shore are pulling so hard on the rope that the four of us are surfing to safety. But wait ...

Whir-Click — Dead ahead, a rusty metal fence post sticks out of the muddy bank like a spear. This close to shore and safety, we don't want to impale anyone and create another emergency. The firefighters on the rope move two steps down the bank and guide us in away from the post.

The victim is unconscious when we hit the mud on the shore. Medics can't get a pulse. They're about to start CPR when his eyes pop wide open. They load him in the Stokes basket, a welded metal and wire litter that's standard in rescues. Leaning into the wind, slipping in the mud, half a dozen fresh firefighters haul him up the hill toward the road and the waiting ambulance. The weather's too awful for medevac to fly.

Whir-Click — Another hand. This one belongs to the gray-haired man from the pond. He charges up to me with his right hand out and a big smile. I clutch his hand. Next thing I know, we have our arms wrapped around each other. Wet, stinking, shivering, we're pounding each other on the back. We're laughing. Or crying. Or both. Yes! We did it! *YES!* We got him out.

They say my dip in the pond lasted about 30 minutes. No wonder I was shivering. Chief Reiss wrapped a wool blanket around me, then a second one. He bundled me into his Jeep, and turned the heater on full blast.

Someone was calling my name. It was Ron Devlin, a reporter friend from *The Morning Call*. Ron was asking me questions. I wanted to answer him. I knew I should answer him, but I couldn't. My teeth were chattering too much. The chief said he'd take me home.

Back at the house, Melanie was worrying. "He's been gone a long time. I don't have a good feeling about this call," she told her friends. A wave of nausea rushed over her. Shaking, she rushed back inside to the bathroom.

As she started back out toward the garage to check on the vegetable packing, Melanie saw a man coming toward the open garage door. She was still disoriented, but instantly recognized the uniform. White shirt. Gold badge. It was ... the Fire Chief.

"Oh, my God!" she gasped. "No!"

She didn't see me scrambling out of the passenger's seat. So I started yelling. "I'm OK! I'm here! I'm OK!"

A look of complete horror covered her face.

She didn't see that Chief Reiss was smiling. He was grinning from ear to ear. And peacock proud of everyone involved in the rescue.

Melanie said she vaguely remembered the chief saying something about my being really cold. Then the fog rolled in, again. She didn't remember me peeling off most of my pond-stinking wet clothes and dropping them in a heap in the rain on the pavement outside the garage door. She remembered me taking a long, HOT shower, saying something about not wanting to go to the hospital, and that her friends were mad at her for coming back out to bag veggies instead of resting. She remembered saying, "Shouldn't you go to the hospital?" and later, "How did your truck get home?" I started to explain how another firefighter drove my truck home, while I was in the shower. Mel just shook her head then crawled into bed.

The nurses and doctors at Lehigh Valley Hospital were expecting at least three victims from the pond, one with unknown but probably massive traumatic injuries and two with acute hypothermia. The ambulance brought only one, the trauma victim. That was probably a good thing because the ER staff had its hands full, and then some, with just him.

His name was Christopher V. Barebo. He was 37, married to Dee, and the father of two young children, 2-year-old Daniel and 5-year-old Robyn. He was a real mess. Chris died three times on the way to the hospital. His blood pH was 6.39, the lowest and most acidic that trauma doctors had ever seen. When deprived of oxygen, muscles release acid into the blood. That can cause serious heart, lung and kidney damage. Almost no one survives at much below a pH of 6.8. His core body temperature plunged to 93.2 F, threatening fatal heart arrhythmia. Tissue damage was so massive that he might lose his right leg. Doctors pegged his chances of survival at less than 50-50.

But I didn't know any of this at the time. I was trying to get my own core body temperature somewhere back up to near normal. I stayed in the shower until we ran out of hot water. Then I piled on warm clothes. Later, after tucking Melanie into bed again, I drove into town to pick up my watch, glasses and pagers at the firehouse.

"How's our guy from the pond?" I asked Emmaus Ambulance Chief Mike Nonnemacher.

"Mmm ... we really don't know much."

So how did all of this happen? It started innocently enough that morning with Chris worrying about the water level rising rapidly in the pond behind his home. He fretted that it might overflow, wash away some of the embankment and flood his downhill neighbors again.

As he left for work, Chris asked his wife, Dee, to call him if it looked like the pond would overflow. Chris was vice president of manufacturing at Otterbine-Barebo, Inc., a company that makes pond aerators two miles away in the village of Vera Cruz. It wasn't long before Dee called Chris at work.

Chris rushed right home. He donned his raincoat and paddled out into the pond on an inflatable raft, something he did all the time. His plan was to remove an 18-inch tall extension on top of a vertical drain pipe in the deep end. Once he removed the extension, the pipe would be shorter, and water would drop to a lower, safer level.

But, thanks to Hurricane Floyd, there was already way too much water in the pond. When Chris pulled the extension off, it created an instant whirlpool. The violent vortex grabbed the plastic raft. The raft exploded, wrapping around Chris' right leg. The deflated raft flushed right down through the pipe. But Chris was too big for the pipe to swallow whole. He was stuck in the eye of the maelstrom with his right leg completely inside the pipe and his left ankle grinding against the sharp lip of the drain. Dee and Chris' father, Charles, 65, tried to free Chris. When they couldn't, Dee called 911. Charles stayed with Chris in the water, trying to keep his son from drowning.

On my way home from the firehouse, I took Fifth Street over South Mountain so I could get another look at the pond. Nearing the pond, I slowed way down, then jammed on the brakes. I couldn't believe my eyes. The pond was completely empty. It was just a muddy crater with a long pipe sticking up out of the brown goo. Where'd the pond go?

It seems that "Pop!" we heard when the pipe finally released Chris was the sound of the pipe cracking at the elbow joint in the bottom of the pond. That instantly released the rushing water's death grip on his leg. It also pulled the plug on the whole pond.

That afternoon, our home phone rang. It was Ron Devlin from *The Morning Call* with "another dumb question from my editors." But I fired off the first question.

"How's our patient?"

"Critical. But the hospital's probably just being cautious," said Ron. Maybe. Maybe not. A few prayers tonight couldn't hurt.

Next morning, I walked our dalmatian, Jethro, down our driveway to pick up the newspaper. Ron's story was on the front page with all the rest of the hurricane news. "They got him out in the nick of time," said State Trooper Joseph A. Campbell, who was investigating the incident. "He was in the water 45 minutes."

Chris was in critical condition. "He's very, very serious," the paper quoted his brother, Charles Jr., as saying.

Critical! I was stunned, devastated. What did I do wrong? I felt like it was all my fault. What could I have done differently, quicker, better, safer, stronger, gentler? Did I have the rope far enough up on his chest when they started pulling? Or was it too low? He was screaming that it was cutting him in half. Did we tear his liver, rupture his spleen? What? It ate away at me all day and into the evening.

What did I do wrong?

Not a blessed thing, his mother reassured me that evening when I called their home. I couldn't help it. I had to call. The suspense was killing me, and Melanie, too.

Turned out Chris' family was thinking about calling me right about that time, too. They had just looked up our number in the phone book. Then someone said, "Nah, he probably does this all the time, and doesn't want to be bothered at home."

Yeah, right! First time I'd ever done something like this. Far as I was concerned, it could be the last time, too.

"He's not out of the woods yet, but he's making progress," said Chris' mother. There was so much massive tissue, vessel and other damage that they may have to amputate part of his right leg. His kidneys were shutting down because his whole body was so overloaded with toxins. By Friday morning, his body temperature was normal and his kidneys were working again.

"Every day he hangs in there, his chances improve 10 percent," she added. "When he comes home, there is going to be the biggest fireworks display on South Mountain that you ever saw."

"I'd love to see that!"

"You'll be the first one we invite," she said.

That was a relief. They weren't mad at me. All day I'd been kicking myself, second-guessing my every move in the pond.

Later that evening, as part of catching up on my day job with Rodale's Russian magazine, I visited *The Moscow Times* website. I froze on a quote from a member of an elite Russian search-and-rescue crew. In just the past month, he had searched rubble for survivors after an earthquake in Turkey and the terrorist bombings of four Russian apartment buildings. From a total stranger in cyberspace, but a fellow firefighter from halfway around the world, came the perfect thought for the day:

"If you risk your life pulling out a dead body you are insane, but if you do it to save a life and succeed you are simply being professional."

All of this happened long before websites such as firehouse.com, firefighternation.com, firerescue1.com, thebravestonline.com, firefighterclosecalls.com, firecritic.com, statter911.com, and even the 12-County-PA-Fire-Wire-News-Page on Facebook began reporting fire and emergency news from around the nation and the world almost as it happened. Despite that, the word still spread. The Associated Press picked up Ron Devlin's article. Response was immediate.

"You damn fool," Steve Bulkley our old boss at *The Dispatch,* e-mailed from Pompano Beach, Florida. "What if there was room in that drain pipe for another foot — yours!!!? Or the suction could have caught your clothing and dragged you in.

"Yeah, I know: You were just running on adrenaline and did what needed doing at the time. That's my kid! Congratulations! What a helluva way to make a livin'." He forgot we're volunteers. We don't get paid but a few bucks to cover expenses for running on fire calls.

"Holy shit, Aquaman!" said my best friend and publishing partner Keith Crotz in Illinois. "Not many people could or would do what you did. If you hadn't gone in when you did, it would have had a very different ending. Send me a copy of the commendation when you get it!!!! Takes a person's breath away, no kidding."

But there was no commendation, never even any official recognition. Emmaus and Vera Cruz don't believe in it. Helping save a life when the opportunity presents itself just comes with the territory. It's what we're supposed to do, plain and simple. Besides, in the military, this was the kind of "bonehead stunt" that might well earn both a commendation and a court-martial, or at least a reduction in rank, like being busted back to buck private.

Jim Kelly, Melanie's former city editor at *The Morning Call,* weighed in with big-picture editorial comments, rightfully praising volunteers everywhere: "Just read the story on Mr. Barebo. God bless you and all the other firefighters and fire police whom we take for granted. What you did yesterday, and what people like you perform every day, is a wonderful gesture of community spirit and concern for the family of man. Great work!"

As Thanksgiving approached that year, writers at both the daily and weekly newspapers got the bright idea to do a Turkey Day feature on someone who was truly thankful for something — like being alive. Ron Devlin of *The Morning Call* interviewed Chris and Dee Barebo. He sent a photographer out to their house. Over the mantle hung a huge banner that read, "WELCOME HOME DADDY. WE LOVE YOU!" Little handprints and other artwork from his children adorned the sign. The banner was in the background of a four-column color photo at the top of the front page. The photo showed Dee planting a big kiss on a smiling Chris. "Holiday takes on new meaning for Upper Milford man, who almost lost his life in Floyd aftermath," the subhead read.

"I appreciate my family, the healers, the firefighters and my friends a lot more. This Thanksgiving, the clichés actually mean something," Chris said in the article.

Corrine Durdock, our friend at *The East Penn Press,* took a different approach. She arranged a face-to-face meeting between Chris and me, two months to the day after we took our dip in the pond. I met Chris in his office in the renovated silk mill in Vera Cruz a quarter-mile from my house. Corrine didn't get many good quotes. Chris and I didn't have too much to say. That wasn't because we didn't want to talk. We just had a hard time saying anything to each other without choking up. We still do. Probably always will. Corrine snapped a photo of the two of us shaking hands.

What brought a lump to my throat was the fact that Chris was walking. He was using a cane, yes. And he was a lot skinnier than I remembered him. But he was alive, standing upright, and walking under his own power — on his very own right leg. He didn't lose it in the pond when we heard that "pop!" and horrible sucking sound. Although doctors feared they might be forced to, they didn't have to amputate.

The next year on Sept. 16, the first anniversary of our adventure in the pond, a delivery van from Macungie's Posey Patch turned up our driveway. The driver dropped off a huge arrangement of flowers. Accenting the bouquet were four of the biggest rolls of "Life Savers" candy they make. The thank you card read, "You're a real Life Saver! Chris Barebo and Family."

I kept the candy, but the flowers rightfully belonged to Melanie. Like Chris Barebo, she will always remember that date as the worst — and best — day of her life.

PART 5

The *Citizen's* Fire Company

CHAPTER TWENTY-ONE

Just Get the Truck to the Fire

When we moved to the Borough of Emmaus in 1981, the Emmaus Fire Department was already a venerable 111 years old. But the fire company in the adjoining township, Upper Milford, hadn't even celebrated its 40th anniversary. Barely 5,000 people lived in the township. Instead of being jammed in on top of each other in row houses, apartments and suburban tract homes, as was the case in much of Emmaus, Upper Milford residents were comfortably spread out over more than 18 square miles of hilly forests and fertile farm fields, far from the madding crowd. Life in the township was slower. Property taxes were lower. It seemed like a great place to raise our two children and lots of organic vegetables, berries and cut flowers for market. We soon bought 20 acres of vacant land that would become our farm. Upper Milford was also where I would serve as a volunteer firefighter for 25 years.

Change came slowly in Upper Milford. The mostly Pennsylvania Dutch people who lived there liked things just the way they were. And they aimed to keep things that way. Alas, like residents of many unincorporated rural areas throughout the United States, the earlier citizens of the township never saw much need to get serious about fire protection — until it was too late.

The date was March 2, 1941. Snow drifts were 4 to 5 feet high. Snowplows had reopened King's Highway South only 12 hours before milkmen Emil Koehler and Albert Dries rolled into the village of Zionsville. They were on their way to collect milk at local dairies when the milkmen discovered the fire. They saw smoke pouring from the east end of a large factory building that adjoined the Zionsville post office, Yeakel's General Store and the storekeeper's home. It was 1:30 a.m. and a Sunday, so the storekeeper and his wife were probably at home and in bed, fast sleep.

The milkmen banged frantically on the front door of the store to wake the couple. There was no answer. The fire was growing. So Koehler and Dries kicked in the rear door and rousted Emanuel and Eva Yeakel from their bed, almost certainly saving their lives.

Since Upper Milford had no fire department, volunteer fire departments miles away in Emmaus and Macungie were called. The Yeakels, meanwhile, hooked up a garden hose and tried to battle the blaze. Emanuel was burned on his hands, face and head. But he managed to carry two bags of mail and six parcel post packages out of the post office before flames forced him to give up the fight.

By the time the volunteers arrived, 60 jobs at the sportswear factory had gone up in smoke. Firefighters could only hose down the burning ruins. Four brick walls and a chimney were all that remained.

Township residents were horrified. Upper Milford needed its own fire company, they all agreed. But where? That's where the agreement ended. One idea was to have a firehouse located in the geographic center of the township in Old Zionsville. But the people from the village of Vera Cruz far to the east said, "No." Then they said, "Hell, no!" Vera Cruz wanted its very own firehouse — in Vera Cruz, not 3 miles away in Old Zionsville. And so, the citizens decided to have two fire companies, one in Old Zionsville (Western District), the other in Vera Cruz (Eastern District).

"That's probably the best thing they could have done," 94-year-old Henry Beitler said about the decision. He was the last surviving charter member of either fire company and a former fire chief in Old Zionsville. From their founding, the two fire companies went their very separate ways. Each raised money, bought new trucks and land, and built its own firehouse. Old Zionsville had fire practice on Thursday night; Vera Cruz on Tuesday night. About the only time the two companies got together was at bad fires, when one needed the other's help.

Old Zionsville quickly signed up 37 members at an organizational meeting on March 26, 1942. But 19 months would pass before its first fire truck went into service. And disaster didn't wait. Just three days after the meeting, fire destroyed the Old Zionsville Hotel. Private Edwin Hillegass, who was home on leave from the Army, and another township resident, Walter Sadrovitz, discovered the fire as they passed by about 11:45 p.m. The men broke open the front door to search for anyone who might be inside, but flames drove them back. As the fire raged, villagers feared the innkeeper's two young sons, ages 2 and 4, and the family's maid were inside the burning building. Turned out the little boys were safe with their grandparents in nearby Hellertown. The maid was away visiting friends on her day off. The only casualties were the family's two dogs, who were trapped in the basement, reported Allentown's *Evening Chronicle*.

Township residents redoubled their efforts to establish two fire companies. Progress was neither quick nor easy. It wasn't cheap, either. The world was at war. Fire trucks and other equipment were scarce. So was money.

First came the pump, on a trailer with steel wheels ...

No one knows what became of the trailer, but the 500-gpm pump found a new home on Vera Cruz' first fire truck. When the truck wore out, firefighters moved the pump to a replacement truck, a 1962 GMC. These days the truck's not in great shape, but the pump still works just fine.

UPPER MILFORD HISTORICAL SOCIETY PHOTOS

But the volunteers in Old Zionsville managed to scrape together $1,400, and in late 1942, they bought the chassis of a 1937 Diamond T coal truck. It was outfitted with a body and a pump in Indiana, and finally went into service in October of 1943. For the next nine years, the pumper was housed in a volunteer's garage until Old Zionsville finally opened its own firehouse.

Three miles to the east, in Vera Cruz, the first fire truck was built by the volunteers themselves. It started with an old Civil Defense pump that came on a trailer with steel wheels. Members mounted the pump on a 1939 International truck chassis, then added a body. Total cost was about $2,800. An old silk mill in the center of the village housed the truck for a few years until firefighters could afford to build a single-bay engine room. "We hauled rocks in from the fencerow with a horse and buggy to fill inside, then poured concrete," said Cyrus Mohr, a Vera Cruz volunteer for 55 years.

Each village installed a fire siren to alert volunteers to emergencies. A "telephone tree" was also set up. When the siren went off, the volunteer living closest to the firehouse started calling around. "I'd get a call: 'The fire siren is going' — that's all we would say. We'd hang up and call the next person," said Bill Stahler, a Vera Cruz volunteer for more than 50 years.

"When the siren went, everybody came running. The first guy there drove the truck. The other guys hung on the sides and back," said Mohr. Fire helmets, coats and boots hung on the side of the truck or on the garage walls. The first volunteers to arrive scrambled for gear. On good days, they found boots that matched and a coat that fit, more or less.

"Just get the truck to the fire. Somebody will follow and be able to help you," former Fire Chief Carl Schell said the old-timers told him when he joined Vera Cruz in 1955. "We just had one truck. A lot of times we had to jump the battery to get it started, because we didn't have the fire calls we have today." Tow ropes or chains also got the truck going.

"Just get the truck to the fire" orders also applied to some of the good women of the Ladies' Auxiliary, which was formed not long after the Citizens' Fire Company was founded. "Sometimes there wasn't a driver available when the alarm went," said Mohr. Chief among female drivers was Joyce Arndt. She lived right across the street from the firehouse. Joyce was usually home during the day. She was outraged at the thought of volunteers already on the scene of a fire having to wait for a driver to bring the fire truck. A founding member of the Ladies' Auxiliary, Joyce drove the fire engine to her share of fire calls.

Fortunately, fires were few and far between. "We had brush fires and barn fires and house fires, same as we do today. We weren't called out to accidents the way we are today. Once in a while, we had a chimney fire.

Vera Cruz firefighters battle a stubborn fire inside the railroad tunnel
beneath the Northeast Extension of the Pennsylvania Turnpike.
UPPER MILFORD HISTORICAL SOCIETY PHOTO

There were quite a few barn fires, a lot of brush fires from passing trains and
people burning off fields," said Mohr. "When we were kids, we didn't have
a fire company. Emmaus had to come out here. But a lot of times, no one
even called the fire company. They didn't have to. A whole bunch of guys
from around the village would come out with rakes and shovels."

One of the worst fires early in Vera Cruz' history was actually deep
underground. It was in the historic Reading Railroad (Perkiomen Branch)
tunnel through a steep hill just south of Vera Cruz. The one-third-mile-

long tunnel was dug in the mid-1870s by some 450 mostly Irish laborers. "Work was done by hand drills and powder, donkey engines and hoists, and 20 horses with dump carts. One man lost his life during construction. A rock above the tunnel entrance bears a white figure that legend has it is the ghostly image of the lost man," according to the Upper Milford Historical Society's photo history of the township.

In December of 1959, more than 80 years after the tunnel was dug, the 12-by-12-inch beams supporting the tunnel's ceiling were dry as a bone. They were also slathered with creosote. Chunks of burning carbon from a passing locomotive's exhaust set the beams on fire about 100 feet inside the tunnel, which passed under the recently completed Northeast Extension of the Pennsylvania Turnpike (then State Route 9).

"Dillinger RR Tunnel Fire Raging Beneath Turnpike," screamed the headline in *The Morning Call*.

"Fifteen firemen from the Vera Cruz Citizens Co. responded to an alarm shortly after 10:30 p.m. last night," the newspaper reported. "They pumped water from natural streams on either side of the track, and reused the water as it drained back into the creeks. The Zionsville Co. arrived at mid-morning ... Debris blocked the flow of the streams, forcing the fire companies to haul water in relays to a nearby bridge from where hoses were run. The distance is about 100 yards."

A photo on the front page showed firefighters attacking blazing beams far above their heads in the smoke-filled tunnel. The men wore hip boots, long rubber raincoats and helmets. There were no air packs. Those didn't appear until years later.

It wasn't the first — or last — time the founding firefighters put themselves in harm's way with little to no protection against known toxic chemicals. In the summer of 1971, a relatively new business in the township went up in flames. It was called "High Quality Polishing and Plating," a fancy name for a place that did really dirty work — electroplating metal. It was located on State Routes 29 and 100, near the geographic center of the township. Although it was just a quarter of a mile down the road from Old Zionsville's firehouse, Vera Cruz, Emmaus and other nearby fire companies were quickly called in on multiple alarms as the stubborn flames grew and grew.

The flames were like nothing even the most experienced firefighters from any department had ever seen before. In addition to the usual red and orange, the leaping flames were blue, green, and purple, among other weird, almost psychedelic, colors. The smoke smelled and tasted funny. That's because the place was full of drums, vats and large tanks containing an array of acids and solutions of copper, chromium, arsenic, silver, lead, nickel, and cyanide. Only a few firefighters had air packs. Despite that, they bravely battled on. They saved the business, but may have paid a terrible price for victory.

When High Quality was abandoned in 1983 after the deaths of its owners, the United States Environmental Protection Agency took over the site. It was a Super Fund site, a toxic wasteland, just 50 feet away from Indian Creek, which feeds into the drinking water supply of the nearby Borough of Red Hill, population 2,382. In 2014, drinking water wells around the site were still tainted with chemicals, environmental officials regularly inspected monitoring wells there, and the whole area was secured by towering chain-link fence.

By then, most of the old-timers who faced the flames were gone. Some were victims of strange cancers and other diseases that friends and family blamed on the High Quality and other long-ago fires.

The fire company itself also developed a troubling malady about the time of the High Quality fire. It was called "founders syndrome," or "founderitis," a condition common in both for-profit and nonprofit corporations, associations and other legal entities. Simply put, this crippling disease sets in when one or even a handful of founders holds all power within the organization, and wants to keep it that way. New blood, new ideas and new ways of doing things are not welcome.

But that malady did not go undetected for decades the way the old smokeaters' diseases did. New members quickly made an important discovery: Some of the old Dutchmen who founded the fire company didn't play well with others. They didn't want to share their "toys," the fire truck they had built and the other firefighting tools they had scrimped and saved to buy. They especially didn't want to share their hard-won firefighting knowledge.

The youngsters grew restive. They wanted to learn more than how to simply "put the wet stuff on the red stuff." Other fire companies had regular, weekly fire practice. Why didn't Vera Cruz? Don't you think that just might be a good idea?

"Well ... we do it this way, because that's the way we've always done it! If it ain't broke, don't fix it.

"And, anyway ... what's to know about hoses? They have two kinds of couplings. One's male, one's female. The male goes to the fire, and the female stays home." That's the way it was taught, back in the day.

"And if you don't like it, too bad. It's MY way ... or the highway!"

The new recruits didn't like it. But they weren't about to hit the road and leave the fire company. No, they were just getting started as firefighters.

They wanted to learn. They needed to learn everything there was to know about:

* Water supply
* Hitting a hydrant
* Drafting water from a pond
* Hoses and hose lays
* Fire behavior
* Fireground size-up and tactics
* Ventilation
* Forcible entry
* And more.

The list was endless. And so, a few young Turks secretly began plotting a revolution. They formulated a crude battle plan, then set a date and a time to launch their attack.

On the appointed Tuesday evening, the conspirators gathered at the engine room. One of them pulled the lone fire truck out of its bay, so it was in full view of everyone passing on the highway, and of anyone who might be out and about in the village.

Then their momentum stalled. They milled around the truck, not quite sure what to do or where to begin. They went over the truck from stem to stern, from top to bottom, opening and closing various compartments, unloading and then reloading fire extinguishers, hose couplings and other pieces of arcane firefighting equipment. They tweaked the siren, tried the truck's flashing red lights and honked the horn, and even looked under the hood. They marveled over various nozzles and adapters, hand tools, the two hard suction hoses and a strainer used for drafting water out of ponds or streams, axes, saws, pike poles, wooden extension ladder, tire chains, and spanner wrenches used to tighten and undo hose couplings.

That was long before my time, of course, more than a decade before I joined the fire company. But some of those who were there say the conversation that night went something like this:

"What's this long pointy thing with a hook on the end?"

"I heard someone call it a 'pike pole.'"

"Whaddaya do with it?"

"You poke holes in ceilings and walls. Then you use the hook to rip things open to find hot spots."

"Oh! Well, whaddaya think this thing does?"

"How should I know?"

"Beats me."

"What's with these big black pipes on the side of the truck? Geez, they weigh a ton!"

"You hook 'em to a fire hydrant."

"Nah! They're for pumping water out of a pond. That strainer goes on one end so you don't suck up a bunch fish or a snapping turtle."

"Dipstick! You can use 'em both ways. They're called hard-suction hoses."

This went on for more than an hour. All the while, the youngsters were secretly being watched. One of the older members of the fire company lived just down the street, within view of the engine room. He kept a close and critical eye on them from a lawn chair on the front porch. Finally, he couldn't stand it anymore. Curiosity was killing him. He got up and walked over to the firehouse to confront the youngsters.

"Whatthehell do you hoofties think you're doing?" he asked.

"We're having fire practice!"

"Oh!"

Probably not a bad idea, he agreed. Then the older man did something surprising: He offered to help.

"I'll drive the truck, but … one of you is going to have to figure out how to run the pump."

So they all piled into and onto the truck, and drove to where there was a good water supply. Compartment doors clanged open. Hoses were unloaded, stretched and reloaded. Then they were reloaded again — the right way. The choke on the gasoline engine that powered the pump slid in and out, in and out. The engine coughed to life, then died. It was restarted, multiple times. Levers on the pump swiveled back and forth. Words were spoken. Many words! Finally, after about an hour, water began flowing. Hose couplings leaked. Water sprayed everywhere, on everything and everyone. But everyone was also very happy.

And so Tuesday-night fire practice became a tradition in Vera Cruz. But it was a blessing and a curse, because it meant that, from then on — every week — the fire chief, or officers, or *someone* had to come up with an idea for something meaningful to do that night for fire practice.

CHAPTER TWENTY-TWO

"Greetings," You're Drafted

The Citizens' Fire Company of Upper Milford Township prided itself on being strictly an all-volunteer fire department. That's true, except for me. I was a draftee.

It all started with our dream to be farmers. Melanie and I wanted to raise organic vegetables, fruit and flowers, and sell them as close as possible to where they were grown. As we prepared to move from South Florida to Pennsylvania in 1981, however, there was no time to find a farm in the Lehigh Valley. We just needed to get a roof over our heads in time for the big move. So we bought a suburban ranch house in town in Emmaus. It was hardly our dream house. But it would do fine, until we found what we wanted.

The urge to get growing was strong. Our first summer in Emmaus, we borrowed a garden tiller from the Rodale Research Center. I worked up the west side of our yard in suburbia for a garden. We planted five long rows of sweet corn. The corn grew headhigh. That was not particularly amusing to some of our new neighbors with perfect — weedless — lawns and neatly trimmed hedges.

Our suburban garden produced excellent yields and delicious dinners. That's when we started looking seriously for a farm. For three years, we scoured the countryside for our dream place. Every chance we got, we piled both kids in the backseat of the station wagon. We prowled the back roads in parts of three counties for hours on end. We didn't want much, just a classic pre-revolutionary stone farmhouse with a huge Pennsylvania Dutch stone bank barn, a spring-fed pond, maybe a springhouse, and fertile fields dotted with fat cattle for as far as the eye could see. We came close a few times, but our hearts were always broken. Our dream house and farm just didn't exist — at least not anywhere close to our price range.

Then on one of our weekend drives, a new "For Sale" sign caught our eye. It was in a field along Acorn Drive. We already knew all about that property. It was a wedge-shaped 21 acres with an old stone house and barn. It was way out of our price range, but it had been on the market a long time.

Maybe they were splitting off five or 10 acres. I jotted down the real estate agent's number. I would call him first thing Monday.

"No, they're not splitting off a field," the salesman said. "Just trying to attract more attention with more signs. But I do have another property, 20 acres of vacant farmland, right around the corner."

"Yeah, we already checked it out," I said. "Too expensive."

"Well, you probably don't know the owner just dropped his price $20,000," he replied.

That was news. Good news! Why the price drop? The owner was old, the realtor explained. His health was failing. He had been trying to sell the land for development, but builders weren't interested. The land was just a little too rolling and too wet in spots to handle the 15 to 20 new homes developers wanted to build there. The owner was tired of it all. He wanted one less thing to worry about. The realtor offered to show us the property whenever we wanted.

Great! How about now?

My next call was home. "Can you meet me out there in 15 minutes?" I asked Melanie. "Oh, and bring the checkbook!"

Mel and I walked over just a bit of the west hayfield. The front field was a little swampy, but the view from a low hill about 600 feet back from the road was simply spectacular. A million-dollar view if ever there was one. Looking due north, across a small valley with a stone farmhouse and bank barn from the 1850s, all you could see was the forested face of South Mountain. Its steep slopes are in conservation zoning. They can never be heavily developed. It was the perfect place for our dream house. We handed the realtor a deposit check for $500.

The land was ours. Our long search was over. We finally had a real farm! Sort of. The land spread out behind 10 single-family homes built right on Main Road. Most of those lots were only 150 feet deep. Our fields ran down to the road between the houses in three spots. There were no buildings, no well, not even a driveway or a farm lane. Just 17 acres of overgrown fields, along with three acres of woods, wetland, and wooded fencerows piled high with fieldstone. There was also a handful of failed "probe holes" left by would-be developers doing "perc tests" for standard septic systems. The tests all failed. We saw an expensive sand-mound septic system in our future, but that was OK.

The good news far outweighed the bad. The land was barely three miles from where we lived in town. It was close to work for both Melanie and me. The mailing address was still Emmaus, even though the land was in the village of Vera Cruz in Upper Milford Township. We were still in the East Penn School District, which was high on our "must-have" list. We could still keep the same phone number. And it was close enough for me to keep running with the Emmaus Fire Department.

We were delighted. Our new neighbors were delighted, too. One of their worst nightmares was having a "house farm" in their backyards. They were perfectly happy with a couple of crazy organic farmers raising vegetables, berries, kids and flowers.

Our nearest neighbors were a 50-ish Pennsylvania Dutch couple, Carl and Jean Meck. Jean was born and raised in the cottage next to the house where she and Carl lived now. Carl was a Justice of the Peace and longtime captain of the local Fire Police. He knew I was a firefighter in Emmaus. "Soon as you move out here," Carl said, "you're joining Station 28, our volunteer fire company here in Vera Cruz." I didn't argue with him. It seemed like the right thing to do, but it would have to wait a few years. We had a farm and a house to build first.

We had $10,000 in the bank. It was money we'd saved from Melanie's newspaper salary. We gave that to the owner as our down payment. He carried the financing on the remaining $20,000 for two years at 10 percent interest. In 1984, that was a pretty good deal.

The next month, we bought a 1946 Ford 2N tractor, a 5-foot Bush Hog rotary mower and a 5-gallon gasoline can. We parked the tractor in our newly acquired field behind the Meck's woodpile. We covered the tractor with a blue poly tarp. Now, instead of prowling the back roads in search of our dream house, every spare hour and dollar went into making our dream come true. The old Ford and I began the task of reclaiming the land from multiflora rose, wild grape vines, poison ivy and brambles. Melanie and the kids planted blueberries, a small garden and flowers, lots of flowers. The place was overrun with pheasants. Every time we went out to the farm we would see and hear pheasants everywhere. We called our little Eden "Pheasant Hill Farm."

But it was tough being absentee farmers. We still lived in town. There was no water at the farm. To keep our newly planted blueberries, fruit trees and raspberries alive, I roped three 55-gallon drums into the back of my pickup and hauled water into the fields. It was a lot of work for me, but a lot of fun for our children. As I bailed water with 5-gallon buckets, 7-year-old Don and 5-year-old Ruth went swimming and splashing in the barrels to escape the 100-degree heat. "Fun … in the barrels!" they sang, while I sweated.

Carl and Jean were good neighbors. They kept a close eye on everything, and on everything we did. When I skipped lunch in a rush to finish roofing our new equipment shed, Carl brought me some leftover stromboli and coffee. He and Jean even recorded our progress with photos. "Our neighbors' new barn," read a handwritten note on the back of a snapshot of our "Traktor Haus," as we'd named the new shed. It was the old Ford's new home.

Then, one weekend, we found our dream home in the Sunday *Morning Call*. It was the Associated Press "House of the Week," a two-story farmhouse design with four bedrooms, 2.5 baths, fireplace and attached two-car garage. We sent off $2 for the mini-blueprints and rushed them to builder Anthony Koneski. We eliminated the spiral stairway, and Melanie and I did all of the painting and staining ourselves. That freed up enough money to put a big screened-in porch on the back of the house. Finally, in late May of 1987, we moved into our dream house.

But Carl didn't forget about drafting me into the local volunteer fire company. We were still unpacking boxes when he nominated me for membership in the Citizens' Fire Company of Upper Milford Township. That was the way things worked in Vera Cruz. Applications for membership had to be accompanied by a $2 application fee and $4 annual dues. Then, after the report of the "investigating committee," applications had to be approved by a vote of the members on two successive readings at the fire company's monthly meetings.

That was what the fire company's constitution and bylaws called for when they were written in 1942. That's exactly the way things still work today.

Carl didn't have to lobby too hard. I had five years of training and practical experience with the Emmaus Fire Department. I already knew a lot of the firefighters in Vera Cruz. And they knew me from "mutual aid" fire calls and occasional fire practices together. Another thing in my favor was that I would be available for daytime fire calls. With Rodale, I worked just three miles from the Vera Cruz firehouse, not half an hour away like so many volunteers. Plus, I had the boss' blessing to run on fire calls when necessary. The rest of the time, I would usually be at home, working around our farm. The members approved my application. The company issued me bunker gear that fit more or less OK. I got an old black helmet from the days long before "political correctness" entered the fire service. The reflective crests on the sides of my helmet bore one word: "Fireman."

Vera Cruz, it turned out, was even more "Dutchie" than Emmaus. The roster included last names like Arndt, Brinker, Bryfogle, Heiserman, Kleinsmith, Kleppinger, Meck, Mohr, Schantz, Schell, Stahler, and Tapler. (The exception to the rule in Vera Cruz was Giuseppe Martellucci, a self-described Old World stone mason.) The main pumper was a "Hahn" — German for rooster. And the Hahn was made in Hamburg ... Pennsylvania, of course.

A curious thing happened to my name when it went on the active roster in Vera Cruz: I was no longer a "DeVault;" I suddenly became a "DeWalt."

When we ordered embroidered jackets for the whole fire company, the seamstress stitched "DeWalt" on the front of mine. But I didn't complain. I took it as something of a compliment, a sign of acceptance as a naturalized Pennsylvania Dutchman. In everyday speech, my first name got a makeover, too. I was now "Georgie DeWalt." Use of the diminutive meant I would do, I was OK, they would keep me around.

There was just one little snag. Both Vera Cruz and Emmaus practiced on Tuesday night. Every week, I had to choose between departments. Usually, Emmaus won. But I made more than my fair share of fire calls with Vera Cruz, especially the daytime calls when volunteers were scarcest. That kept me current with the tools, trucks and procedures in Vera Cruz. So the chief tolerated my training in Emmaus.

When I joined Vera Cruz, there were only stop signs for north-south traffic at the intersection in the center of the village. That created some real traffic hazards when there was a fire call and volunteers rushed to the firehouse from all directions. To protect life and property when the fire siren roared to life, our fire police sprang into action. Two of them lived in the village center. Whoever was home at the time immediately took command of the intersection. Wearing a crossing guard's white cape with the legally mandated "badge of authority" and a policeman's hat and waving a flashlight with an orange traffic cone, they controlled traffic. For many years, Elaine Heiserman protected the intersection. Then Joe Miller took over.

Trouble was, they were volunteers. They were not always around to direct traffic. That was the case when I almost got T-boned — by another firefighter — while responding to a Turnpike fire call. Both vehicles entered the intersection at exactly the same time. I had the right-of-way, but that didn't mean anything as the other guy blew around a line of cars waiting at the stop sign. While he completed his left turn and went on to the firehouse, I jammed on the brakes and swerved to the right, skidding to a stop in front of the Vera Cruz Tavern, where a line of Harleys usually stood.

When I got to the firehouse, the other driver was already behind the wheel of our pumper. I scrambled into a jump seat behind him, still shaking from the near miss, swearing like a sailor. We pulled up to the edge of the Turnpike and waited for orders. We sat in the hot sun, waiting, and waiting some more. The longer we waited, the more my blood boiled. Finally, we were recalled and released. State Police radioed that fire trucks were not needed, thank you.

That did it. I nearly got creamed — by one of our own guys — for nothing. So, what's the fire chief going to do or say to the other driver for pulling such a bonehead stunt?

Nothing? Nope. Not when the other driver is the head of one of the leading families in the village, a longtime member, and a former fire chief, himself.

"That does it!" I said. Life's too short to almost get killed my one of your own men for a stupid Turnpike recall. "I quit!"

"I'll need the fire company license plate off the front of your truck," was all the chief said as I stormed out of the engine room.

"Got a screwdriver?"

He didn't. I told the chief I'd unscrew his precious license plate once I got home, then drop it off at the station later with some other gear.

But before I could do that, the other driver apologized. I cooled down. And the two of us went on to answer scores of fire calls together over the years.

That was just the first of two narrow escapes I had while responding to fire calls. The second happened while I was heading downhill toward Emmaus for a reported car fire. I was assistant chief in Vera Cruz at the time. My red lights were flashing, siren wailing. But a young fire police officer coming the other direction still crowded the center line. Our driver's side sideview mirrors kissed — at 40 miles an hour. Our windows were down. Glass flew everywhere. Luckily, no one was hurt.

Once again, the fire chief didn't step in. After all, I was still an "auslander," an outsider … "from away." And, besides, he didn't want to do anything to possibly offend the other driver, who might vote for him in the next election for chief. The kid did apologize, though, and he bought a new mirror for my truck.

Upper Milford Township and Emmaus are exact opposites. For example, Emmaus has a 100-foot aerial ladder. The longest ladder in the township is a 35-foot extension ladder. Emmaus has a well-equipped heavy rescue truck. The township has the Jaws of Life, but not much else to go with it. Emmaus has its own police force. The township relies on the Pennsylvania State Police. There are just two stoplights in the whole township. Emmaus has some 350 fire hydrants to protect everything from six-story apartment buildings and lots of old row homes to neatly spaced suburban tract homes. The only water we have in the township is what we carry on our trucks. And in tankers, sometimes endless lines of tankers from Old Zionsville, Hereford, Limeport, Alburtis, and other surrounding departments. The tankers refill from ponds, creeks, swimming pools, distant hydrants in town, whatever water source is available. The township allows open burning of household trash, leaves and brush. Open burning has been banned in Emmaus since 1960. But that doesn't keep the wind from blowing smoke from the township downhill into the borough. Urban-rural clashes are common.

While Emmaus lies on a gentle plain on the north side of South Mountain, Upper Milford spreads out over wild uplands to the south. "Flat land does not exist in Upper Milford," said the township's Park, Recreation, Open Space and Environmental Plan. "Steep slopes, narrow stream valleys, and rolling hillsides flow from one to the next, like waves across a wind-blown pond." It's similar to the Hocking Hills of Southeastern Ohio and the "driftless" area of the upper Mississippi River valley in Illinois, Iowa, Minnesota and Wisconsin.

Upper Milford feeds the headwaters of at least three different water-sheds that drain into the Schuylkill and Lehigh Rivers. Five of the eight major creeks are "high quality coldwater fisheries," according to the Pennsylvania Fish and Game Commission. Leibert Creek, the stream that drains our farm, has the added distinction of having a naturally reproducing brown trout population.

The township has more than 50 cultural and historic sites. They range from old grist mills with huge waterwheels to ancient jasper quarries. Native Americans from throughout the mid-Atlantic area trekked here to mine jasper as early as 8,000 B.C. Alas, construction crews blasted right through the middle of the largest native quarry when they built the Northeast Extension of the Pennsylvania Turnpike in the mid-1950s. The Turnpike plans to chew up even more history to widen the road to 6 lanes by 2025.

The village of Vera Cruz grew up at the intersection of two state highways, Vera Cruz Road, north and south, and Main Road, east and west. On the northwestern corner is the Vera Cruz Tavern, which dates back to the 1730s. They say it's the oldest tavern in Lehigh County. Both roads are narrow. Some two dozen brick and frame homes grew up on all sides of the intersection from about the 1840s through the early 1900s. Corroded bronze plaques on a bridge over a stream on Main Road West bear the date 1917. The bridge is a tight squeeze for two cars at the same time. On the north side of the road, there's just enough room for one car to park, lengthwise, between the front steps and the edge of the pavement. There's no parking on the south side, just a few feet of muddy berm. There are no sidewalks, no curbs or gutters. Most days, six or seven American flags fly from front porches. Here and there, a Marine Corps flag adds a splash of red and yellow. There's a hand-painted sign for "Dave's Small Engine Repair," and another that reads, "Audit The Fed. Where's the money?" One yard sign warns, "Protected by Smith & Wesson."

So how did a crossroads village in Pennsylvania Dutch country get a Hispanic-sounding name like Vera Cruz? Legend has it that back in 1851, some men were hanging out at the general store in the center of the village when bloodcurdling screams filled the air. They rushed outside to investigate. There, in the middle of the dirt road, two local "characters" — regulars at the stone tavern on the opposite corner — were rolling around on the ground, fighting. Finally, one man nearly bit off the other man's thumb. After the entertainment ended, the villagers went back into the store. There, an open newspaper bore the headline, "Revolt in Vera Cruz (Mexico): 12 Killed, 20 Injured." And Alexander Weaver, the wisenheimer of the group, said something like, "Oi, cheese! We've got our own little Vera Cruz right here!" Being Pennsylvania Dutch, Weaver pronounced it "Wear-a-Krutz." The name stuck.

Firefighting in Vera Cruz was always a family and community activity. Hopefully, it always will be. Sons followed their fathers into the fire department. So did wives, brothers, sisters, aunts and uncles. There were in-laws and even an occasional outlaw.

More than four decades passed before Vera Cruz bought its first factory-built fire truck. That was the 1983 Hahn pumper. It carried up to three firefighters in the cab. Two more sat in the rear-facing jump seats with air packs behind the cab. A jump seat is my favorite place on any fire truck, even though now we're locked in by spring-loaded metal safety gates to keep us from falling out and under the wheels of our truck or other vehicles. In its early years, the Hahn also carried up to four firefighters on the tailboard, the wide rear step on the very back of the truck. Each firefighter had a safety strap with a seat belt-like loop that buckled around your waist. For added safety, there were handrails and a signal button on the left side of the hose bed.

We don't ride the tailboard, anymore. Haven't for years. It's simply too dangerous, even though it was a ton of fun. That's just as well because the trucks and volunteers are constantly on the go today, running on hundreds of calls a year. Thankfully, actual fires account for only a small percentage of those calls. What keeps volunteers busiest are auto accidents, automatic alarms and medical emergencies.

As always, we help a lot of township residents and total strangers from out of the area. But, over the years, we also helped a lot of fellow firefighters. Here are a few examples:

* Firefighter Arnie Mohr slipped on the open floor joists of the log cabin he was building near his parents' and brothers' houses in the woods at the base of South Mountain. He tumbled into the basement pit below and landed — flat on his back — in the mud and construction debris below. We eased him onto a backboard, then slogged our way through the muck to a waiting ambulance. He was banged up, but soon recovered.
* A runaway car with an elderly driver at the wheel plowed through the

arborvitae hedge behind Roxy and Matt Fatzinger's house. Roxy was our
fire police lieutenant. She was also a "Proud Marine Mom." Her bright red
sweatshirt said so. Her only child, Michael Dries, served two tours in Af-
ghanistan, while she and Matt, also a fire police officer, protected the Homeland. Roxy and Matt were not hurt, but the car totally destroyed their hot
tub. We were lucky. The car just missed their house and a 100-gallon propane tank.

* Drainage, or the lack of drainage, has always been a serious problem in the
village of Vera Cruz. Many homeowners there have two sump pumps. They
often run constantly. But when torrential rains come, they're not enough.
And when the power goes out, some basements fill to the floor joists, sub-
merging washers and dryers, furnaces, and electrical panels. If heating oil
tanks aren't full of fuel, they break free and float against the ceiling. We saw
all that and more while repeatedly pumping out the basement of our late
Chaplain Willis Brinker.

* Like a lot of township residents, fire police officer Joe Miller heated his
century-old wood frame home in the center of the village with wood. One
day, a fire erupted in his chimney. His house filled with smoke. The fire was
so hot the masonry cracked. Another time, Joe's pickup hit a patch of ice
on Mill Road at the Turnpike overpass. The truck skidded out of control.
It landed on its side against the Turnpike embankment, trapping Joe and
his mother inside the cab for about 15 minutes until we could free them.
Fortunately, their injuries were not too serious.

* Late one winter afternoon, there was a call of a house fire south of the village. A neighbor reported heavy black smoke "puffing" out from around the
air conditioner. It was Firefighter Larry Stahler's house. When our pumper pulled into the driveway, Larry met us at the door. He said he thought
the fire was in the kitchen. "Just go straight down the hallway to the end.
You'll run right into the kitchen," Larry said. Good thing he was there to
give us directions. Made our job a lot easier, because you couldn't see anything inside the house. Thick smoke banked all the way down to the floor.
We spotted a dull orange glow at about the height of a kitchen counter on
the right. One short burst from the hose had it out in seconds, but serious
damage was already done. Black soot covered everything throughout the
two-story house.

Then, one day, it was our turn ...

CHAPTER TWENTY-THREE

Fire Hits Home

Unusual subzero weather socked the Lehigh Valley in late January, 2003. A water pipe in our garage wall froze. The attached garage was built for two cars, but Mel's car and my pickup never saw the inside of the garage because it was full of stainless steel sinks, tables and an 8-by-10-foot walk-in cooler for storing our vegetables and flowers. Shelves and the attic above the garage were completely full of our farming supplies, salad spinners and lettuce sleeves, cases of berry and tomato boxes, waxed produce boxes, pop-up market awnings, and plastic bags. Quite a "fire load," as the experts say, if the garage ever caught fire. Dan Mohr, the plumber and township supervisor who lives just east of us, easily repaired the burst pipe. He advised adding heat tape to keep the pipe from freezing again. I called all the hardware stores and building supply centers, but everyone was already sold out of heat tape.

To tide us over until we could track down heat tape, I dusted off a small ceramic heater. The cord was not long enough to get it anywhere near the pipes we were trying to protect, so I plugged the heater into the first extension cord I found. It was the cord I used to power the block heater on my tractor. Should be OK, I figured.

The next day, our son, Don, insisted on having pizza for lunch. The refrigerator was full of leftovers, but he called for pizza, anyway. When he went outside to get into his car, Don smelled something burning. Smelled like plastic. Maybe a neighbor was burning trash. When Don got home with his pizza and climbed out of the car, he smelled smoke, again. It was a lot stronger. Then he *saw* smoke. Thick, angry black smoke. It was puffing out of the eaves of our garage.

"The garage is on fire! The garage is on fire!" Don screamed as he burst in through the back door. I was at the computer in my office down in the basement. I heard the ruckus upstairs, but couldn't make out what anyone was saying. Didn't sound good, so I ran upstairs.

Mel greeted me at the top of the stairs. "The garage is on fire! The garage is on fire!" she said. I opened the laundry room door into the garage, but just a crack. Everything was black. From floor to ceiling, wall to wall, there was nothing but black smoke. I slammed the door shut. I felt sick. "That damn cord!" That had to be the problem. Couldn't be anything else.

"Mel, you and Don get the dogs outside. Put them in your car, and stay with them," I said. "Ruth, call 911. Tell them the garage is on fire. I'm going to turn off the power. Meet you outside." I ran back down into the basement, and threw the main circuit breaker, killing power to the whole house. We have an electric garage door opener. How would we get the garage door up? We'd worry about that later.

Mel, the kids and I hunkered down outside beside the cars. A mile to the west, the fire siren wailed. We waited for what seemed like ... forever. Actually, it was only a few minutes. All the while, we kept a nervous watch on the garage. Black smoke still pushed out from the eave vents. It didn't seem to be getting any worse. But, it wasn't getting any better, either.

Soon, we heard sirens in the distance. Then 2821, the big red pumper/tanker, slowed down at the end of our driveway. It coasted past the driveway, then backed up and turned into our lane. Jim Kellar was driving. Behind him was 2822, our tanker with 3,300-gallons of water. Kevin Kleinsmith was at the wheel. Kevin took over the control panel on the pumper while Chris Rickert connected a supply hose from the tanker to the pumper. That gave us 5,300 gallons of water, should we need it. I prayed we didn't. While Kevin got the pump going, Jim put on an air pack. His wife, Kris, was already packed up.

While all that was going on, I filled Chief Jason Tapler in on the situation. He agreed. The extension cord was probably the culprit. When the chief said everyone was ready, I ran back into the basement and turned on the power. Mel hit the remote. The garage door rumbled up. Black smoke billowed out. Kris and Jim lugged the heavy hose into the garage. They disappeared into the darkness. All we could see was their legs from the knees down. We heard water gushing. Jim and Kris got a jolt of electricity as their hose stream hit the burning cord and wall outlet. Smoke quickly turned from black to steamy white. Our walk-in cooler was cooked. The garage, and everything in it, was a horrible mess. But the fire was out. The house was safe.

When it was all over, Chief Tapler said something I couldn't believe: "I'm sure glad it was your house."

"What? Thanks a lot, pal!"

"No, I'm serious. Anybody else would have opened the garage door to let the smoke out. Flames would've been through the roof by the time we got here."

Kris and Jim stripped off their air packs. As the volunteers drained the hose, Bob Rodale's commonsense policy on leaving work to respond to fire calls came back to me: "Do what you have to do. It might be *my* house. It might be *your* house." Today, it was *my* house. And the volunteers — friends and neighbors who dropped whatever they were doing when the alarm sounded — saved our dream house.

God bless them all!

CHAPTER TWENTY-FOUR

Requiem for an Old Fire Truck

Eight volunteer firefighters live just down the road from our new house in the country. Whenever we have a fire call, Main Road East immediately fills with pickups and cars heading to the firehouse in a column of flashing blue lights.

But not tonight. There's nothing and no one in sight. Good thing, too, because my pickup spins sideways across the road as I reach the bottom of our driveway. It's snowing like crazy. Pavement under the snow is as slick as ice. Snow is so thick it bounces my headlights right back into my eyes. I can barely see. It's Thanksgiving Eve, 1988, the second Thanksgiving in our new farmhouse out in the country. I'm roasting a holiday goose we bought from a farmer friend and basking in the penetrating warmth of our woodstove — until the fire call comes in.

Speed limit is 30 miles per hour. The best I can do after I straighten out my pickup is 10, maybe 15 mph, tops. It's only one mile to the firehouse in Vera Cruz, but the drive seems to take forever. That's bad, because both Vera Cruz and Emmaus are being dispatched to this house fire.

When I finally pull in beside the firehouse, only one other vehicle is in the parking lot. Firefighter Carl Schell opens one of the tall garage doors and slides behind the wheel of Engine 2811, lovingly known as "Eleven." It's our oldest fire truck. He motions me into the passenger's seat.

Carl is one of our most senior members (fire chief in 1962-1963), but he's more than just a firefighter. He's also a diehard Pennsylvania Dutchman, a card-carrying member of a nearby Grundsow Lodge. Carl and his wife, Ruth Ann, are chicken farmers. For decades, they've run the landmark "Schell's Egg Ranch" on the south side of the village. Both are active in the Vera Cruz Community Association. Carl is also the fire company's Santa Claus. With white hair and a thick white beard, Carl rides atop a pumper at the end of the annual Vera Cruz Halloween parade, waving and throwing candy to the hundreds of children along the parade route. He makes a right jolly old elf.

But there's nothing jolly about Carl tonight. He has about as much

Christmas spirit as the Grinch. Carl pulls the truck out onto the apron to wait for more firefighters. We wait, and wait some more.

"Whatthehell!" says Carl. "Where is everybody?"

Good question, but we don't have a good answer. All we know is that they're not here. Snow swirls across the empty parking lot as the fire siren wails. We're on our own.

The burning house is right around the corner, just a few hundred yards from the firehouse. "Let's go!" Carl finally says. He jams the stubborn stick shift into gear and we roll out into the storm. The old-fashioned rotating red light on the roof of Eleven's cab paints the snow an eerie crimson.

Eleven is a genuine oldie but a goodie, a 1962 GMC 5000 with a mighty V-6 gasoline engine. It cost the fire company $7,680, new. Eleven is a classic medium-duty truck with tandem rear wheels, just like the old truck seen in a few episodes of "The Dukes of Hazzard" TV series. They don't build them like that anymore. Haven't for decades. Eleven has a bench seat in the cab. The emergency brake is a hand lever on the floor next to the stick shift. Also on the floor is a foot-operated dimmer switch for the headlights. There's a manual choke. The gasoline tank is completely inside the cab. It stands upright between the back of the driver's seat and the rear wall of the cab. The fuel fill is outside, just to the right of the driver's door handle. Mounted on the frame, directly behind the cab, is a huge gasoline-powered pump that's more than twice as old as the truck. The 500-gallon-per-minute pump is military surplus from the late 1930s. It arrived at the firehouse early in World War II on a trailer with steel wheels. The founding firefighters mounted it on our first truck, a 1939 International truck chassis. "All the work was done by members of the company at the Vera Cruz silk mill. The cost of the truck and building it into a fire engine amounted to $2,800," according to the fire department history. When the International wore out years later, the thrifty Dutchmen salvaged the pump. They added it to the brand new 1962 truck, and Engine 2811 was born.

Behind the pump is a 500-gallon water tank and hose bed, all of which could come crashing forward into the gas tank and the cab in a serious accident. Eleven can carry a crew of up to seven. It seats three in the cab, provided the person in the middle of the bench seat is a half-pint who doesn't mind straddling the gearshift. The other four ride on the tailboard at the rear, using safety belts and handrails. There are no seat belts in the cab, no "Nader bolts" to keep the doors from flying open in a collision. Ralph Nader might not love this old truck, but it's the darling — the first love — of everyone at Station 28. Many of our middle-aged firefighters learned to drive on Eleven. While we have a newer, much more powerful and modern pumper that's only 5 years old, Eleven is still the truck everyone instinctively turns to when there's a fire call.

Carl and I don't have far to go for this call. Left out of the station, under the Turnpike and up the second driveway on the right. There isn't even time to get the old-fashioned siren cranked up or shift out of third before we reach the house. In the same radio transmission, we tell the dispatcher that 2811 is responding — and on scene.

What a scene it is. Carl guns the old truck up a steep, curving asphalt driveway. The snow is no problem for Eleven. We briefly see smoke billowing out of the front of the house as we round the middle of the driveway's reverse-S. Carl continues to the very end of the drive and jams on the brakes. There are no cars in the driveway. No one seems to be home.

Usually, the first thing you ask yourself when you get off the truck is, "Where's the fire?" This time, it's, "Where's the house?" On our way up the driveway, it has disappeared. I look to the right where the house should be. It's not there. At least that's the way it seems, at first. Instead of the walls and windows of the upper story, all we see is a carpet of thick grass covered with snow. Turns out, that is the roof. This is a new passive solar house on the side of a low hill. It's built into the ground, not on top of it. The building tunnels straight back into the hillside. All you can see from the front is the patio entryway and large plate glass windows on either side of the front door. The rest of the house is buried. A foot of soil and sod replaces roof shingles. The only thing resembling a house up top, where we are, is a row of south-facing windows that run the whole width of the house.

Thick black smoke belches from large cracks in one of the middle windows. While Carl gets the pump going, I pull a hose from the rack just behind the cab. There's no air pack in the front seat of Eleven. Maybe there's a pack squirreled away somewhere in one of the truck's many compartments. We don't take time to root around for it, because this baby's about to take off. We need to get some water on the fire — now! We only have 500 gallons of water on the truck. Pumping 100 gallons a minute, that'll last all of five minutes. If help doesn't arrive soon, we're sunk.

I stretch the hose across the roof to the middle windows by the time Carl starts pumping water. But we still can't get at the fire. These windows aren't made to open. About two feet tall, their thick double panes are sealed with caulking and wood strips nailed into heavy wooden frames. All the windows are black on the inside. One is cracked from the heat of the fire. Black smoke pours through the cracks. A dull red glow looms below.

I take off my helmet and slam it against the cracked window. My helmet just bounces back off of the glass. Even cracked by superheated air, this glass is still tough stuff. So I pull my left arm all the way back and deliver a smashing backhand with my helmet. The first pane crumbles, then the next.

Pent-up smoke and heat belch around my head. Fresh air rushes in, feeding the fire. The dull red glow inside turns cherry red.

Quickly, before the fire roars to life, I hold my breath and lean in through the broken window, then open the nozzle, full blast. It's set on narrow fog so I can cover a wider area inside without precise aiming. The smoke quickly turns from thick brown-black to grayish white. Water turns to steam, which scorches my cheeks. But I don't mind. The steam tells me I'm hitting the heart of the fire.

Can't hold my breath forever, though. I keep my arms and the open nozzle inside the window, while I lean back to gulp fresh air. My eyes are watering, nose is running. I can't see. Holding my breath again, I stick my head back through the window and press the attack. Minutes tick by.

Suddenly, two other firefighters materialize right beside me out of the swirling snow. They're fresh from fighting another battle just to get here. Both the Emmaus and Vera Cruz fire departments were at Emmaus High School for the homecoming bonfire. They were only three miles away, but the roads are so bad they had trouble fighting their way up South Mountain and into Vera Cruz. The new arrivals wear air packs. They kneel down at the opposite end of the broken window and feed their hose inside. Just one problem. They don't have water yet. I have a hose and water, but no air pack. So we swap. More firefighters arrive, more trucks. The fire is dying.

I'm done, too. My fingers and toes are frozen. While fresh troops knock down the hot spots, I trudge down the hill looking for someplace warm. I snuggle up beside the rusty muffler of a gasoline-powered generator on one of the fire trucks. Despite the noise and stinking exhaust fumes, it's just the place to warm my fingers. Not my wonderful woodstove at home, but, for now, it'll do.

That was one of 2811's last big hurrahs. A few years later, we got another new truck, a 2001 Central States pumper/tanker that carries 2,000 gallons. That's four times the water Eleven holds. The new truck is not as nimble as Eleven on our narrow, twisting township roads that meander through the upland hills and valleys. It can't go off-road in the fields and forest like Eleven. But, with four air packs built into the jump seats in a fully enclosed cab, the new truck is a lot safer. And so, the old warhorse went into mothballs. We stored it here and there, wherever there was room, until Eleven finally ended up back where it started life, in the original single-bay engine room attached to the social hall.

At the monthly meetings over the next decade, there was talk of restoring Eleven, and putting it back into service, at least on a limited basis.

"It'd make a great brush truck (for fighting wildfires)," someone said.

"Or a backup pumper in emergencies."

"Could be really cool in parades."

One member bought a pair of fenders and a hood from another 1962 GMC to replace Eleven's parts that had terminal body cancer.

But there was never enough money to finish the job. The fire company needed new bunker gear, new air packs, new radios. Our "new" trucks started wearing out, even though we were still paying off their loans. We had no apparatus-replacement fund. New pumpers now started at more than $300,000. It was always something. The replacement front end wound up out in a leaky metal storage shed, drawing moisture and rusting, too. Eleven's master brake cylinder went dry. The battery died. Dust piled up on the truck's faded red paint and dull gold trim.

A couple of members added a new rough-sawn oak rack to the hose bed, but the inspection sticker expired. One day, we refilled the brake cylinder, topped off the gas tank and gingerly drove Eleven to a local garage for inspection. The mechanic was a fellow firefighter. He loves old fire trucks. But he couldn't — he wouldn't — slap a new inspection sticker on the windshield.

"You need to replace the rear brake line," he said. "Looks like original equipment from 1962." There was also a bad oil leak in the left rear wheel. The clutch slave cylinder was badly corroded; the tubing, too. It all needed replacement. The rear inner tire on the driver's side was wearing unevenly. That indicated some kind of a problem, although it was not an inspection issue. But the rotting — missing — floor behind the cab and in compartments elsewhere certainly was. Sorry, guys. No can do.

What was all of that going to cost? No one would give us a solid estimate, but we knew it was going to be plenty. And, so, the old pumper sat, loved but lonely, in the dark engine room. Eleven can still put out a fire, if it has to. The pump fires right up, as long as it has fresh gasoline. So does the engine, provided the battery charger stays plugged in.

What worries everyone is the fact that 2811 now has an even higher calling. Five of our longtime members, men with more than 50 years of service each, say they want to take their last rides — respond to the last fire calls — with their caskets on the hose bed of the truck that they helped cobble together when they were firefighters once ... and young.

CHAPTER TWENTY-FIVE

The Longest Fire Call
(Letter from Iraq)

One of the first casualties of Operation Iraqi Freedom, the U.S.-led invasion of Iraq in 2003, was the Citizens' Fire Company of Upper Milford Township. After many weeks of rumor and speculation, it became official: We were losing our deputy chief, George Heiserman. His Army Reserve unit was among the first going off to war.

But this was not just any old rifle company that orders activated on Feb. 10, 2003. It was a unit of elite Army firefighters. Assignment: Baghdad International Airport, the very heart of the war against dictator Saddam Hussein. Working as a "joint fire service" with the Air Force firefighters, the Army unit would provide fire protection and suppression for the constant stream of planes bringing supplies and personnel into the Iraqi capital. The troops figured they would be gone for one year, maybe longer.

"Georgie," as we all call him, is an outstanding young man, one of our best and brightest. Everyone in the fire company hated to see him go. So when we finally heard that he had e-mail in Iraq, we jumped online. We sent him jokes, news of our fire calls in Vera Cruz, and more jokes.

A lot of people throughout Vera Cruz knew and liked Georgie, his parents, and sister, too. They kept asking, "How's he doing? What's he doing? When's he coming home?" To bring the community up to date, Fire Company President Kevin Kleinsmith got the bright idea to interview Georgie and write an article about his life in Iraq. But he needed a volunteer. Since I was our resident scribe, and was also serving as deputy chief in Georgie's absence, Mr. President volunteered me.

Fine. I was as curious as anyone about what Georgie and our troops were going through. Lest we forget, our fighting men and women were being sent into battle without proper protective gear. Their supposedly "bulletproof" vests were so poor that troops reportedly repositioned crotch protectors in their armpits to close fatal gaps in government-issue vests. Others bought their own body armor that was a whole lot better than what the government was providing. Many Humvees had canvas sides and tops, which did absolutely nothing to stop bullets or rocket-propelled grenades. Thin metal floorboards couldn't withstand roadside bombs. Soldiers scrambled to fortify their unprotected Humvees with everything from plywood and sandbags to old boiler plates while Washington studied the problem.

"So what the hell's really going on over there, Georgie?" I asked in an e-mail.

For security reasons, he couldn't reveal too many details. And he was not quite sure what we wanted to do in the way of an article. So I fired off lists of general questions, and offered to ghostwrite a "Letter from Iraq" if he would just give me some basic information to massage. He was game. That took a big burden off of his back. And so began a long series of e-mails back and forth between Vera Cruz, Pennsylvania, USA, and Baghdad, Iraq.

"How weird is this?" I wondered as we swapped e-mails. Cue the theme for "The Twilight Zone." I could hear Rod Serling now. "Imagine, if you will, two firefighters on opposite sides of the world ..." Here I was sitting safely at my keyboard in Pennsylvania, while Georgie was 5,000 miles away in one of the hottest parts of a war zone. At any moment, either or both of us might have to drop what we were doing to answer a fire call. Yet we were just shooting the breeze about the weather, the food and fire calls like it was the most normal thing in the world.

So, in a salute to all of our veterans, here's the result of our dozens of e-mails. A staple on the Vera Cruz Fire Company website for nearly 10 years, it's Georgie's "Letter from Iraq."

Letter from Iraq, Feb. 16, 2004

Rockets, Mortars and Desert Heat
Add to Everyday Dangers of Firefighting

BAGHDAD, Iraq — "Marhaban," friends and neighbors. That's Arabic for "Hello." And "ahlan washlan" — welcome — to Iraq! My name is George Heiserman. In real life, I'm a 22-year-old volunteer firefighter from Vera Cruz, Pennsylvania. But for almost the last year, I've been serving as a U.S. Army firefighter stationed at Baghdad International Airport.

We don't really have a printable pet name for this place. Hell, maybe. I measured outside temperatures as high as 137F last summer. It's even hotter inside a tent or building. Just sitting around in a T-shirt and shorts, we sweat like crazy. It is almost always windy. There is not much rain, but when it does rain it is quite heavy and makes a muddy mess out of everything.

When a fire call comes in we put on our heavy bunker gear, air pack and attack a fire in a burning tent, building or aircraft. Talk about HOT! We just can't drink enough water to stay hydrated. Our drinking water is all bottled.

We shave and shower with tap water, but only after it is tested and treated.

The Baghdad airport is roughly the same size as Philadelphia International, but without all of the fancy walkways, parking decks, escalators and other modern conveniences, of course.

The airport is very big and crowded. Thousands of military personnel from America, Australia, Poland and other countries live and work here. There are two active runways. Air traffic is mainly military flights, but there are also a few civilian aircraft. Most are cargo flights, but there are also troops coming in and out pretty regularly.

The perimeter is fairly secure. When we first arrived here last May (2003) we could sit out at night and watch tracer rounds flying through the air. We don't see that too much anymore. Our biggest problem is the rockets and mortar rounds launched into the airport. We hear and feel those explosions and see the smoke. When incoming rounds touch off a fire, we respond to fight the fire, rescue the wounded and investigate. We also hear American artillery returning fire and the Explosive Ordinance Disposal team detonating confiscated explosives.

How did I get here? Firefighting runs in my family. Both my parents were active with Citizens' Fire Company (Station 28) in Vera Cruz for years. My mother, Elaine, was a fire police. My father, George, was a firefighter. My older sister, Jen, is an active firefighter with Vera Cruz. My uncle and three cousins are also volunteer firefighters in Conestoga, Pennsylvania.

When I was a child, every time the Vera Cruz fire siren went off my friend Chris Groller and I would run down to the intersection of Vera Cruz Road and Main Road to watch all the fire trucks go by. From that and going to the firehouse with my parents, I sensed the excitement and brotherhood involved in being a firefighter. I knew that I wanted to be a firefighter when I got old enough. As soon as I turned 16, I applied for membership in Citizens' Fire Company. My application was approved, and my dream came true: I was finally a firefighter. After starting as a junior firefighter I am now deputy chief at Vera Cruz.

When I graduated from Emmaus High School in 1999, I joined the Army Reserves — as a firefighter, of course. After basic training, I was sent to Goodfellow Air Force Base, in San Angelo, Texas, and attended the Louis F. Garland Fire Academy, the training center for all military firefighters. I was certified as Firefighter 1 and 2 and trained in hazardous materials operations, first aid/CPR, and aircraft rescue and firefighting. In civilian life, I work for the Pennsylvania Bureau of Forestry as a Forest Patrolman responsible for wildland fire prevention, suppression and investigation.

My reserve unit, the 369th Engineer Detachment, arrived in Kuwait in April 2003. We advanced to Baghdad in May. Since then we have been quartered in an old Iraqi firehouse that was abandoned during the first Gulf War in 1991. It was a dump when we first moved in. Our toilet was a plywood outhouse. The shower was gravity-fed from an overhead tank. Living conditions are steadily getting much better, though. We now have more things to make life a little easier, including a nice, pressurized shower, porta-johns, weight room, a dayroom with TV, microwave, toaster oven and refrigerators. We are able to watch the news to see what is going on over here.

For firefighting, we have four engines, two 6,000-gallon water tankers and five Hummers. Two of the Hummers are rescue vehicles equipped with the "Jaws of Life" and other hydraulic rescue tools.

We work 24-hour shifts, one day on, one day off. Shift change is at 8 a.m. every day. That's when we have a briefing and receive any new orders or intelligence for the day. We do maintenance checks on our vehicles and gear, so we are always ready for a call, have cleaning details and conduct regular fire inspections in all the tents. On our off days we are pretty much free to do whatever we want, unless there is a major fire or some military detail.

Things are still a mess in Iraq. Baghdad is a dangerous city, a whole different world outside the gates. We don't leave the base much.

We have plenty to do at the airport. We respond to a variety of different calls such as structure fires, tent fires, vehicle fires, spills, hazmat incidents, vehicle accidents, brush fires, aircraft emergencies, fuel fires, mortar and rocket strikes and standbys at incidents possibly involving explosives. Then there is constant training. We conduct live structural burns and train in the shutdown and rescue procedures of the different types of aircraft we have to deal with. We also do rescue training on scrap vehicles, popping and removing doors and roofs. Besides all of that, we have helped to train Iraqi firefighters.

Back home in Vera Cruz, we average about 150 fire calls a year. We had about that many calls in just our first two months in Baghdad. We were pulling our hair out in the beginning. That was good because it helped the time to go by quicker. Things have slowed down a little, but the attacks are still frequent and, in my eyes, they are getting a little worse.

Our toughest call was a fire in a huge aircraft hangar. The fire was too big and intense for us to do much with, considering we don't have all the resources and constant water supply. We did the best we could, though. Part of the hangar collapsed. Luckily, nobody was injured. We did manage to save a lot of aircraft parts worth millions of dollars.

We were at a fire call when President Bush came to visit for Thanksgiving. It was a room and contents fire in the hangar that burned earlier.

The food here is edible. It is not the best, but it is better then eating MREs ("Meal Ready to Eat"). When we first arrived, that's all we ate. Over the holidays they did a good job preparing special meals to make us feel a little more like at home.

Home — and everything about it — is what I miss most. Fortunately, we have good contact with our families and friends through e-mail. There is not much letter writing anymore because snail mail takes about two weeks. Still, it is amazing the amount of care packages and letters of support that we all receive from a variety of people, the majority of whom we don't even know. We have telephone access. It is limited, but it sure is nice to hear our loved ones' voices over the phone. All of that really helps to boost our morale and makes us feel a little better.

As it stands now, we are expecting to come home toward the end of April 2004. I can't wait.

Well, I must get going. Thank you ("shokran lak") to the Vera Cruz Fire Department and everyone else who supports us. Take care, and keep in touch.

See you later ("araka lahikan"),

Georgie

Homecoming!

But the 369th didn't make it home in April. In true Army tradition, they hurried up ... and waited. It was early May before the unit finally returned to its base in Pennsylvania. The unit formed up in a shopping mall parking lot in King of Prussia in suburban Philadelphia. Family, friends and fire trucks from throughout the area surrounded the soldiers in their sandy camo desert fatigues. Also on hand were fellow firefighters from the soldiers' hometown fire companies in Pennsylvania, Delaware and New Jersey. When an officer dismissed the company, the soldiers rushed into the arms of family and friends. Hugs and kisses abounded.

Then the troops piled into the fire trucks for a welcoming parade right up the main streets. I was driving Vera Cruz' brush truck near the front of the parade. Our new tanker/pumper, 2821, was ahead of me. Looking in my sideview mirrors, the parade seemed to stretch on forever. The line of flashing red and white lights extended as far as I could see. Sirens and yelpers on every truck were going full blast. Airhorns blared almost non-stop. It was deafening and delightful. Civilians on sidewalks and in cars stopped and gawked, then waved and cheered. Motorcycle cops leapfrogged around

200 Years of Volunteers – Celebrating a combined 200 years of service with the Citizens' Fire Company of Vera Cruz, Pennsylvania are, from left to right, Kenneth Arndt, Cyrus Mohr, Willis Brinker and William Stahler.

Back from Iraq – Deputy Fire Chief George Heiserman, center, presents a framed certificate and American flag that flew over Baghdad International Airport to fire company President Kevin Kleinsmith, left, and Fire Chief Jason Tapler.

PHOTOS BY GEORGE DEVAULT

the procession, stopping traffic at every intersection for almost nine miles. Finally, we turned in at the North Penn Memorial Army Reserve Center at 1625 Berks Road in Norristown.

The unit formed ranks again. Lt. Col. Howard B. Gartland gave a short speech for the returning heroes, their families and friends. "The 369th saw more action than the rest of the 4th Brigade combined," he said. Averaging two emergency calls a day — for one year — they responded when the enemy shot down a cargo jet at Baghdad International Airport, routinely extinguished raging hangar fires, put out tents set ablaze by rocket and mortar fire, and went on "air mobile missions."

"Each time, they saved lives," the colonel said. There was not a dry eye in the crowd.

A few days later, back in Vera Cruz, the Citizens' Fire Company held its 45th banquet in the Social Hall beside the Turnpike. Georgie was the guest of honor.

"When you come from a small community, there is a special significance when one of your own goes overseas, is in harm's way and comes back home safely. It represents the best of what we like to have in Vera Cruz and the Lehigh Valley," said State Rep. Douglas Reichley. He gave Georgie a commendation in honor of his service.

Fighting back emotion, Georgie thanked Reichley and the 80 other people filling the Social Hall. He presented the fire company with a neatly folded and framed American flag that flew over Baghdad International on March 14, 2004. "Please," he said, "keep all of our military men and women in your prayers. They're going through a rough time, and it's getting worse."

Later, Georgie passed out gifts from Iraq to the firefighters in Vera Cruz, commemorative T-shirts with the 369th's "Black Sheep" logo, and 4-inch square embroidered Maltese Cross unit patches that read, "Crash, Fire, Rescue, Baghdad, Iraq." They were gifts we would always treasure.

From the fire company, each of us also received a coffee mug. It had the Vera Cruz Maltese Cross logo on one side. The other side read, "Thank you for your support! May 15th, 2004."

More than 10 years later, after hundreds of runs through the dishwasher, the red paint on the cup has faded badly. But it's still my favorite coffee cup. It always brings me joy, because it makes me think of one of the happiest days in my 30 years of fire calls — the day Georgie and the entire 369th came home safely from what I call the longest fire call.

PART 6

"Light Duty"

CHAPTER TWENTY-SIX

Hat Trick

This is a working house fire, and a tricky one. It's in a neighboring township. At first, the chief there calls for only our tanker. Then he orders a full response. The attached two-car garage is a mass of flames. Hit the fire with a hose from the wrong direction, and you'll drive the blaze into the rest of the house.

That's why firefighters on the outside aim their attack lines through the side windows of the garage. Another hose team goes down and left in the bi-level's foyer. They're fighting the fire from the inside out, pushing flames back toward the garage. Vera Cruz Firefighter Mike Edmonds and I are on the upper floor. We're wearing air packs and have a charged hoseline, but the hose is just a precaution. We're on a search-and-rescue mission.

"They're in a back bedroom!" an officer says as he orders us inside.

"They" would be victims, emphasis on the plural. But, how many? Where? He doesn't know.

Our job is to find them — wherever they might be — and get them safely outside before it's too late.

There is a closed door on the left, at the head of the hallway, the end farthest from the fire. Not much smoke has gotten past the closed door. It's a bathroom. All clear. We move on, crawling toward the burning end of the house.

The hallway leads to another closed door. Mike feels the door with the back of his hand, then turns the doorknob. It's a big room, a bedroom that runs the whole width of the house. The burning garage is on the other side of the far wall.

There's smoke, but not enough to defeat our flashlights. We do a quick search. The far wall is hot, especially near the ceiling, but there is no fire. There are no victims, either.

Where are they? This is a race against time. So far, we're losing.

Mike starts opening windows to let smoke and heat out. I return to the hallway and open the first door on the left. It's another bedroom, about half the size of the first one.

There is no sign of fire, just smoke and heat. Still on my hands and knees, I check behind the door, inside the closet and begin a left-hand sweep around the room.

Her eyes are the first thing I see. They're wide open, scared, unblinking. Then, through the smoke, I see her body. She is sprawled on the floor at the foot of the bed. She is old, frail, with white hair. She's not moving. Flecks of white foam hang from her pale lips.

I scoop her up in my arms. She weighs next to nothing. At the front door, I hand her off to an officer in a white helmet.

"Yeah!" a couple of firefighters cheer. They sprawl around the front yard. It's littered with helmets, gloves, air tanks and exhausted firefighters. They're beat from the fight. Face masks hang from their necks. Their hair is matted, wet with sweat. Steam rises into the cool night air from each head.

"Supposed to be three inside. Keep looking!" says the officer.

I crawl back to the bedroom. A few seconds later, I find her lying on her left side, just behind where I found the first one. She's black. I barely notice her on the dark carpet in the smoke. Then she turns her head slightly and rolls her eyes. She's alive! But barely.

I hand her off to the officer at the front door. "There's one more in there. Check under the bed."

Soaked with sweat, huffing and puffing, I lumber back into the bedroom. Smoke is clearing now. I lay down flat on the floor and shine my flashlight under the bed. The space is crammed with stuff.

A small head rises from the middle of the clutter. A pair of eyes pop open. They stare right at me, but they don't move or blink.

Turning on one side, I slide my right arm under the bed. I can just barely reach her, but I can't get a good grip. I scoot deeper under the bed, banging my helmet on the metal bed frame. Twisting, turning, I grab a handful of hair and slide her forward. It's only a few inches, but it's enough. I get a firm grip on the back of her neck and ease her out from under the bed.

She's in bad shape, too. I hand her off to the officer at the front door. He rushes her to a nearby ambulance. I go back inside to help Mike with ventilation. We pull down and extend the folding stairs from the ceiling to make sure there is no fire in the attic. It's a shame about all of the smoke inside. This is a nice house, comfortable, clean, new furniture. There are lots of pictures on the once-white walls, mostly cats, everything from little tabby cats to sleek, spotted leopards prowling the jungle, plus figurines of cats here and cats there. Cats are everywhere.

"Somebody sure likes cats," says Mike. Not me. I'm a confirmed dog person.

With only a haze of smoke left in the house, we finally head outside and strip off our air masks. "Where are they?" I ask an officer.

"Back of the ambulance. Squad's giving them oxygen."

"How are they?"

"Uh ... they took in an awful lot of smoke," he hedges. My heart sinks. I should have found them sooner! He sees my frown, then adds, "But they're OK! Vet says they'll be fine."

CHAPTER TWENTY-SEVEN

A Nice *Romantic* Meal

"Can we maybe go out for breakfast before I have to work tomorrow?" Melanie asked.

"Sure, as long as we go early enough," I said. "The cable guy is coming tomorrow. Sometime. They can't say when, so someone has to be home all day."

"Oh," Mel said. "Never mind."

"No, wait. Why don't we stay here, have steak and eggs for breakfast? I'll cook the steaks out on the grill in the backyard. It's still plenty warm outside." It's winter, but we were having a January thaw with highs in the 50s.

"Oh," she said. "We can have a nice *romantic* meal."

"Why not?"

So, that evening I went to the liquor store and picked up a small bottle of Korbel brut champagne. Then I stopped by the supermarket for two strip steaks. We packed them in the fridge about 9 p.m.

What was the occasion? Nothing special. It was just a dreary, gray winter in the North. And we were reciting the punch line from Florida travel ads, "We need it, bad!"

We were also still getting used to being "empty nesters." Don was away at Penn State. He wouldn't be home until Friday. Our daughter, Ruth, and a friend from College of the Atlantic were visiting Steve Bulkley, our old night city editor in South Florida. We had the whole house to ourselves.

Mel had been saving a bottle of Chambord, a strong, black raspberry-flavored French liqueur, to bake Chambord brownies sometime this week, but Chambord-champagne cocktails came first.

Next morning, I put a little too much Chambord in the bottom of two champagne flutes, but the resulting drinks still tasted good. Melanie started cooking up a pan of potatoes and onions from our garden. The kitchen filled with a heavenly aroma.

Outside, I was just putting a match to the charcoal in the Weber kettle when my Emmaus pager went off.

"*Station 7. Wentz Hardware, 221 Main St., cross street Second. A structure. 08:04 hours.*"

Never failed. Every time we had something special planned and had completely forgotten about the fire department, we got a fire call.

I hustle into my bunker gear stashed in the closet, and turn on the radio in my pickup truck. Engine 712 is already on the scene. *"You'll need air packs,"* the driver radios. Heavy smoke in a hardware store? This doesn't sound good.

It isn't. As I fight my way through downtown rush-hour traffic, my pager goes off, again. Emmaus is calling for help. Second alarm! Dirty brown smoke pours from the front door of the hardware store as I swing into the bank parking lot next door.

"What do you need, Chief?"

"Men in air packs!"

I grab the last air pack from Squad 751 and follow a blue fire hose in through the side door. Fire's in the basement. The crew downstairs needs relief.

Smoke is thick. The basement ceiling is low. Piles of merchandise litter the floor, making it doubly difficult to maneuver the heavy hose. Alarms that signal just a few minutes of air left in air packs are already going off in the darkness ahead of me.

The seat of the fire is an oil-burning furnace. The stench of heating oil quickly works its way past our air masks. Firefighter Bob Grantham is ripping out metal cowling with a Halligan bar as I take up the nozzle. We hose down smoldering two-by-fours and plywood, then check everything over with a thermal detector called a "hot spotter."

Once we're sure the fire is out, we open all of the doors and turn on powerful fans to clear the smoke. The smell of heating oil will linger for days.

By the time I got back to the house, Mel had already eaten and left for work. The champagne in the glasses on the kitchen counter was flat. The open bottle was in the fridge, topped with a plastic bag and a rubber band.

I called Mel at work. "We'll have the steaks for dinner tonight, and a nice *romantic* meal," I promised. Sounded like a plan.

That evening, when the steaks were done just so, mushrooms were fried to a golden brown and little rolls were piled high with crushed garlic, I popped the cork on a new bottle of champagne. This time, only a teaspoonful of Chambord went in the bottom of each glass. But I had left the champagne in the freezer too long. It was half-frozen. White foam gushed out of the top of the bottle as I tipped it toward the glasses. I was just topping off the second glass when ...

"Stations 63, 62, second unit, and 7. Weis Market, 1220 Chestnut St., cross street 12th St. Emmaus borough. Rescue! 17:53 hours."

No!

Melanie and I looked at each other in disbelief. What could cause a "rescue" at a supermarket? A child stuck in the automatic door? A butcher with a hand caught in a meat grinder? A pedestrian wedged under a car in the parking lot? Or, maybe someone trapped on the railroad tracks that run beside the store? Who knew?

We'd soon find out. I geared up, again, then fired up my truck and tore into town, again.

"Fingers stuck in a shopping cart," reports the driver of Engine 712 as I pull into the parking lot.

The officer in charge sends the heavy rescue truck back to the station, then calls for a hand saw from the pumper's toolbox. Our victim is a chubby young fellow with one gold earring. He's wearing a blaze-orange hunting cap, a ragged flannel shirt and blood-streaked white sneakers.

He had stumbled, and his meaty fingers had slipped right through the inch-wide, hexagonal holes in the thick plastic side of the shopping cart. Now they won't come out. And they're turning blue. Medics spray the fingers with vegetable oil. It doesn't work. Ice doesn't help. The man's not in pain, he's just good and stuck. Finally, Firefighter Bob Grantham revs up our battery-powered Milwaukee Sawzall.

"Now, this won't hurt a bit," Bob says.

The victim's eyes go wide with fright.

Then, like a surgeon, Bob cuts a neat half circle out of the side of the cart around the man's hand, and we send him off to the emergency room for more delicate procedures.

When I got home my steak was in the oven. Melanie had already eaten. She was on her second glass of champagne, but not because she was mad at me. Dan Rather was on TV. American cruise missiles were raining down on Baghdad. We were at war. And there was only half a glass left in the bottle.

So much for our nice *romantic* meal.

CHAPTER TWENTY-EIGHT

Midnight Run to a Cathouse

Not even four-wheel drive works on ice. My tires have plenty of tread, but the truck doesn't hold very well on the sloping pavement, not with a quarter-inch of ice making the road as smooth as glass. I have to straddle the double yellow line in the center of the road to keep from sliding into the ditch on my way to the Vera Cruz firehouse.

The urgency in the dispatcher's voice — *"Homeowner reports a chemical problem"* — makes me want to floor it. But I barely touch the gas pedal and still I fight to stay on the road.

"What kind of chemical?" I wonder. What common household chemicals could raise such an alarm? Chlorine? Maybe. Or some kind of potent insecticide. The possibilities are endless. Is it a leak, a spill, an explosion or a fire? Maybe all four. Has to be something serious for dispatchers to summon two fire companies and two ambulances in the middle of an ice storm on the worst night in years.

My brakes are almost useless. My pickup slides at least 6 feet before stopping just short of the firehouse wall. Engine 2811 is already on the concrete pad in front of the station. It's a 1962 GMC, our oldest pumper. There is only room for two people on the bench seat in the cab. There are no jump seats, so we start strapping ourselves in on the tailboard on the rear of the truck.

I love riding the tailboard. It's a near-religious experience. Bravely facing into the wind and charging off to save the day with red lights flashing and siren wailing is what children of all ages dream of when they think of fire trucks. The tailboard is heaven on a warm summer evening. But on a night like this, it's going to be pure frozen hell.

Freezing rain is still falling as the last of four firefighters climb onto the tailboard. Our coats, helmets, boots and gloves are already starting to glaze with ice. The entire truck is becoming a giant ice cube.

Every inch of exposed space on the truck is slick. That includes grab bars, handholds, the safety straps around our waists and the tailboard under our feet. The big challenge is to keep from falling off of the truck.

Thank goodness for our safety straps. If the worst happens and one of us loses our footing, the strap will catch us under the arms and keep us from breaking our necks as we bounce down the street. At least, that's the way it's supposed to work. There is always the chance that the seat belt-style buckle on the strap will pop open under pressure. Or that we'll slide right through the loop in the belt and fall under the wheels of an oncoming truck.

But we're not thinking about that. We focus on the wheels of our own truck. They're bound with heavy tire chains, which are at their best in 6 inches of snow. On ice, chains rattle the roots of your teeth.

"All strapped in?" yells a firefighter on the far left side of the tailboard. That's where the buzzer connected to the cab is mounted. Two hits on the buzzer means "Go!" Three, "Back up." One long buzz means "Stop. Now!"

He hits the buzzer twice. 2811 rolls out onto the highway with red lights flashing, siren wailing and chains chattering like a machine gun. The road curves to the right, then makes a hard left through a narrow bridge over a creek. The bridge was plenty big when it was built in 1917. Back then, Main Road carried mostly horses and a few horseless carriages. Today, the same concrete span is barely wide enough to allow two cars to pass at the same time. We cross the bridge sliding sideways, taking up all of both lanes.

Approaching the intersection in the center of the village, the driver slows. He begins turning the wheel to the right to turn up the hill. But nothing happens. The truck is sliding, skidding sideways toward a big ditch.

"Hang on!" someone yells. OK, but maybe not for long. If we start into the ditch and the truck rolls, we're diving off the other way. No one wants to end up under 11 tons of steel.

At the last second, the chains dig in. The truck straightens out. We make the turn, then start up the long hill past Schell's Egg Ranch. The chains hold on the bridge over the Northeast Extension of the Pennsylvania Turnpike and through the curves at the old seed farm. Then we start down, down, down. The driver is tapping the brakes, downshifting gently to keep us from spinning out. We swing left onto Churchview Road. At the hard right onto Dillingersville Road it's down, down, down another hill.

"Whoa! Hang on!" someone yells as we bounce across the railroad tracks. We flex our knees to absorb the shock, and tighten our grip. "Everybody still here?"

We are. The truck picks up more and more speed as we skate down the hill. By the time we reach the bottom, trees on both sides of the road are just a blur. Wind tears at our helmets. Rain stings our eyes. We crouch behind the hose bed seeking shelter.

We rocket up the next hill. But, halfway up, the truck slows to a crawl. We're almost in Granny gear now, and we're still not there yet. "Whereinhell is this place?" someone asks.

Not far now. Another left onto another hilly, winding road and we're almost there. Exactly 3.1 miles from the firehouse, we turn into the driveway of a new, two-story Tudor-style house on a hill in the next township.

There are no flames. No smoke. Just a few raindrops passing through the floodlights on the fire engine already on the scene. A township police cruiser sits in the gravel driveway, red lights flashing. The driver's door is wide open. An ambulance parks on the road behind us. Other red lights and sirens are pouring in from the north and the south.

This looks to have the makings of a major disaster, but our officer motions us to stay put on the tailboard. He goes inside the house to see what's happening.

Radios crackle. Officers in white helmets storm into and then out of the house. The crowd of white hats grows. The township cop appears. Everyone starts yelling.

"STUPID! Stupid, goddamn dumb son-of-a-bitch!"

"Can't lock somebody up for that. Stupidity's not a crime."

"Well, it sure as hell ought to be!"

"What's going on?" we finally get a chance to ask our chief.

"We're goin' home."

"What? You gotta be kiddin'."

He isn't. Our driver turns the truck around, and we start back over 3.1 miles of icy roads.

This fire call's a big, fat nothing. There's no chemical leak, no spill, no explosion. No suffocating victims to rescue. Nothing. Just a house full of cats — a lot of cats — that haven't been outside in weeks, maybe even months. It's been even longer since anyone cleaned their litter boxes. Just what we don't need in the middle of an ice storm, a midnight run to a cathouse.

CHAPTER TWENTY-NINE

99 Bottles

A tower of smoke fills the night sky as I arrive at Rumors Bar & Restaurant with the third-alarm companies. I strap on an air pack, then turn to the chief for an assignment. "Where do you need help, Bobby?"

"Inside with Jimmy," says Chief Reiss. "He's in the front, to the left somewhere. By himself. There's another crew in the back. But Jimmy's all alone. Be careful when you go in. Stay away from that electrical box. It's hot yet."

Uh, oh. One man inside, alone on a hose. Not a good thing. Neither is playing dodgeball with an arcing electric meter dangling from the wall.

That side of the building is pitch-black. I follow two white hoses to the side door. One turns to the right. It snakes down a long hallway and into the kitchen where the fire started. The crew on that hose is in the attic now, where the fire still hangs on stubbornly. The other hose turns left toward the main dining room where the chief's son is alone on the nozzle. I start to follow that hose.

"Boom!" As I step toward the door, a blinding flash of white-hot light explodes 3 feet in front of my face. A clap of angry thunder buzzes past my ears. I jump back, falling on my butt in the mud.

No kidding, the "electrical box is hot yet." It's arcing like crazy. On my hands and knees now, I hug the side of the door frame and scoot inside.

"Chug-a-lug! Where are you?"

"Over here. Who's that?"

"It's me, George."

"Good. I'm in the middle of the room."

"OK. I see you now. You OK?"

"Yeah," he says. "Not much going on here now. Just some hot spots."

Jim is in the middle of the dining room, kneeling on the floor in a pool of water. He's surrounded by piles of charred debris. Smoke is starting to clear through the holes in the roof. Flickering flames dance here and there around the floor, walls and sagging rafters.

Suddenly, the whole room lights up. The top of the far wall erupts in flames. Jim hits it with the hose. Everything goes dark and quiet.

Then a loud alarm bell starts ringing. It's the low-air alarm on Jim's air pack. He only has a few minutes of air left. "Go on out, Jim," I say. "Get some air. And watch that electric meter on your way out."

Jim doesn't argue. He's tired. He passes me the nozzle and follows the hose back toward the door. As he disappears in the darkness, he says, "I'll send somebody back in to stay with you."

I kneel on the floor, holding the nozzle at the ready. I scan the charred ceiling, rafters and walls for fresh flames. Nothing showing, just wispy smoke and steam. Breathing slowly to conserve my air, I fall into kind of a daze as I watch the hoses beat back the last of the flames at the rear of the building. It's quiet, peaceful.

Then someone starts shouting from outside. "Fire under the eaves!"

As I whirl around, flames explode from the the wall behind me. A curling wave of fire rolls out of the top of the wall. Flames shoot out of the gaps between boards.

I yank the handle on the nozzle all the way back, releasing 100 pounds of water pressure per square inch. The hose bucks as I rake the nozzle back and forth across, then up and down the wall.

"*Crash!*" The sound of breaking glass drowns the noise of my nozzle. It's not the gentle tinkling of toppled stemware or a cracking window, but an avalanche of destruction. Sounds like a recycling dump truck full of bottles just dumped its entire load.

"Jeeze-a'mighty!" someone yells from outside. "The hell's going on in there? You all right?"

"Yeah! But the bar's not."

The restaurant owners are going to have a hard time drowning their sorrows after the fire is finally out. Every bottle of booze from the bar is blown to bits.

CHAPTER THIRTY

Flight of the Amazing Fire Bed

While not entirely the figment of a Hollywood screenwriter's vivid imagination, the constant camaraderie and carousing of firefighters in movies wouldn't exactly be an accurate portrayal of the Emmaus Fire Department.

A handful of us did do some things together away from the firehouse, sure. We occasionally went boating or camping, hunting or fishing together. But for the most part, we were busy with our day jobs, daily lives and young families. Most of us saw quite enough of each other at weekly fire practice, weekend fire classes, work details and the steadily growing number of fire calls.

"We really have to stop meeting like this. People will talk!" everyone said when we showed up at the firehouse on a fire call.

"Aw, I didn't know you cared, sweetie."

There were exceptions to every rule, of course. One of them was when a bunch of us had an opportunity to really show off in public — to make a real spectacle of ourselves, some might say. That was especially true when it was for a good cause such as raising money for the local Muscular Dystrophy Association. The opportunity was a race. Not just any old foot race, but a bed race.

"Who's got a bed? asked ringleader Randall Murray.

"I do," said Randy "Moose" Miller.

"Groovy!" gloated our mad scientist, Wayne Ernst. Wayne's brother, Dave, was also a firefighter in Emmaus. To keep them straight, we called Wayne "Wernst," and Dave "Dernst."

The hot rod-to-be was Moose's childhood berth, a simple single bed with a folding metal frame and wooden head- and footboards with turned spindles. It was going to take a lot to turn it into a real racing machine. The transformation started with wheels. But how to attach 6-inch high solid rubber wheels to the bed?

Break out the torch! After stiffening the bed frame with his welder, Wernst clamped the wheels in place. "More amps, Igor!" Wernst yelled to Moose. "More amps!" Smoke engulfed the bed. Sparks flew.

Next came 42 feet of copper pipe, copper elbows and Ts, a roll of black electrician's tape, a bag of zip ties, a propane torch, solder and flux, saws and sandpaper, speaker wire, electrical wire, and more. The creative team fashioned the pipe into Gothic arches, one at each end of the bed. We added side rails and top braces. Uprights on each arch, originally meant to hold a ladder, became a mount for four flashing red lights. Safety concerns ruled out adding a ladder and a fire axe.

Once the glossy, fire-engine-red paint dried on the pipes, the crew wired the bed for sound. We bolted on a big dry cell battery, an 8-track tape deck, stereo speakers and a siren. Next came plumbing, a water tank, electric pump and scaled-down fire hose.

A hand-painted metal sign on the rear of the fire bed warned the world: "Keep back 500 feet." On the front was a little box that held a fire extinguisher. Its cover was marked, "In case of fire, break glass."

When the smoke cleared, it was time for a road test. We wheeled the fire bed out onto the country road in front of Moose's house. Ready, set ... GO! The lights really flashed. The siren screamed. The tape deck blasted music as loudly as any boombox. The pump worked. And the hose sprayed water on anyone within 20 feet.

That was a whole lot of extra weight, but our gonzo gladiators didn't really care. Unlike the more serious commercial entries from local businesses, our hearts weren't set on winning. Oh, sure, a trophy would be nice. But having a good time and entertaining the crowds came first.

Early on race day, we carefully loaded the fire bed into the back of my pickup. We hauled it to Hamilton Boulevard in the center of Allentown and unveiled our secret weapon. The other racers' eyes popped. Jaws dropped. Spectators swooned.

"Turn it up!" commanded Wernst. From his perch on the bed, Randall Murray flipped on the lights, siren and stereo. We rolled toward the starting line to the blasting beat of "Gonna Fly Now," the theme from the movie "Rocky;" then Survivor's "Eye of the Tiger"; and Queen's "We Are the Champions." Hundreds lined the sidewalk on this sunny May morning. They were easy targets for Randall, who also manned the hose.

Then we saw our competition. Our hearts sank. The other beds were sleek, aerodynamic. They had large, inflatable tires that rolled easily and faster. Instead of an empty ladder rack, their "pushers" had real handles to grip. They were lean, mean racing machines ready to roll right over us.

At the starter's signal, the crowd went wild. Wernst, Moose, firefighter Mike Koenig and I gave it our all. Randall, our mandatory rider, cheered us on from his perch on the mattress. We surprised even ourselves. With war cries and war faces, the amazing fire bed flew down Hamilton Boulevard.

But the bed from Rothrock Motors flew even faster. We lost by a nose.

So it goes. Trophies gather dust. Memories don't. Months later, nobody remembered the winner of the race, but no one there that day forgot the amazing fire bed and those wacky firefighters who got everybody all wet.

PART 7

Apocalypse ... *On Call!*

CHAPTER THIRTY-ONE

Fire Call!

"How often do you get a fire call?" People ask that all the time. I hate the question. There are too many answers. Not one of them does the subject justice.

"How often do you get a fire call?"

Often enough for my grandson, Forest, to use it as the perfect excuse to leave the dinner table whenever he felt like it when he was 3.

"And where do you think you're going?" his mother (our daughter, Ruth) asked as little Forest started to slither out of his chair halfway through lunch.

"I have a fire call," Forest announced. Melanie and I instantly choked.

"Don't laugh!" Ruth whispered with a hand over her mouth. We couldn't help but lose it. "You stay where you are. We're not done eating yet."

"I have a *fire call!*"

"You get back in that chair, right now! Do you want a time out? That's one, that's two ..."

Forest was indignant. He planted his hands firmly on his hips, then yelled, *"I have a FIRE CALL, Mama!"*

Even at his tender age, little Forest completely understood the primal urgency of a fire call. He knew it was a command to action that must be obeyed regardless of circumstances, without question or fail. But, like most people today, he was blissfully ignorant of its true meaning.

"Fire call." Those two words are as powerful as they are simple. Without warning, they bring daily life to a screeching stop, then send it careening off in unexpected and often dangerous directions.

In our house, "fire call" always meant, "I gotta go. Now! Someone's in trouble. They need help." Over 30 years as a volunteer firefighter, I answered that call more than 5,000 times.

I never knew where I was going, exactly.

I never knew exactly what I might end up doing.

I never knew when — or if — I would return.

Fire gear and traffic cones help grandson, Forest, learn to be a better driver.

PHOTO BY MELANIE DEVAULT

We never spoke of the "or if" part, of course. That would invite bad luck. But I know my wife thought it more times than she would ever admit. And, I must confess, "or if" flashed through my mind on a few fire calls.

But, happily, Melanie never had to rush to my bedside in the emergency room because of a fire call, although I probably should have gone to the ER at least a time or two.

"How often do you get a fire call?" Honestly, there is no way to say. Days, even a week or more, might pass without a fire call. You'll check your pager, again and again, to make sure the battery hasn't died. Then you'll get two fire calls in 30 minutes. One time, we were busy tearing open a wall in a smoke-filled house at 1:30 a.m. to reach the seat of an electrical fire. Then the pager screamed to life, again. A few miles down the road, a man had just ridden his motorcycle into a utility pole, head-on.

Other times, we were in exactly the right place at exactly the right time. Two days before Christmas, four of us responded to an automatic fire alarm at about noon. Turned out to be nothing, an accidental trip. As we pulled away from the house, though, our driver noticed that the fuel gauge was just a hair below half. When that happens, SOP is to top off the tank. So we reluctantly drove clear across town to Harned-Durham, our fleet fueling station. As the diesel pump clicked off, I looked out the windshield and saw a weak column of smoke start rising from a house along the nearest road.

"Sure hope that guy is just starting up his woodstove," I said to no one in particular. A couple of other firefighters turned their heads toward the house and gritted their teeth. Time to go. The smoke kept getting thicker, darker. We were halfway down the driveway when our pagers went off.

"Station 28. Dwelling fire. 4723 Buckeye Road." It was no woodstove.

We flip on the red lights and siren, then turn left onto Buckeye. We only have a few hundred yards to go. Firefighter Kris Kellar and I are in the rear jump seats. We started strapping on air packs and masks. Assistant Chief Jim Kellar, Kris' husband, is in the officer's seat up front. He picks up the radio mic and, in one breath says, *"Lehigh County. 2821 responding, and on scene. Two-story dwelling. Working fire. Give me a second alarm."* By now, heavy dark smoke is pouring out of a second-floor bedroom window at the front of the house. We don't see any flames, yet. But the heat has already broken out the front window. The fire is gulping in fresh air. This blaze is seconds away from roaring to life.

Kris and I are all packed up and ready to go when we step off of the truck. We pull a hose from the side of the truck facing the fire. Jerry Schantz puts the 1,250-gpm pump in gear. He pulls a lever. Water surges through the hose. We blast a stream through the broken window, banking water off of the ceiling, so it acts like a giant sprinkler head covering the whole room. The muddy brown smoke goes white as our water turns to steam. Jim leans a ladder against the porch roof. Kris and I drag the hose up the ladder. We lean in through the window and give the room a good soaking. The fire is out long before the next fire truck turns onto Buckeye Road. We've spoiled all of their fun. You just never know with fire calls.

"How often do you get a fire call?"

So often that in our house, "Fire call!" evolved as our shorthand for whatever bad news just came across the pager. When you're scrambling out of bed and throwing on whatever clothes are handy, there's no time to repeat the dispatcher's detailed message: *"Station 28, Rescue 741. I-476, Northeast Extension of the Pennsylvania Turnpike. Mile marker 47.9, southbound. Delta response. Motor vehicle accident with rescue. Multiple victims."*

"Fire call … bad accident on the pike" was about all I could manage on my way out the bedroom.

"You be careful! It's a jungle out there!" my wife said. Translation: "I love you! Come back in one piece — or I'll kill you."

"Always!" I answered. I planned to be careful in all ways, always. I wanted me to come back in one piece, too.

Many nights, Mel couldn't go back to sleep after the pager went off. When I'd come home, hours later, our bedroom lights would be on. In fact, all the lights in the house might be on. She'd be reading.

Other nights, Mel did manage to go back to sleep, but not before locking the bedroom door. Never mind that there were two big dogs in the bedroom. She doesn't like being alone at night. That created a problem when I got home. If I knocked on the bedroom door, the dogs would go postal. Then, Mel would wake up again and often couldn't get back to sleep for hours.

That's why, after more than a few late-night fire calls, I'd just fix a cup of coffee and hunker down at my computer. I'd check e-mail and write up a short account of what just happened, while the details were still fresh in my mind. Then, if there was time, I would cover up in my recliner by the woodstove for whatever was left of the night.

"How often do you get a fire call?"

Statistically speaking, our rural, volunteer fire department in Vera Cruz gets a call every 2.2 days, or about every 50 hours. That's according to our 10-year average from 2001 through 2010.

But numbers lie. Without any context, they don't really mean anything. Statistics don't take into account all of the little things that really matter, such as time of day, the day of the week, the season of the year — or the weather. After all, what's the point of having a fire call if it's not 3 a.m., or 104 degrees in the shade, or 10 below zero, or the middle of a blizzard — or a hurricane?

"How often do you get a fire call?" Let me count the ways:
  * Every time I sit down to a meal.
  "Eat fast — before you get a fire call," is my wife's standard line.
  Holidays are the worst. I'm no Scrooge, but I almost dread holidays, when meals and guests are timed to the minute.

Suddenly cutting out of a holiday meal for a fire call creates what sociologists politely call "dynamic tensions." No wonder the divorce rate for firefighters is triple that of the general population and second only to that of the military, according to *Fire Engineering* magazine. It gets worse. The nonprofit Stronger Families, a counseling group in Washington state, reports that in some fire departments, the divorce rate is as high as 80 percent.
  * Every time I stretch out in my recliner in front of the woodstove for a long winter's nap.

There's no escape. Melanie and I managed once to go on a rare after-work "date" and the specter of fire calls still got in the way. We went to TGI Friday's. The main restaurant was crowded and noisy, so we sat in the bar at a small table facing the outside wall of windows. We were treating ourselves after a long weekend of work for Melanie and 16-hour vehicle rescue class at Bucks County Community College for me. The class was intense, a prerequisite for Firefighter I certification. It involved long hours of hands-on work freeing trapped victims from mangled cars, learning to "roll" the dashboard with chains and winches, pop open doors with powerful hydraulic rams and the "Jaws of Life," and completely remove the cars' roofs. I was pensively sipping a pint of Guinness, gazing out over the parking lot. I was a million miles away when Melanie asked, "What are you thinking?" In a script written by one of the Noras — Roberts or Ephron — this would have been the perfect opening for a classic romantic line about how lovely she is, or how lucky I am to have such a caring, understanding wife. What was I thinking? I wasn't. That became obvious the minute I opened my mouth: "Oh, nothing ... just the best way to cut the roof off of that brand-new Beamer out there in the parking lot."

"How often do you get a fire call?"
  Often enough to give spouses tunnel vision, too. Not long after I joined the Emmaus Fire Department, I was at home one Saturday taking care of the kids while Melanie was out grocery shopping. Everything was nice and quiet on the home front until two minutes past noon when Melanie sud-

denly burst through the front door, yelling: "You can go on your fire call!"

"What fire call?"

"You have a fire call! I was at the Emmaus Bakery, waiting in line, and the air horn on borough hall went off. You have a fire call. Go!"

"What day is it?" I asked.

"Saturday."

"What time is it?"

"Noon. But you have a fire ca ... Oooh," Melanie said. Then she remembered. Every Saturday, promptly at noon, Emmaus tests its air horn, the fire alarm atop Borough Hall — one block from the bakery.

Even our children were not immune from fire call fallout. In 1994, when I was promoted to lieutenant in Emmaus, the hit movie that summer was "Forrest Gump." Suddenly, I had a new title at home: "LEW-tenant DAD!"

"How often do you get a fire call?"

* Every time I sit down to watch a good movie.

* Every time I stretch out in a nice hot bath.

* Every time we get 6 inches of snow and I haven't plowed our 600-foot driveway.

Of course, my pager didn't go off every time I had something else to do. But it's happened often enough that, to be on the safe side, I've always felt pressured to have a "Plan B." That can put a strain on your marriage because it often means changing plans at the last minute, and even taking separate vehicles to a party or a restaurant — just in case there was a fire call and I had to bug out.

Returning from fire calls creates other complications. A few days after Christmas one year, I came home from a two-alarm house fire and flopped down in my recliner in front of the woodstove. All I could think about was getting warm. My clothes were sweaty. My jeans were wet from crawling through 4 inches of water in the smoke-filled basement.

"Something is wrong with the woodstove," Melanie said. "I smell smoke!" She was sitting about 3 feet away from me, directly in front of the stove.

"Really? I don't smell a thing."

"No, really," she insisted. "I smell smoke, like something is burning."

But it couldn't be the woodstove, I was sure. I had cleaned the catalytic converter, tightened the door latches and gaskets, and vacuumed out the flue a few days ago. The stove was just fine, but I was busted.

"Maybe it's me," I finally admitted.

Mel walked over to my chair and buried her nose in my sweatshirt. "Oh, yeah! It's YOU!" My clothes had to go. All of them. Standing beside the washing machine, I peeled off my sweatshirt, turtleneck and T-shirt. I emptied my pockets onto the kitchen table and stripped off my jeans. "I'm even going to give you my socks. I suppose you want my skivvies, too."

My shorts followed the socks into the washer. "I'm going to take a bath now, if you don't mind," I announced with as much dignity as a naked man could muster.

"Please, DO!"

But as water started filling the tub, I remembered my pager. It was downstairs on the kitchen table with the contents of my pockets. What if I got a fire call?

Newly liberated of clothing and all inhibitions, I ran back downstairs to grab my pager before the tub overflowed. "You like parading around the house naked, don't you?" Mel teased from her perch back under the reading lamp beside the Christmas tree.

Bathed in the glow of the Christmas lights on the stairs, all I could do was start singing, "Santa baby ... hurry down the chimney tonight."

"How often do you get a fire call?" Here are the statistics for Vera Cruz:

Year	Fire Calls
2001	146
2002	146
2003	144
2004	156
2005	197

"If we're at 199 on New Year's Eve, I'm going to call in an alarm, myself," joked Company President Kevin Kleinsmith near the end of 2005.

2006	187

At the time, 2006 was our second busiest year ever. But what the statistics didn't reflect was how many other important things were going on in the volunteers' lives. Between the pressures of home, family and business, something had to give. By September, it was too much. Both our fire chief and assistant chief abruptly quit. As deputy chief, I was left holding the bag. We called an emergency meeting of the fire company, elected new officers and soldiered on, with me wearing the Vera Cruz fire chief's helmet — and two fewer firefighters responding to fire calls.

2007	174
2008	161
2009	162
2010	147

We were almost back to where we started 10 years before. The downward trend was encouraging. Then along came 2011. All of the averages went right into the trash. This recap of fire calls for just the last week of June is a snapshot, just one small segment of what turned into our busiest year ever:

Saturday, June 25

My day started at 5 a.m. I was a full-time farmer now. I loaded my pickup with fresh-cut flower bouquets, vegetables and blueberries and hit the road by 7 a.m., heading for the Easton Farmers' Market 22 miles away.

It was another long, hot day. The market ran from 9 a.m. to 1 p.m. When I got home mid-afternoon, I unloaded the coolers, folding tables, boxes and canopies from my pickup. I was looking forward to a late lunch, a whole pitcher of iced tea and maybe a quick nap in air-conditioned comfort — before harvesting more vegetables for our second farmers' market on Sunday. Then my pager went off.

Call # 77 — 3:41 p.m. — Electrical Emergency

Smoke and sparks are coming from the electrical service of a house on a back road a few miles away, the dispatcher said. I don't want to go on a fire call. But the chief is at his cabin in the Pocono Mountains. So, as assistant chief, I hit the red lights and siren on my pickup and head to the scene.

The fireworks are over by the time we arrive. Black scorch marks on the side of the house are the only sign of trouble. The homeowner and I go down into the basement to check out the main electrical panel. Everything looks good, until I see daylight underneath the wall. It's not just a half-dollar-sized hole that can be filled with Great Stuff expanding foam. This is a broad band of daylight that runs all the way around the foundation in the corner by the electrical service.

"Oh, *that!* " the homeowner says. "You see, it's a fairly new house, but this corner settled some."

So, "Mr. Fix-It" dragged out a big bottle jack, a long 6-by-6 timber and a few 2-by-4s. All he wanted to do was even up that corner, just a wee bit. So he braced the lumber under the floor joists, and pumped away on the jack until ... *be-ZAP!* Bolts of white hot lightning shot past his head. Sparks flew everywhere. Smoke filled the air. That corner of the house was now at least 2 inches off of the foundation. Stretched beyond its limits, the underground electric line was arcing at the meter. "Hello, 911."

The power is off now. There is no fire. Nothing we can do, except head home and wonder ... about the size of the bill "Mr. Fix-It" will get from Pennsylvania Power & Light. We already knew "Mrs. Fix-It's" mood. If looks could kill, we'd be releasing the scene to the coroner.

Call # 78 — 7:37 p.m. — Auto Accident, Multiple Injuries

This is the vegetable farmer's precious, last hour before dark. I am out back behind the big greenhouse cutting baby zucchini — with edible blossoms — for tomorrow's market.

"Car into a yard ... multiple injuries," my pager cries. The first ambulance crew on the scene has called for a second ambulance with advance life support capabilities. Speeding into an S-curve on a narrow, winding road, the driver missed the beginning of the first curve. His car clipped a utility pole, took down three big arborvitaes, bounced down an embankment and plowed into a backyard beside Leibert Creek about 1 mile from our farm.

We have two victims. Neither man speaks English. The only Spanish I can remember from my new language tape is two basic questions: "¿Estuviste tomando?" (Have you been drinking?), and "¿Estas embarazada?" (Are you pregnant?). No need to ask either question. The answers were obvious. The driver is staggering around, feeling no pain. His passenger, however, is rolling around on the ground, covered with blood. He is also talking continuously on his cell phone, making call after call, like he is saying good-bye to everyone he knows in the whole world. The man keeps speed-dialing and frantically talking until a medic finally rips the phone out of his hand. "No teléfono! No más!"

We strap him onto a backboard and apply a cervical collar. We are just wheeling him into the back of the ambulance when two pickups and a car skid to a stop at the fire police barricades. A dozen people pile out into the street. The women are hysterical, screaming, sobbing. One woman throws herself onto the victim as the gurney glides into the ambulance. We have to pull her off of him.

It is almost dark when I get back to our farm. But magically, or so it seems, the baby zukes are all cut. Melanie has cut scores of zukes and arranged them neatly in a big bread tray. They are waiting in the long shadows for me to lug them into the walk-in cooler.

"I didn't know when you'd be home," Melanie says. She'd worked late into the night and is still making floral bouquets at 10 p.m., all because of my fire call.

Sunday, June 26

Not a single fire call. Good! A true day of rest. We're going to need it.

Monday, June 27

Call # 79 — 10:58 p.m. — Working Structure Fire

Heavy black smoke and orange flames fill the night sky more than a mile ahead to the northwest as our convoy of four fire trucks with a dozen firefighters races downhill toward the blaze. A commercial-scale carport and picnic pavilion are fully engulfed in flames. It is a total loss. So is about $50,000 worth of gasoline-powered equipment, including a new tractor, seven BBQ-size propane tanks and at least 20 gallons of gasoline in metal and plastic cans. We pump about 4,600 gallons of water and fall into bed at about 3 a.m.

Tuesday, June 28, 7 p.m.

At our regular, weekly "fire practice," we cleaned up some more from the night before. We washed hoses and trucks, and turned in early, hoping for a good night's sleep. Dream on.

Call # 80 — 10:59 p.m. — 2-Alarm Commercial Structure Fire

Heavy black smoke and orange flames fill the night sky more than a mile ahead. It is "Groundhog Day," a rerun, almost 24 hours to the minute, of the night before. Only this time at the bottom of Leibert's Gap we jog right and veer to the northeast into the borough of Emmaus. A six-bay, two-story commercial garage is fully engulfed in flames. In the middle of the building is the source of the stubborn orange flames and black smoke — a tank truck loaded with 1,200 gallons of home heating oil.

All of the fire hydrants closest to the fire are already taken by Emmaus pumpers. As the second-alarm company, we have to suck hind teat, literally. Firefighter Kevin Kleinsmith is behind the wheel of 2821. Following radio orders from the incident commander, he deftly maneuvers our huge 2,000-gallon pumper/tanker into the narrow grassy strip between a large picnic pavilion in Furnace Dam Park and the half-acre Furnace Dam pond. The pond is our water supply.

Kevin and Firefighter Georgie Heiserman muscle the large suction hoses off of the truck and into the pond, while Deputy Chief Brian Kleppinger and I pull a 150-foot pre-connect hose from the other side of the truck, the side closest to the fire. The edge of the pond is steep, slippery. Georgie's feet go right out from under him. He slides down the bank and up to his waist in the pond. His bunker pants and boots fill with funky pond water.

Brian and I snake the hose through the line of towering arborvitaes to the back corner of the burning building. The metal sides of the building glow red hot. The roof collapses. Firebrands and orange flames soar into the sky. We have just enough hose to shoot a water stream in through a side door. Brian is an old Navy firefighter, a good man to have beside you in a firefight. A firefighter in any branch of the military is a genuine superhero, but Navy firefighters seem special. Maybe that's because on a ship, there's no retreat. You can't swim home. I always feel a little safer fighting a fire with Brian, Dean Seibert, Steve Erbrick and other swabbies.

We don't even think about going into the burning building. No one is going inside. There's no reason to. The building and everything in it are already a total loss, and everyone knows it. So, this time, we risk little to save little.

But the safety officer worries about the walls collapsing. Brian and I are on the edge of the collapse zone. Safety orders us to fall back to a safer position. Behind us, we hear the roar of heavy equipment. A bulldozer is scooping up gravel from the driveway and using it to build a low dam to keep fuel-laced runoff from getting into nearby streams. HazMat teams are suiting up to join the fight. We dig in and pour 5,000 gallons of pond water onto the inferno. A thick blanket of foam finally quenches the blaze.

Officially, 11 of our firefighters and four trucks were tied up on the call for five hours and 13 minutes. Our last truck clears the scene at 4:12 a.m. Everyone gets home sometime around 5 a.m. and wrestles with the same question: Do I go back to bed for even one hour before work, or do I put on a pot of coffee? For me, coffee wins. The sun is already lighting up the sky. I need to get to work on the farm early to beat the heat and humidity.

Wednesday, June 29
Call #81 — 7:58 p.m. — Man Pinned under Tractor

After a short night and a long, hot day in the fields, Melanie and I take a few hours off. We drove into Allentown to have dinner at our favorite Mexican restaurant, Amigo Mio. I was just finishing my second Negra Modelo and a coconut rum-raisin flan when my pager goes off.

"Man pinned under a tractor," says the dispatcher. We are a good 20 minutes away. And I have been drinking, so I am no use on this call. But nine volunteers and two trucks do respond. It's a quick call. The man wasn't trapped too badly. His injuries are minor. The crew clears the scene as we turn into our driveway.

Friday, July 1
Call # 82 — 9:48 a.m. — Truck Fire, Pennsylvania Turnpike

A flatbed truck carrying industrial materials is on fire at mile marker 48.2, north. That's only two miles south of our station, but it's on the wrong side of the divided super highway. To reach the truck, we first have to drive past the fire — 7 miles to the south — then turn around at the Quakertown interchange and head back north.

You can see the column of thick black smoke half a mile away. "Working fire," I radio, as I drive past the truck, heading south in my pickup. The truck is already a total loss. A few extra minutes getting water on the blaze won't make any difference.

A pumper from Station 57 in neighboring Bucks County reaches the scene first. It stops in front of the burning truck. Firefighters in air packs attack the fire with two handlines. They are almost out of water when our

2,000-gallon pumper/tanker pulls in behind. We take over the battle. It's a stubborn fire. The truck was carrying 7,000 pounds of heavy-gauge copper wire. The wire held the heat. Insulation keeps burning.

Before the fire is even out, the scrap dealer who owns the truck says, "I want to give you guys a donation!" Yeah, right. We'll be lucky to get a check for $25 in a couple of months, the cynic in me mused. "I'm going to give you all of the money I have," he says, reaching into his pants pocket. He pulls out a wad of cash and starts peeling off $100 bills. One, two, three, four ... plus two $50s for good measure. Ka-CHING!

The cash goes right into a cargo pocket of my bunker pants until I can turn it over to our treasurer. With the truck still smoking, I write out a receipt to the owner for his generous donation. We will follow that up later with a formal thank-you letter, so the man can deduct the charitable gift on his taxes.

The owner is delighted. Turns out he had a good reason. Without insulation, scrap copper wire is worth $1 more per pound. The value of his load just increased by about $7,000. Maybe that's why the state trooper on the scene was so keen on determining the cause of the fire. But it was obviously accidental, mechanical. Locked rear brakes overheated, setting the wooden truck bed ablaze, confirms Firefighter Jim Kellar, who happens to be an ace mechanic.

Call # 83 — 1:28 p.m. — Truck Fire, Pennsylvania Turnpike

Déjà vu, all over again! It's the same truck we put out a few hours ago. Only now it's on the back of a flatbed wrecker and sitting right at our gate to the northbound lanes. Rekindle. We hate it when that happens. But, from time to time, it happens to the best of us.

There are no flames this time, only what looks like a little smoke coming off of the pile of scrap wire. It could be steam, too. The wrecker driver isn't sure, just cautious. He saw "something" coming off of the truck as he got up to speed on the Turnpike and called 911 to be on the safe side. We dumped a few hundred more gallons of water onto the pile, and all is well.

Call # 84 — 3:19 p.m. — Wires

A tree is hanging down on telephone wires. With only a few hours of daylight left to harvest vegetables for our farmers' market tomorrow, the boss, my wife, gives me "The Look," as my pager goes off and a fire siren wails in the distance. The Look says it all: "We have bills to pay. You've done enough this week. Besides, the fire chief and other volunteers are home from work now." They handle the call just fine.

A day later, the Vera Cruz fire chief breaks a leg jumping out of a runaway dump truck at his cabin in the Poconos. Doctors say he'll be out of commission for at least a couple of months. "Poor guy!" my wife says when I break the news. "And my condolences — Acting Chief."

I'm glad I retired from the Emmaus Fire Department three years earlier. Responding with just one fire company keeps me plenty busy.

"How often do you get a fire call?"

That depends a lot on Mother Nature. She has an uncanny way of keeping us in our place by regularly kicking our butts. She's always full of surprises, like the earthquake that rolled up the East Coast on Aug. 23 — without setting off a single automatic fire alarm in our fire district.

"That was close. What was next?" we wondered.

Aug. 28-29, 2011 — Meet Irene

Hurricane Irene is swirling up the East Coast, leaving billions of dollars of damage in her wake. Heavy rain and high wind are forecast for the weekend. The ground is already saturated from what will turn out to be the wettest August on record. With nothing solid to hold their roots, trees throughout the township topple without warning. It rains all day Friday (1.64 inches) and all day Saturday (3.37 inches). Governor Tom Corbett declares a state of emergency for Philadelphia and surrounding counties. Philadelphia International Airport closes at 10:30 p.m. Commuter rail service is suspended after midnight. We go to bed early that night, expecting the worst. We don't have long to wait.

The power goes out some time after midnight. Sump pumps quit working. Rain keeps falling. Basements throughout the area start filling with water. The first call, number 113 for the year, comes in at 12:58 a.m. on Sunday, Aug. 28. And the calls just keep coming — 1:05 a.m., 1:29 a.m., 2:49 a.m., 3 a.m., 3:45 a.m., 4:13 a.m., 4:40 a.m., 5 a.m., 5:04 a.m., 5:05 a.m., 5:42 a.m., 6:05 a.m., 7:20 a.m.

The rain is relentless. Gutters overflow. Storm drains clog with debris. Ditches and streams overflow their banks. Streets become rivers, backyards, oceans. Water pours into homes and businesses throughout the township. Our pagers don't shut up for the next 41 hours.

We scramble. The firehouse doesn't have power. Our garage door openers don't work when we arrive at the station for the first call. The telephone and radios there are dead. A portable generator provides light to most of the station, plus the garage doors.

The pager keeps screaming. Most calls are pump outs. But we also have trees into electric lines, trees across the road. There is a tree into a house. The only two traffic lights are out; they're at major intersections. Indian Creek Road is two feet under water.

We only have 10 firefighters to go around. We can't be everywhere at once, so the officers in their personal vehicles start doing triage, checking out each call and assigning priorities.

How much water is in the basement? Those with just a few inches will have to wait. Homes with a few feet of water come first. Is water into the electrical panel yet? A fuel oil tank is on its side and floating in one basement. Another basement has six feet of water.

Which home needs just a generator? Which needs just a pump? Which needs both? Who can we spare? We have more than enough hose, but there are only so many pumps and generators to go around. A few homeowners have their own generator or a pump. Most don't. Where can we scrounge another generator or pump? We yank a 50-year-old generator and an even older pump off of our 1962 pumper in mothballs. Both engines fire up on just the second pull.

Pumps and generators run continuously through the night. By dawn, all of the portable equipment needs refueling. Our 5-gallon fuel cans are empty. But where can we fill up? Who has working gasoline pumps?

Around dawn, four more firefighters join the fight. They relieve volunteers who then stop home briefly to manage water in their own basements, start or refuel a generator, change into dry clothes and grab a quick bite to eat. Firefighters are running on empty, too. We need food, rest. We are saved by a firefighter's wife. When daylight returns, Tina DiBlasio Schantz empties her refrigerator and freezer and turns on her gas stove. Tina keeps us supplied with egg-sausage muffins, then hot dogs and hamburger barbecue. Dropping food off at the firehouse also lets her check on husband, Jerry, a 30-year firefighter and former fire chief, and her 18-year-old son, Dylan. Late Sunday, a young couple who had six feet of water in their basement drops six pizzas off at the firehouse.

And so it goes through another night and the next day. We log our last hurricane call at 5:41 p.m. on Monday, Aug. 29. It's call number 185. Just the day before, we were at number 113. Irene jams five average month's worth of calls into 41 hours.

What's Next?

We're still drying out from Irene when the next disaster arrives. Tropical Storm Lee dumps up to 7 inches of rain on our area from Sept. 5 to Sept. 8. Everyone is better prepared this time. We only have three pump outs, one wires call and one railroad boxcar on fire in Emmaus. Many homeowners who were flooded during Irene put the week after the hurricane to good use. Those without sump pumps bought pumps. People with puny pumps bought bigger pumps and backup pumps — in case one burned out. Some even bought battery backups for the pumps. Many who Irene left for days without lights, water and power for cooking and refrigeration bought the biggest generators they could find.

Piles of wet carpet, moldy drywall, paneling, toys, games, clothing, and ruined washers, dryers and other appliances line the streets. The rain continues, 2.33 inches on Labor Day, 2.01 inches on Tuesday, 1.49 inches on Wednesday, and 1.17 inches on Thursday.

It's so wet inside the firehouse that mildew grows overnight on all of our bunker gear, coveralls and gloves and even inside our fire helmets. The month ends as the wettest September on record.

Call # 198 — Wires

The record-breaking call comes when a clump of large trees loses its grip on the soggy soil and topples onto the high-voltage electric lines, completely blocking Churchview Road and almost smashing a house. The wires still carry a full load of electricity. They are arcing, smoking and flopping around in the middle of the road in a blinding white fireball. All we can do is keep a respectful distance, block traffic in both directions and radio for the electric company to "expedite" its response.

A PPL supervisor soon arrives in a pickup truck. He takes one look and mutters something that rhymes with truck. All he can do is relay a message to kill the power and wait for line crews with bucket trucks and chain saws.

It is Sept.15. We still have a long way to go to the end of the year. Lucky us.

Enter "Snowmageddon"
Oct. 29-30, 2011

Two days before Halloween is much too early for snow, at least in southeastern Pennsylvania. All of the leaves are still on the trees. But that doesn't stop an early Nor'easter from slamming the Northeast on Oct. 29.

As our farmer friend Nate Thomas rolls up our driveway about 9 a.m. with his pig roaster in tow, it starts snowing. Hard. Fast. Visibility drops to a few hundred yards. Big, heavy, wet flakes quickly pile up on the farmer, the pig and the two bags of charcoal we were trying to light inside the roaster. But this is a paying job. Farmer Nate has promised a whole, roasted pig for a big party in town that evening. The roast must go on! And so it will. Farmer Nate is dressed for the weather — in snow boots — and shorts.

Matches and a lighter are useless. Wet snow dilutes the lighter fluid as quickly as Nate squirts it on the charcoal. Nate heads into town for more lighter fluid. I crack two highway flares, toss them inside the roaster and slam the lid, then open one of our pop-up farmers' market canopies to shelter the roaster.

By the time Nate returns, we have fire in the hole. The pig goes into the roaster. Soon, sweet smoke fills the air, but so does thick snow. It quickly piles up on everything. The canopy sags and groans under the growing weight. My 150 blueberry bushes are still covered with bird netting. The netting catches the snow. The 6-foot-tall bushes droop, then bend to the ground. While Nate tends to his pig, I tear away netting to keep the blueberry bushes from being broken into matchsticks.

The snow only gets heavier. Soon, all up and down our little valley, tree branches start cracking like rifle shots. I use a broom to knock some snow off of our prize dogwood trees. It is a losing battle. Throughout the township, branches come crashing down by the hundreds. The constant cracking sounds like the rattle of small arms fire. It is punctuated by the crash of heavy artillery, as larger branches and tree trunks break and fall on phone wires, electric lines, roads, houses, and cars. Electrical power goes out everywhere.

Our first fire call comes in at 12:53 p.m. Wires down. Then a tree goes into wires at 1:01 p.m. More trees are down at 1:14 p.m. Then more wires at 2:15 p.m., 2:22 p.m., 2:45 p.m., 2:56 p.m., 3:16 p.m., 3:21 p.m., 3:24 p.m. A motorist is reported stranded at 3:49 p.m. one mile west of our firehouse. No one is there when I arrive. Wires calls come in at 4:01 p.m. and 4:04 p.m.

Then, at 4:28 p.m., with firefighters and trucks scattered all over our district, comes the call we have been dreading: Motor vehicle accident — with injuries. The location is the same treacherous S-curve where the two Hispanic men wiped out last June. But this time the road is slick with deep snow. Nearly bald tires couldn't hang on. The black Jeep Cherokee wiped out on the first curve and T-boned an oncoming pickup.

Pulling up to the scene, I immediately recognize the Jeep. It belongs to one of our youngest and newest firefighters. He is miles away on a wires call. His girlfriend was behind the wheel. Three other people were inside the Jeep. A man and his son were in the pickup. No one is seriously hurt, but it was a close call. As we lift one of the girls out of the Jeep on a backboard, snow-laden branches crash down on top of the Jeep. Then a tree trunk falls into the nearby house, punching a hole in the roof and smashing a dormer window. The girlfriend's mother arrives in the only ride she could arrange in haste, a friend's van loaded with medical equipment, including tanks of oxygen. As the van's driver backs up to turn around and leave, he gets stuck in the snow. He is spinning his tires, rocking the van, when white hot light explodes in the trees just behind the van. He makes a mad dash out of the van as an electric transformer blows up.

The state trooper on scene is fuming. She has a wrecker "en route,"

Oh, the weather outside may be frightful, but the farmer's pig roast –
and responding to fire calls – must go on. Let it snow! It did.

PHOTO BY MELANIE DEVAULT

but there are so many accidents everywhere, it might take hours for one to arrive. That's when neighbor Dave Kaiser saves the day. A building contractor, he has a front-end loader with a backhoe at home just two doors away. Dave pulls the van out of the snow, maneuvers the Jeep off of the road and into a wide driveway, then piles branches and tree trunks beside the road. The ambulances leave. The highway is finally open. We go back to chasing more downed wires and trees. The roar of generators, crashing branches and chain saws fill the night.

For a few hours, we get a break. Then, at 12:59 a.m., when everyone is enjoying some much needed sleep, the pager goes off again. It is Call #236, a "medic assist." A 70-year-old woman got up to go to the bathroom. She lost her way in the dark house with no power. She opened the basement door by mistake and tumbled down the stairs. When we arrive, Grandma is lying on the cold concrete floor, bleeding from a nasty gash on her head. We strap her into a wrap-around backboard. Four of us muscle her up the stairs. Deputy Chief Brian Kleppinger almost breaks a finger as we stand her upright to make the tight turn into the hallway. It's another call that hit close to home. The woman is an in-law of Jay Welter, our fire police captain.

When it's finally over, "Snowmageddon" leaves 13 dead and some 1.6 million homes without power in the Northeast. Our area has 15 to 18 inches of snow. We are lucky. Other parts of the Northeast have almost twice as much.

Although the pace slowed somewhat the rest of the year, fire calls kept coming. We had 14 in November (nothing on Thanksgiving, for a change). There were only 10 in December, but they included three working house fires in Emmaus and a head-on auto accident with injuries at 10:47 p.m. on Christmas Eve. No silent night for us.

We finally finished 2011 with a record 268 fire calls. (Also a record 71.72 inches of precipitation, beating the old record, set in 1952, by more than 4 inches.) That's an average of 22.25 fire calls every month, five fire calls per week, a fire call every 1.4 days, or one fire call every 30 hours. But who was counting, anymore? What was the point? The numbers were meaningless.

No matter how you look at them, they just don't answer the original question: *"How often do you get a fire call?"* There is only one correct answer: "Too often." That's not because of any personal inconvenience it may cause first responders or their families, but because, for the people calling 911, it's probably the worst day of their lives.

On foul-weather fire calls, ice coats everything – and everybody.
PHOTO BY GEORGE DEVAULT

CHAPTER THIRTY TWO

Highway from Hell

A gray SUV sideswipes a guardrail at about 70 miles per hour. The 23-year-old driver loses control. Her vehicle rockets up a steep embankment, then flips and rolls completely over at least once. The SUV comes to rest on its side. The driver is unconscious inside it.

A Chevy Cavalier swerves to avoid the SUV. Then a bus from New Jersey Safety Tour clips the swerving Cavalier. A second tour bus from the same company rams the first bus from behind. Most of the people in both buses whack their heads on the seat in front of them.

Drivers behind the buses jam on their brakes. Traffic in the northbound lanes of I-476 screeches to a halt. Southbound traffic slows. Everybody wants to see what's going on. There's plenty to see.

It's about 9 p.m. on a Friday when my Vera Cruz pager goes off. Our volunteer fire company covers I-476 – the Northeast Extension of the Pennsylvania Turnpike – from mile marker 43 at the Quakertown interchange north to mile 55.9, which is just shy of the Lehigh Valley Service Plaza. The gates that we use to enter and exit the Turnpike are barely 100 yards from our firehouse at mile marker 50.3.

Tonight's accident is about half-a-mile south of the firehouse — but in the northbound lanes. That's a really bad thing. It means we have to drive past the accident and go 7 miles south to Quakertown. Only then can we "flop" at the interchange and fight our way back north for almost 7 more miles through all of the stopped traffic to reach the accident scene. We're not allowed to stop in the southbound lanes and work over the concrete barrier that divides the superhighway. That snarls traffic in both directions.

"You may be getting a lot more calls about this ... buses involved," Fire Chief Joe Sherman says on the fire radio as I hop in my pickup and head for the firehouse.

The crash scene is chaotic as we drive past. I'm a firefighter in a jump seat of our pumper. I'm sitting high enough above the road to have a clear view. In addition to the totaled SUV, the Cavalier has heavy front-end damage. Broken glass is everywhere. It includes two cases of longneck beer bot-

That tractor-trailer in the background is on the Northeast Extension
of the Pennsylvania Turnpike (I-476), a stone's throw from
the firehouse in Vera Cruz, Pennsylvania.

PHOTO BY KEN KLEPPERT

tles that flew out of some vehicle. Most of the bottles are shattered. The highway is covered with beer, glass and other debris.

When our fire truck finally pulls in behind the last bus, we begin helping the injured. There are a lot of them. Too many. First estimate places the number of injured at about 50. Turns out that's low. Dispatchers scramble ambulances from four counties. Injuries total 61.

But all the wounded aren't the biggest concern of Turnpike officials. They want to keep northbound traffic moving. Troopers order Chief Sherman to get at least one lane open so paying customers can be on their merry way, despite the mayhem. He refuses. No way! Not with four damaged vehicles, debris covering the highway, scores of injured — even if most of them are walking wounded — and ambulances and other emergency vehicles rushing in from all directions. Troopers threaten to arrest him. The chief stands his ground. The cops back down.

"It appears to me that traffic control is their number one problem. They're in the business of keeping traffic moving, but to me, patient care comes first," *The Morning Call* quotes Chief Sherman as saying. "We had maybe 40 ambulances. How can you have all that going on and keep two lanes open and not get somebody hit by a vehicle?" The chief threatens to

View from the northbound entrance/exit gate to the Northeast Extension
of the Pennsylvania Turnpike. The short ramp at the gate faces south.
That forces emergency vehicles heading north to make a 180-degree
turn and usually start into high-speed traffic from a dead stop.

PHOTO BY KEN KLEPPERT

quit responding to calls on the Turnpike if the Turnpike doesn't change its
priorities and policies to improve safety.

The northbound lanes are completely shut down. It's official, they're
going to stay that way until it's safe to reopen the Turnpike. That now means
ambulances have a clear, short shot at the scene. They can come in the gate
by our firehouse and go south in the northbound lanes without fear of getting hit by oncoming traffic. The Turnpike calls that "Plan X." The Turnpike
hates "Plan X." We firefighters love it because it makes our job so much
easier and safer.

So how do we get people complaining of possible head, neck and spinal
injuries out of a Greyhound-size bus? Very carefully. Because of the delicate
nature of their possible injuries, we can't have them just stand up and walk
out. Suppose they trip and fall in the narrow aisle, or they tumble down the
bus steps in the dark. Instant lawsuit! Never mind that some of the passengers have been drinking. Isn't that what you're supposed to do on a skiing
and vacation bus trip to Mount Airy Lodge in the Pocono Mountains?

Medics slip a high plastic cervical collar or neck brace onto each passenger. Then we ease each person onto a backboard and immobilize the
head with foam blocks and velcro straps. Adjustable straps that look and

work like seat belts secure the patient to the backboard at the ankles, waist and shoulders. Only when all of those preparations are complete can the patient be safely moved.

The easiest way to get a loaded backboard out of a tour bus is through a big side window. That's why firefighter Mike Edmonds and I are standing on a folding ladder outside near the back of the bus. The ladder is configured to form a large, stable work platform. Teams inside the bus pass backboards to us through the window. We ease them down to crews on the ground. The only problem is keeping the heavy window up until we find something to brace it open. The windows are hinged at the top. I'm 6-foot-4. My fire boots and helmet add about four inches to that, which is why I usually bang my head on chandeliers when I walk into a house in bunker gear. Working from the ladder platform, I'm just the right height to hold the bus window up with my head as we shuttle backboards. Fortunately, I don't have to do that for long. We throw some ropes over the top of the bus, then tie them off on the other side and secure the windows.

It's a long, cold night. But, for a change, Melanie doesn't have to wonder where I am and what I'm doing. All she has to do is look out the back door at the four news helicopters circling over the Turnpike a mile away from our house. And, at 11 o'clock, she can go inside and turn on any of the Philadelphia TV stations to see exactly what I'm doing.

The Turnpike finally reopens about 1:30 a.m. I get to bed about 2 a.m. Melanie and I are up again at 5:30 a.m. At least it's not for another fire call. We have to spend all day manning a booth at an upstate farming conference.

Prophetic Words

Just two days later, on March 9, 1998, Chief Sherman's warning proves prophetic. During a heavy rainstorm northwest of Philadelphia, a woman's red Pontiac runs off the main East-West Turnpike (I-276), trapping her in a ditch. Volunteer firefighters from Lionville Fire Company and Uwchlan Ambulance Corps medics are loading the driver into an ambulance. A Pennsylvania Department of Transportation dump truck with a flashing yellow arrow directs traffic into one lane around emergency vehicles.

Then a tractor-trailer's brakes lock up. The semi flips on its left side and slides across the highway. The rig clips and flips a landscaper's dump truck, hits a parked pickup and then the ambulance. The 18-wheeler pushes all three vehicles more than 300 feet down the road, according to *The Philadelphia Inquirer*.

"People were tossed in the air when they were hit. I went inside and prayed," the newspaper quotes eyewitness Willie Cuebas as saying. He's the manager of a nearby auto dealership. His car lot becomes a triage area and landing site for a medical evacuation helicopter.

The crash kills one volunteer firefighter and injures 10 other people. Dead is David Good, 36, a five-year member of the Lionville Fire Company, married with two teenage sons. Mourners at his funeral number in the thousands. Most are uniformed firefighters from several different states. Some 350 fire trucks accompany Good's funeral procession.

Shortly after the crash, Bill Wohl, president of the Chester County Emergency Medical Services Council, emerges from the Lionville firehouse. He tells *The Inquirer*, "They left their jobs for a routine auto-accident call, and it turned into a terrible tragedy."

It may be a cliché. But there really is no such thing as a "routine call," especially on what some of us firefighters affectionately refer to as the Highway from Hell.

Hazardous Cargo

We know we're not supposed to do it, but one night we do it, anyway. If we don't, we know even more people might die. The "it" is stopping our fire truck on one side of the divided superhighway to fight a fire on the opposite side of the tall concrete barrier in the median.

Two 18-wheelers are in flames. One is a double-decker car carrier, the other a Federal Express semi pulling two trailers. The accident happened when the driver of the empty car carrier pulled onto the berm and stopped. But the rear of his trailer still hung a few feet out into the northbound travel lane. It's late at night. The highway there is not lighted. The driver of the FedEx truck didn't see the trailer until it was too late. The high-speed impact blew both trucks apart. The cabs exploded into pieces and flames. State Police say both drivers died on impact.

We can see the fire from half a mile away. It's bad, and getting worse. Large pieces of flaming wreckage litter the highway. Fire is greedily gobbling up what's left of the first FedEx trailer. It's starting to feed on the second trailer. We slow way down, then stop to study the situation. That's when we see the placards on the rear trailer.

"HAZARDOUS."

"DANGEROUS."

Our stomachs sink. Although vague, the placards are a big red flag. They mean we may have a real mess on our hands. They hint of a witches' brew of potentially flammable, toxic and even explosive materials. By themselves, the contents of the trailer may be completely harmless. But mix 'em up, shake 'em up, then heat 'em up, and all that changes. Suddenly, you may have all the ingredients and perfect conditions for what the U.S. Department of Transportation calls a "mass explosion," which "affects almost the entire load virtually instantaneously."

We don't know what's in the burning trailers. We can't ask the drivers. They're dead. By law, shipping papers that tell exactly what's in the trailers must be kept in the truck's cab. The papers also contain an emergency response telephone number that federal regulations say, "must be monitored at all times while the shipment is in transit." Shipping papers are a wealth of information. They describe the hazardous material, its immediate health hazards, immediate methods for handling small or large fires and spills or leaks, and preliminary first aid measures. Just one problem. There are no cabs anymore. What is left of the cabs looks like they've been torn apart by a roadside bomb. Shipping papers, if they still exist, could be anywhere.

"Screw protocol!" says Fire Chief Jason Tapler from the front officer's seat. We're on scene at the fire now, even though we're on the wrong side of the road. If we follow procedure and drive all the way down to the Quakertown Interchange, then make a U-turn and drive back through a massive traffic backlog, it'll take at least 15 minutes — if we're lucky. Sometimes we're not. Traffic is so heavy and space is so tight at overpasses on this stretch of the Turnpike that sometimes fire trucks simply can't fight their way through the hundreds of cars and trucks clogging the road. Lord only knows what could happen if we get shut out at one of those bottlenecks.

Driver Kevin Kleinsmith backs the truck up a respectful distance. We pile out of the jump seats wearing air packs, and drag hoses over the concrete barriers in the middle of the highway. We train our hoses on the fire working its way into the front of the second trailer. It's a long shot. We're at the end of our hoses and water pressure. It's one of those gut-wrenching, edgy moments when the tide of battle could go either way, and you can't help but wonder if it's all going to blow up in our faces.

Then help arrives. With the northbound lanes completely closed, "Plan X" goes into effect. Firefighter Jim Kellar brings our next pumper south in the northbound lanes. Our tankers and other trucks are quick to arrive. Finally, the fire is out.

And not a moment too soon, a hazardous materials expert says later. He never reveals the contents of the trailer. But he does say that if the fire reached the heart of that rear trailer, the result might have been a 40-foot wide crater in the middle of the road.

Once again, we're lucky. We get to go home this morning. Elsewhere, on other eerily similar fire calls, many other firefighters are not so fortunate. In Texas, on the evening of April 17, 2013, firefighters and medics from the West Volunteer Fire Department responded to a growing plume of smoke from the West Fertilizer Company. They knew the facility contained a mountain of ammonium nitrate, the same explosive fertilizer that killed

Willie Nelson has a heart of gold when it comes to helping farmers —
and volunteer firefighters. Since 1985, his annual Farm Aid concert has raised
more than $45 million to help America's family farmers and grow the Good Food
Movement. Besides helping a worthy cause, Farm Aid allows music fans
like Melanie to get on stage (almost) with Kenny Chesney.

PHOTO BY GEORGE DEVAULT

168 (including 19 children less than 6 years old) and injured 680 in the
1995 terrorist bombing of the Oklahoma City federal building. An off-duty
Dallas fire-rescue captain and two community supporters accompanied the
West volunteers. At 7:50 p.m., an explosion that registered as a small earthquake leveled nearly half the town. The blast killed nine firefighters from
five departments, plus an Emergency Medical Technician and five local residents. The dead included five of West's 33 members and three of the 15 firefighters from the nearby town of Abbott, Texas, Willie Nelson's hometown.

Country music fans know what's near and dear to Willie through songs
like "My Heroes Have Always Been Cowboys." Everyone knows Willie as the
founder of Farm Aid in 1985. But few people know that he also has a very
special place in his Texas-sized heart for volunteer firefighters. Immediately
after the explosion, Willie announced that he was turning his 80th birthday
concert into a fundraiser for West. He collected more than $120,000. "West
is like our backyard," Willie later told *Country Music Television*. "It's where I
grew up. I rode my bike from Abbott to West and back all the time on that
road where all this stuff happened." A decade earlier, Willie footed the bill

for building West's firehouse. In 2013, he donated $81,000 from his birthday bash to the West Volunteer Fire Department and $40,000 to the town of Abbott.

Others gave what they could. On the East Coast, volunteer firefighters in Berwyn, Pennsylvania, were getting ready to retire a 30-year-old pumper for use as a training vehicle. When they heard that the explosion wiped out West's firehouse and many of its fire trucks, they transferred the truck to Texas.

"Even if they can just use this truck for a year, it's worth it to us. We need to look out for each other. It was a no-brainer for us to do this," Berwyn Assistant Chief Eamon Brazunas told the CBS affiliate in Dallas-Ft. Worth. "Whether you're a first responder or not, when you can do these things it's just nice to do it. Again, our hearts are with West and the people of Texas as they continue to recover from this thing."

The year 2013 was a disastrous one for the fire service in general, and for Texas in particular. In addition to the nine firefighter deaths in West, four firefighters died in the line of duty in Houston, and two lost their lives in Bryan, Texas. A wildfire in Arizona later that year killed 19 elite "hotshot" firefighters, bringing to 97 the number of firefighters who died in the line of duty that dreadful year. Forty-one of the fallen were volunteers, according to the NFPA. The other deaths included 25 career firefighters, 19 municipal wildland firefighters, five federal employees, three federal contractors, two state contractors, one state employee and one prison inmate.

Distracted Driving

In the early years of the 21st century, more and more motorists use E-ZPass to drive the Pennsylvania Turnpike. Not me, at least not when I'm responding to a fire call on the Turnpike. I use an old-fashioned metal key. It hangs, always within easy reach, from a binder clip on the passenger's side visor of my pickup. The key opens the two gates, each about 100 yards away from our firehouse on either side of the pike. One gate is for northbound lanes, the other for southbound.

"Cool!" you say. "Your very own key to the Turnpike!"

Oh, yeah! Très cool. Now, just imagine how cool it is trying to get onto — and then off of — the Turnpike without the benefit of entrance and exit ramps. That's not so cool. Anyone whoever pulled to the side of any interstate highway for any reason has some idea of how positively uncool it is. If there's much traffic, getting back onto the highway is a little like playing Russian roulette. That's because not a few motorists on the Turnpike are just plain nuts. They seem to think they're NASCAR drivers. And many believe their toll ticket is a license to fly, that the green "GO" light at the tollbooth means, "Punch it! We're off to the races!"

The posted speed limit on most of the Turnpike is a relatively safe, sane 65 mph. Few people actually drive that slowly. Many immediately kick it up to about 75. And a few, the ones who want to fly for NASA, drive a whole lot faster. They constantly tailgate, riding the bumper of the car or truck in front, as if that will make the other driver go faster. They cut in and out of heavy traffic without using their turn signals, constantly weaving from lane to lane. They're part of the reason why, in the worst years, we get a fire call on the Turnpike about every 10 days.

Our gates are at mile marker 50.3. That's a level half-mile strip of highway with steep banks on both sides. Visibility is limited. Northbound traffic is on a slight downward approach, curving gently to the right. Southbounders top a gentle rise, then lean slightly right. If there's traffic in both lanes, as is often the case, no one can move over into the passing lane for you to enter the highway. Could be worse, though.

Back in the late '80s, we only had one Turnpike gate. It was on the northbound side. Getting on the pike for calls north of the gate was a breeze, relatively speaking. Southbound calls were another story. Our only "entrance" to southbound lanes was a gap in the concrete barrier in the median. How did we cross four lanes of high-speed traffic in a fire truck? Very carefully, and at just the right time, we hoped. Fire truck drivers had to watch traffic from both directions, twice. Then, with red lights flashing, sirens and air horns blaring, they picked a likely opening in four lanes of two-way traffic — and punched it. Trouble was a 21-ton fire truck doesn't exactly leap off the line. Acceleration stinks, especially when you're making 90-degree left-hand turns ahead of oncoming traffic. The last thing you want to do with a fire truck is roll it.

The window of opportunity is small and fickle. With traffic coming from both directions at 70-plus miles an hour, civilian drivers don't have much time to respond, or room to maneuver. For anyone driving an emergency vehicle, entering and exiting the Turnpike there seems a little like taking off from and landing on the bouncing flight deck of an aircraft carrier — without benefit of a catapult, a tailhook and arresting cable, or a control tower.

Exiting southbound at the Quakertown Interchange is always a piece of cake. When northbound traffic is hopelessly snarled and our assignment is complete, we just breeze through the E-ZPass gate and take the winding back roads home to the firehouse. But exiting the northbound lanes at our gate gets a little dicey. That's why we switch on our red lights and turn signals long before we reach the gate. As we approach the gate, we slow as much as we dare. Then we suddenly swerve off of the road to the right and hit the brakes. That's OK, as long as you have brakes. One night, the old rescue truck didn't. When Brian Kleppinger hit the brake pedal, it went to the floor. Next thing he knew, the guardrail was sticking through the front and side of the truck. The result was thousands of dollars worth of damage. Miraculously, there were no injuries.

Not all of us drive a fire truck on the Turnpike, however. "Chief officers," whoever is fire chief, assistant chief and deputy chief and on-duty at the time, respond in their personal vehicles, usually full-size pickup trucks with V-8 engines. That evens the odds a little. Red lights and sirens help, too. The Turnpike doesn't allow personal emergency vehicles on the highway without red emergency lights visible from 360 degrees and a siren. Actually, I have four sirens in my truck. Two toggle switches on the dashboard produce four different siren tones — wail, yelp, phaser and air horn. They all work well, so I usually cycle through the whole range when responding on Turnpike calls. Laying on the air horn is especially helpful as I run up the berm past hundreds of stopped cars and semis to reach an emergency scene.

My red light is an old Streethawk light bar off of a police cruiser. It's four feet wide and stands a foot tall. I paid $75 for it. The light bar has four bright lights with rotating mirrors inside two red plastic domes. On the front, it also has two "takedown" lights, bright mini-spotlights. At accident scenes, they turn night into day. On each end of the light bar is an "alley light" for lighting up alleyways, dark gaps between buildings, and areas along the sides of highways. That many spotlights may seem like overkill, but when you're the first one on the scene, you definitely need to see and be seen by motorists and other first responders. The lights also come in handy for spotting vehicles over the guardrail and down an embankment. Two flashing yellow warning lights on the back of the Streethawk help protect me from the rear. I operate the lights with a line of toggle switches on a center console.

Good communications are essential on any fire call, but especially on the Turnpike. That's why I also have two radios mounted in my truck. One is set to Lehigh County's Fire South channel, the other to Vera Cruz, so I can talk to the station, our fire trucks and other officers. I carry two walkie-talkies in the chest pockets of my bunker coat. On a Turnpike call, first thing I do is switch one walkie to the Turnpike frequency. That puts me in direct contact with "Highspire," the Turnpike's communications center. I tell the comm center that county is dispatching us to whatever the call and location may be, and that we're responding. I also ask for additional information, since a Turnpike crew or state trooper may already be on the scene. We don't want to scramble the whole station, put all of our trucks and people in harm's way, if the reported "car fire" is only a blown radiator hose. Responding to anything on the Turnpike is, by far, the most dangerous thing we do on a regular basis. Usually, when all three radios are going at once, my cell phone rings. Don't care who it is, I ignore the phone, and keep flipping siren switches and mic buttons and watching traffic.

My bunker gear, complete with reflective safety vest and air mask, is always within easy reach on the backseat. So are three-ring binders that list all of the streets and house numbers in the township, plus ponds and other possible sources of water. Also in the cab of my truck is a rechargeable flashlight with an orange cone for directing traffic, a red plastic canister with a dozen highway flares, a medium-duty first aid kit, half a dozen pairs of surgical gloves, and a 10-pound dry chemical fire extinguisher. My lock-blade Smith & Wesson rescue knife has a razor-sharp serrated blade for slicing through seat belts and a spring-loaded center punch that takes out car windows with the flip of a lever. Eight orange traffic cones for scene safety are handy in the truck bed.

All of that safety gear may make me feel safer, but I can never forget for a moment that it in no way guarantees my safety. Loganville Fire Co. Fire Chief Rodney Miller was using all of that and probably more about 12:30 a.m. on Saturday, April 27, 2013, while directing traffic at the scene of an auto accident on I-83 near the Glen Rock exit in York County, Pennsylvania. That didn't stop the 32-year-old driver of an SUV from barreling past the flashing lights on Miller's truck and hitting the 45-year-old chief. The driver kept right on going, until he was quickly stopped by state police — and charged with drunk driving.

A few days later, more than 2,500 people, most of them area firefighters, attended Chief Miller's funeral, according to *The York Dispatch*. There were nearly 2,000 vehicles in the funeral procession, including many dozens of fire trucks draped in black.

In a brief written statement, the chief's family said, "We wish to express our sincere appreciation for the devotion of the first responders in our community who daily serve our communities by giving tirelessly of themselves to help those in need. Rodney's life was one marked with a passion to serve our community and to the individuals who live here. We urge everyone to follow Rodney's example by seeking to serve others just as he did." Well said.

One Never Knows ...

One of the first things they teach in fire school is, "Expect the unexpected." You never really know what a fire call is going to involve until you get on the scene. And, even then, conditions can change by the minute. One night, Kevin Kleinsmith and I are in our tanker, answering a call for water from another fire company that's fighting a tractor-trailer fire miles north of our usual coverage area on the Turnpike. Next thing we know, the fire chief in charge at the scene radios that he needs more firefighters — in air packs. Great. Our air packs are not in jump seats inside the cab. They're hanging on the outside of the truck in zippered cases. We'll have to wait to pack up until we reach the scene. When we finally stop the truck, thick smoke is everywhere. Wind pushes it into the narrow gorge where the highway cuts through a big hill. We're just climbing out of the truck and going for air packs when the chief radios again. Get out of the smoke, he warns. The burning truck's carrying hazardous chemicals. Drive upwind, past the burning truck, and lay a supply line to the nearest pumper. Suddenly, a routine water haul turns into a major hazmat incident.

My first Turnpike call as fire chief in Vera Cruz is another classic example of Murphy's Law in action. It's 6:45 a.m. I'm about two sips into my first cup of coffee when a man from Philadelphia stops his 15-passenger van on the shoulder of the Turnpike. When he tries to get back onto the highway, he pulls out in front of a tractor-trailer. The trucker swerves into the left lane, but still slams the back of the van. Another truck hits the tractor-trailer. The van careens into an embankment. There are seven people in the van. Only one is wearing a seat belt, so we're lucky that only two passengers go flying through the air. The rest tumble around inside. No one in the van speaks English, just their native Southeast Asian dialect.

Dispatchers summon our station, a small army of ambulances, and the heavy rescue truck from Emmaus. I'm on the Turnpike for less than a mile before I see another serious problem. Traffic! Northbound traffic is backing up as far as I can see. I grab the county radio mic. *"Any units not already on the pike, use the Indian Creek Road gate."* That's the next gate to the north, and much closer to the accident. *"We have a 2-mile backup northbound."*

When we finally fight our way through traffic to the scene, the paramedic in charge of triage is calling for the medical helicopter. A woman from the van has what appears to be a serious head injury. My next radio message is from the medevac pilot. He wants to know the location of his landing zone. The Turnpike is not going to be happy about it, but the closest, most level and safest space for an LZ is right in the middle of the northbound lanes near the crash site.

My morning starts out as a firefighter. It ends as an air traffic controller.

"Oh, dear! Deer!"

"Station 28, Rescue 741. I-476, Northeast Extension of the Pennsylvania Turnpike. Mile marker 47.9, southbound. Delta response. Motor vehicle accident — with rescue. Multiple victims."

Sounds like a bad one, so we scramble everything. We're expecting major mayhem. But, when we reach the scene, there's only one car. It's sitting upright, with all four wheels on the ground for a change. That's always a good sign. The roof's nice and level, not caved in. Windows are all intact. The front end doesn't resemble a junk pile. Also very good signs.

But there are still four people inside the car, a woman, her two young boys, and their grandmother. The boys are securely strapped into car seats in the back seat. Fortunately, no one is "trapped." All four doors open easily. The occupants of the brand new, gleaming white Volvo SUV are just badly shaken. The worst is the boys' mother. She still sees the herd of 11 deer running right out in front of her when she's doing 70 mph. No way she can miss them. Crunch!

After barreling through the deer, she ran off the road, up a small rise, and brought the SUV to a perfect four-point landing in a grassy swale just outside a wire fence and a line of trees. It was a good landing. The women walk away from it, but we carry the boys to waiting ambulances. While the medics check the adults, we let the boys play with our fire helmets and clip-on flashlights. The kids don't want to give them back.

As the ambulances leave, an anxious firefighter approaches the state trooper, and asks, "What about the bodies?"

"What about 'em?" the trooper says. He's busy filling out his report.

"Well, what do you want us to do with 'em?"

"Don't care what you do with 'em," the trooper replies.

The questioner's eyes light up. "Can we keep 'em?"

"Whatever," the trooper says, barely looking up from his paperwork.

Four firefighters swoop down on the carcasses like a pack of hungry wolves. They lug them to the rear of the pumper, then heft them up onto the tailboard. Bungee cords appear from a side compartment. Quick hands strap the two stacked bodies to the back of the rig.

All of the way down to the Quakertown Interchange and then for the 7 miles back to our gate by the firehouse, the squad truck rides the pumper's bumper. The idea is to hide the evidence. Or, at least make it difficult for some yahoo with a cell phone camera to get a clear shot of the deer, so he won't be able to post the video on YouTube.

The bodies go in the back of a firefighter's pickup, then home. They're good-sized doe. They'll fill up his freezer nicely.

CHAPTER THIRTY-THREE

Mystery of the Burning Bus

With red lights flashing and siren wailing, we're responding to a report of a "bus fire" on the Turnpike. That's all we know about the blaze at the moment, except that it's a bad one. We can see a huge column of thick, black smoke from half a mile away. It towers over the trees lining the highway. The closer we get, the taller the black cloud looms until the smoke almost blocks out the afternoon sun. It looks like a volcano blowing its top.

Jason Tapler, fire chief in Vera Cruz at the time, is behind the wheel of 2821, our pumper/tanker. He's straddling the centerline of the southbound lanes to make sure no one passes the fire truck. Why anyone would want to get to a fire, an accident or other emergency before a fire truck "wonders me," as the Pennsylvania Dutch say. But it happens all the time on the Turnpike.

In the front passenger's seat, the officer's seat, is Capt. Jim Kellar. He's running the siren and the airhorn and juggling two radio microphones, trying to make sense out of what the Lehigh County dispatcher, state police, Turnpike officials and other firefighters are saying all at the same time. None of it sounds very good.

In the jump seats behind them are two firefighters, Kristin Kellar and me. Kris is Jim's wife. They have a 9-year-old daughter, Kourtney, and run a thriving auto repair shop in Emmaus. Kris is a trim, attractive 38-year-old identical twin with shoulder-length brown hair. She likes the music of James Taylor, is a pretty fair shot with a pistol and holds a red belt in karate. Growing up, she watched "Emergency!" on TV. "It looked pretty cool," Kris says. Then the show went off the air, and she forgot all about those dashing paramedics John Gage and Roy DeSoto until many years later, when her husband joined the local volunteer fire company.

The newest firefighter on our team, Kris is about to wear an air pack into a real fire for the very first time. She doesn't know quite what to expect. She's nervous, but she trusts that her training, her gear and her fellow firefighters will see her safely through whatever dangers lie ahead.

I share that trust. I've fought many fires with women firefighters before.

Although they may not have the height and strength advantage of many men, the other female firefighters I've worked with over the years — Victoria Schadler, Sara Wildman, April Lubenetski, Angela Neff, Katy Dickman, Laura Danner, and Jennifer Heiserman — always seemed more level-headed than many of their male counterparts. No female firefighter I worked with ever panicked, dropped the nozzle and ran out leaving me to possibly die in a burning building.

Besides, I helped train Kris, purposely putting her through physical and mental tortures meant to break people made of lesser stuff. She didn't even bend under pressure. After one grueling training session, Kris said, "I'd follow you anywhere." The feeling is mutual, sister. I'll go into a burning building with you any day.

Now, bundled from head to toe in our protective firefighting gear, Kris and I wriggle into the shoulder straps and masks of our air packs as our truck nears the burning bus.

"What kind of bus?" I wonder. School bus? Church bus? Tour bus? Or, maybe it's Arlo Guthrie and his red VW microbus with half a ton of garbage, shovels, rakes and implements of destruction. On the Turnpike, you never know. Sooner or later, we seem to get 'em all.

How many passengers? Was there an accident? Is someone hurt, maybe trapped? Or did they all get out OK? Is the bus upright or tipped over? Is there a fuel spill? Are there any other vehicles involved? Where is the fire? Is it in the front or the back? We talking gasoline or diesel engine? Hybrid or propane? Where is the fuel tank?

Even more questions race through our minds as we near the scene. But we can't talk very well through our air masks. So I just raise my right hand toward Kris, stick the thumb of my thick leather glove high in the air and give it an emphatic shake. Thumbs up! One gesture says it all: I'm good to go! You? I also smile, even though the nose cup inside my air mask completely hides my mouth. All we can see is each other's eyes. Our eyes lock. Kris flashes me a thumbs up in return. Good, because in a few seconds all of our questions about the fire — and about ourselves — will be answered.

Rounding the last curve, we finally see the fire. Orange flames leap 30 feet in the air. The bus is a "Big Rig," a Greyhound-size tour bus, the back half of which is one big ball of fire.

The bus sits off to the side on the berm. A large crowd of people stares in awe at the fire from the embankment above. Must be the passengers. I hope everyone is off the bus.

Chief Tapler stops our engine about 75 feet behind the bus. The fire is so hot and fierce we don't dare get any closer. He sets the air brake, puts the powerful pump in gear. 2821 is designed specifically for fighting fires on the

15 miles of the Turnpike that run through our fire district. It has a pump discharge and hose compartment built into the massive front bumper, so we can pull a hose straight off of the truck and attack a fire without flopping hose into high-speed traffic that refuses to stop for thick smoke, flames or firefighters. The truck cost $210,000 when it was new in 2001. 2821 is 11 feet tall and 36.5 feet long and weighs 46,000 pounds, or 23 tons. It's a battleship.

Kris and I scramble out of the jump seats in the enclosed cab. We both exit on the passenger's side, the side *away* from traffic. We're wearing our full bunker gear — rubber boots, heavy pants and coats, leather gloves, fireproof hoods like race drivers wear, helmets — and air packs, but that's no protection from cars and tractor-trailers traveling 70 miles per hour an arm's length away from us.

Thankfully, drivers see the smoke and flames from far away. They slow down to maybe half their normal breakneck speed — this time.

Facing the flames, we pull the 150-foot pre-connect hoseline out of its bin on the front bumper. I take the nozzle and head toward the bus. Kris stretches out the hose, then falls in behind me. We brace ourselves for a surge of water.

Twenty feet away from the bus, the roar of the crackling flames is deafening. Heat cuts through into our bunker gear. We're already soaking wet with sweat, breathing heavily inside of our air masks. We need water to fight back with, and we need it NOW! I swirl my right hand high in the air, signaling that we're ready for water.

Chief Tapler slams the control levers on the pump panel. Water roars into the rubber hose. The limp hose suddenly snaps tight, thrashing on the ground like a big yellow snake.

The chief is pumping 150 pounds per square inch. It's almost too much. The pressure nearly knocks Kris and me off our feet.

I yank the handle on the nozzle all the way back. A solid stream of water tears into the flames. We stagger backward, recover our balance, then steadily move closer to the burning bus.

But bus walls block our hose stream. We can only do so much from the roadway. We need to get to higher ground and attack the fire from above. Kris and I drag the heavy hose around behind the bus. In our heavy gear and air packs, we scramble, slipping and sliding under the weight of the hose, struggling up the steep embankment beside the bus. The soil is loose, rocky.

Finally, we reach the top. Worried-looking passengers edge closer to us. Their faces are grim. They look almost like something important — or someone — is still on the bus. I sure hope not.

Kris and I renew the attack from above. I throw the nozzle wide open.

The hose kicks. Hundreds of gallons of water pour down into the back of the bus. We rake the flames with the hose stream. The water turns instantly to steam, robbing the fire of heat and air.

Jim and other firefighters in air packs now have a second hoseline in action. They attack the fire in the rear engine compartment. We're not "Waiting for the Next Explosion," as the old song goes.

The fire's stubborn, but we're steadily gaining ground. The smoke is not as thick or as black as it was just a minute ago. Flames are only about half the size they were in the beginning.

As we press the attack with both hoselines, a loud cheer goes up from some passengers lining the embankment. Others applaud wildly. They're a curious bunch. It's early September, but it's not that warm. Yet they're all wearing Bermuda shorts, Aloha shirts and Hawaiian leis, like they're heading to a luau on Maui or a clambake in Key West. Some of the men sport a "pencil thin mustache." A few act like they may have been drinking. One or two are definitely smashed, but that's not unheard of on a tour bus. After all, "It's Five O'Clock Somewhere," and "The Tiki Bar Is Open." So, we don't give it a second thought. We just keep pouring water on the fire.

Soon, there's nothing showing, just smoke and steam rising from the burned-out back of the bus. Kris and I haul the hose toward the front door of the bus. We're going inside to search out hot spots. But passengers want to come inside with us. They want their backpacks, purses, cameras and coolers.

"No!" we insist. "Tell us what it is, where it is. We'll try to find it. But no one goes in without firefighting gear and an air pack." No one has been hurt. We want to keep it that way. The passengers aren't happy about it, but they don't argue. They seem licensed to chill.

Inside the bus, the scene is near-total devastation. What isn't completely burned up is scorched or melted almost beyond recognition. Backpacks are lumps of smoldering nylon. Coolers are mounds of goopy plastic. Most are welded solidly to the floor. Beer cans are burst or bulging. In the overhead bins toward the front of the bus, we discover what look like mini-bales of hay. Some are still smoking heavily. They smell weird. We salvage what little remains, mostly metal keys, wallets and a few cameras that somehow survived the inferno.

Outside, we hear other firefighters banging on the sides of the bus. They're opening the big cargo bays underneath. Out come huge coolers full of sloshing water, ice and clunking cans. Passengers explode in wild applause, song and even dance.

"What's with these people?" I ask Kris, who has been talking with some of the passengers.

"They're Parrotheads."

What? Jimmy Buffett fans. Three buses full of Parrotheads were on their way from Wilkes-Barre, Pennsylvania, to the Buffett concert tonight near Philadelphia. This is the bus to "Margaritaville." The tiny hay bales are grass skirts, not Maui Wowie. And, everyone was enjoying the ride, looking ahead to a "Cheeseburger in Paradise," when the rear brakes locked up and the bus started smoking like a "Volcano."

The last driver in the caravan saw smoke. He motioned the crippled bus over just in time for everyone to get off before the volcano erupted.

Now the fire is over. The Parrotheads pile onto a replacement bus. One grateful concertgoer ceremoniously presents Kris with an official Parrothead flag. Then they're off again, "Sailing to Philadelphia," minus their grass skirts, imagining the "Stories We Could Tell" at the concert. Meanwhile, we cruise on back to the firehouse, wondering what other "Apocalypso" may lie waiting for us on the interstate ... behind "Door Number Three," so to speak.

CHAPTER THIRTY-FOUR

The Children of 9/11

Tuesday, Sept. 11, 2001 — **"Dad! Dad!"** yelled my son, Don, as he ran out of the house toward our chicken coop. "Janon (a neighbor) just called. A plane hit the World Trade Center!"

"What?" I was on top of an 8-foot stepladder, just nailing the first rafter of a new equipment shed in place.

It was a little before 9 a.m., a beautiful September morning. Until that moment, my biggest worry was trying not to smash my thumb with a hammer. Then we switched on CNN. Heavy black smoke and flames billowed from the north tower of the World Trade Center about 90 miles east of our Pennsylvania farm. Details were sketchy. A twin engine plane just hit the tower. No! It was a jet, probably a commercial plane, possibly a 737, witnesses told CNN. The sounds of sirens and air horns on responding fire trucks filled the air as CNN interviewed passing pedestrians in the area.

Horrified, we stared at the tube in utter disbelief.

"Would you go into that building?" I finally asked my kids. "Would you order men into that building?"

We already knew the answers. Hundreds of New York's bravest were racing to the upper floors to evacuate civilians and fight the raging inferno right then.

Blame my many years of working for Rodale Press in Russia, but I immediately thought of Chernobyl. The first firefighters on the scene there faced almost certain death. "We were told there was a high level of radiation. We knew about this," the incident commander, Lt. Col. Leonid P. Telyatnikov, told *The New York Times* nearly one year after the 1986 nuclear explosion. "But we saw lots of flames — that was our main job. We are firemen. We are supposed to fight fires." Six of his firefighters, the ones who dragged hoses onto the burning roof above the blown-out reactor, were dead within days from extreme radiation poisoning. The colonel himself nearly died. Cancer finally claimed him a few years later.

"Fierce devotion," Maya Angelou called the response in Manhattan in "Extravagant Spirits," a piece she wrote later for *LIFE* magazine.

On TV, we could tell many people were already dead in and around the tower. Many more were going to die, including probably more than a few firefighters. I couldn't watch. Picking up my hammer, I went back to my ladder. A second rafter was almost in place when Don ran back outside, screaming. It was a few minutes after 9 a.m. A second plane was burning furiously in the second tower. This was no coincidence, no accident. This had to be deliberate. Was it a terrorist attack? What was going on?

At 9:28 a.m., my Vera Cruz pager went off. I jumped, and I almost fell off of my ladder. *"Medic assist,"* the dispatcher said. Emmaus medics needed help to move an invalid.

Then, at 9:41 a.m., a third jetliner nosedived into the Pentagon. Nine minutes later, the south tower of the World Trade Center collapsed in a huge cloud of dust, smoke and flame. Like the rest of the world, we stared in horror as the New York landmark collapsed and the Pentagon erupted in flames.

All of the major TV networks quickly switched to continuous — "wall-to-wall," they call it — news coverage of the attacks. For the next 93 hours, nearly four full days and nights, there were no commercials or entertainment programs. It was the country's first all-news blanket since the assassination of President Kennedy in 1963. Hollywood scrambled to cut scenes of the World Trade Center from "Spider-Man," "The Bourne Identity," "Men in Black II" and other movies in the making.

Like probably every firefighter in the entire country, my first instinct was to grab my gear and rush to the scene of the unfolding catastrophe. Normally, Manhattan is about a two-hour drive from our farm. With the blue light on top of my truck and an overdose of adrenaline, I could get there in record time this morning. I didn't know what I might do, exactly, but I knew I could do something to help. I had to do something. Anything! I couldn't just stand idly by and watch as hundreds, maybe thousands, of helpless people died.

Instead, I throttled back my emotions and immediately called the firehouse. I was a captain with the Emmaus Fire Department. Our ambulance corps was on standby, said the assistant chief. But no firefighters from other states were being summoned to Manhattan, at least not yet. New York City authorities said they already had too many people in too little space. They would call if they needed more help. Stand by.

10 a.m. — United Airlines Flight 93 crashed near Shanksville, about 80 miles southeast of Pittsburgh.

And, on TV, the planes kept hitting the buildings.

There are now scads of books about the terrorist attacks of 9/11. Most, not surprisingly, deal with the collapse of the Twin Towers and the aftermath. Not so many detail the attack on the Pentagon. And even fewer focus on Flight 93.

The whole world knows how the heroic passengers and crew of Flight 93 tried to take the plane back from the hijackers, but only a few thousand people know the story of what happened on the ground after the crash — or that the first fire trucks to reach the scene were manned by volunteers. Those lucky enough to have read an independently published book have learned the rest of the story. "Courage After the Crash" (SAJ Publishing, 2002) is a 200-page hardcover described as "an oral and pictorial chronicle" that features some 100 first-person accounts of those on the ground who dealt with the aftermath of the crash. The writer, editor and publisher is Glenn J. Kashurba, M.D., a nationally recognized child and adolescent psychiatrist, who volunteered with the Red Cross and worked with the victims' families. He accompanied them to the crash site and the memorial services that followed. Proceeds from the book, first published in 2002, help support 9/11 charities. (In 2006, Dr. Kashurba expanded and updated his coverage of Flight 93 with the publication of "Quiet Courage.")

In Chapter 1, "Where Were You?" readers first meet Rick King. He was the assistant fire chief at Station 627, and was on the phone with his sister, Jody, when a big plane roared low overhead. He was also about to enter the twilight zone of every volunteer fire officer's worst nightmare — "The BIG One" — on a weekday morning when the fewest volunteers are available.

Then the ground shook. As King ran from home toward the firehouse, the fire siren went off. In the distance, a mushroom cloud of thick black smoke billowed into the clear blue sky.

"There were only four of us who came to the station," the book quotes King as saying. "Besides me, there was Keith Custer, Robert Kelly and Merle Flick. ... I drove. I looked at Keith and he looked back at the other two guys and said, 'Get ready, guys. This is like nothing we have ever seen before. Be prepared for anything.'"

But nothing could prepare them for what they found, which was almost nothing. Just a big hole in the ground, a lot of smoke and a few bits of flaming wreckage scattered here and there. Flight 93, a Boeing 757 with a seating capacity of 182, went down nose first — and upside down — at 563 miles per hour. The soft earth of a reclaimed strip mine swallowed the plane in one gulp. The plane carried 33 passengers and a crew of seven. There were no survivors.

I shudder every time I think about the four volunteers on that first responding pumper. There were 2,354 volunteer fire companies in Pennsylvania. Flight 93 flew over many of their stations as it traveled the length of Pennsylvania, looped around Akron, Ohio, and then swung southeast past Pittsburgh. But it came in low over only one, the Shanksville Volunteer Fire Department, Station 627, in Shanksville, population 250. Suppose we ever got a fire call for a jetliner crash. In the middle of a Tuesday morning, the turnout is apt to be slim. Same goes for any volunteer fire department anywhere in the state or the country at that time and day.

And, on TV, the planes kept hitting the buildings.

10:28 a.m. — The north tower collapsed.

4 p.m. — By then, Emmaus Public Library Children's Librarian Martha Vines had had her fill of TV news. When she entered the library, two women stood at the checkout counter. One was a library volunteer, the other, Martha called a "distraught mother." They were patting each other's hands, trying to comfort each other. Library volunteer Marilyn Kolb was Jewish. The other woman was Muslim.

7 p.m. — Fire practice that evening was a lackluster affair. With thousands missing and feared dead, no one could focus on much of anything. We all hungered for news of the hundreds of missing New York firefighters. But there was no real news, only speculation, rumor and worry. I didn't hang around after practice. I had a long drive tomorrow, and an even longer day and night ahead of me.

Wednesday, Sept. 12 — On the road just after dawn, I started fiddling with the radio. I had about 100 miles to go, and didn't want to miss any possible new developments from New York City. I was heading for John Hopkins' Forks Farm north of Bloomsburg, Pennsylvania. John was an old friend. We served together on the board of directors of the Pennsylvania Association for Sustainable Agriculture (PASA). John was a pioneer in producing grass-fed beef, lamb, poultry and pork. PASA was sponsoring a field day at his farm today. The featured speaker was another old friend, Joel Salatin, who ran Polyface Farm in Virginia. I was covering the field day in words and photos for Rodale's Russian *New Farmer* magazine.

John also happened to be a former wildland firefighter with three summers of service under his belt from college days in Montana. We got along well, despite the fact that wildland firefighters think structural fire firefighters like me are absolutely out of our minds. "Go blindly into a burning building where there may be no escape? You gotta be crazy!" And structural firefighters think wildland firefighters like John are absolutely out of their minds. "Face a 100-foot high wall of flames that can run up a hill twice as fast as any human? You gotta be crazy?"

But farmers — not firefighters — were today's link with the terrorist attacks. The pilot of American Airlines Flight 11, the plane that hit the north tower, was a farmer, an organic farmer, a member of the same organic farming group that certified our farm organic in 2001, in fact.

His name was John Ogonowski, a husband and the father of three children. His family farmed in one of the few remaining rural areas north of Boston, Massachusetts. He was one of the founding farmers in the New Entry Sustainable Farming Project, which helped Cambodian refugees begin new lives in America as farmers.

"He was so committed to helping immigrant farmers, to assist new immigrants from war-torn Asia to make a better life farming in America. I just think how ironic it is that someone who worked so hard to help victims of terrorism should be brought down by an act of terrorism himself," another old friend, August "Gus" Schumacher, Jr., said later in eulogizing the farmer-pilot.

On the morning of Sept. 11, other farmers were at the World Trade Center, too. A dozen farmers were selling fresh produce at one of New York's regular green markets in the spacious plaza around the Twin Towers when the attacks came. The farmers barely escaped with their lives. Their vehicles, produce and money were buried when the towers collapsed. Green markets throughout New York City were immediately shut down. And, suddenly, the terrorists' terrible tentacles stretched into our little valley in southeastern Pennsylvania.

Jeffrey Frank, a friend and neighbor, sold his produce every Wednesday at the green market at the United Nations building in Manhattan. He and his wife, Kristin Illick, were harvesting produce for that market when they heard about the attacks on the radio. That put a quick end to the day's harvest. No point in picking when there was no place to sell it.

Growers immediately started thinking more and more about establishing new markets much closer to home. Regional food security was now a big concern. What would happen, people asked, if bio-terrorists disrupted food supplies from California, Mexico or Florida? Pennsylvania can — and must — provide more of its own food, responded the scores of farmers at the PASA field day. Small farms and home gardens are the foundation of a safe and secure food supply, not just in the United States but also throughout the world. When people have their own land and plenty of good food, the words of political or religious fanatics become much less dangerous.

Talk of the terrorist attacks blended quickly with the finer points of rotational grazing, sustainable forestry and direct marketing as we walked around John Hopkins' lush pastures. We can't let the terrorists break our spirit or resolve, the farmers agreed. We must rise above the politics and destruction. Through it all, we must keep on building. New farms. New markets. New barns. The great losses in New York, Washington and Pennsylvania brought tears to our eyes, but they also filled us with an even greater resolve and a renewed hope for the future.

Reluctantly, I had to leave the field day just after lunch. I was on duty tonight at the Emmaus firehouse, captain on the 5 p.m. to 11 p.m. shift. On the two-hour drive home through the mountains, my truck radio picked up NPR and a few all-news stations, making the long drive seem even longer.

When I punched in at the firehouse a few hours later, it was a totally different world from yesterday. Paper and tape completely covered the row of windows in the overhead doors of the engine room. We were not trying to black out the station. The sheets of computer paper bore the names of those missing in the collapse of the towers. A small but growing number of people in the Emmaus area commute to work in New York. Many more have friends and relatives who work or live in the city. The town was frantic for any news about everyone's safety.

Into the early evening, a small but steady crowd milled in front of the firehouse. Couples strolled up and down Sixth Street. Kids zoomed by on bikes and skateboards. We left the front door open for visitors. People wandered in and out in a fog. They variously scanned the lists, gazed at the shiny fire trucks and chatted with the uniformed firefighters. Everyone said how sorry they were about the hundreds of missing New York firefighters.

An old man wandered in, a puzzled expression on his face. He seemed lost, a little confused. "Why," he asked me, "didn't they use chairs to carry people down out of the towers?" It was a rescue carry from his childhood, something he learned many decades earlier as a Boy Scout. "Good idea," I said. "We learned that in Scouts, too. I'll have to tell someone." I didn't know who I could tell or what difference it would make. The towers were now mountains of burning rubble — but it made the old man happy. I guess he felt he was contributing to the rescue effort in some small way.

And, on TV, in our firehouse crewroom and in living rooms throughout the country, the planes kept hitting the buildings.

Thursday, Sept. 13 — On CNN, first lady Laura Bush warned parents: Turn off your TVs. Or at least keep your children, especially very young children, from watching the crashes and tower collapses over and over. It was too frightening, even worse than images of the bombing of the federal building in Oklahoma City six years earlier. For many, her warning came too late.

Sometime that afternoon a harried mom barged into the Emmaus Public Library with her 4-year-old son.

"I had to get him away from the TV set," she told Children's Librarian Martha Vines. "He just told me, 'Everyone who takes care of me is dead because *the planes keep hitting the buildings.*'"

Martha immediately called the Emmaus police. This had to stop! Someone had to do something, the fiery redhead decided.

Then she e-mailed Emmaus Borough Council member Joyce Marin, another fiery redhead. "Can we get a police car, a fire truck and an ambulance to the library for just one hour?" asked Martha.

"Sure! Why not?" said Joyce.

"How many cruisers would you like?" asked dispatcher Cindy Pandol.

We'll call it "Hometown Heroes." People can come to the library and meet our "first responders," the police, firefighters, and ambulance crews. We'll start at 6 p.m. to get the children — and parents — away from the TV and the evening news.

But when? If we wanted a lot of people to show up, and Martha did, it was going to take time to let everyone know about the event. The date was set for Oct. 3, 2001. Martha contacted the superintendent of the East Penn School District. She got notices sent out to all of the elementary schools in the district and contacted the local newspapers, radio and TV stations. She talked up the event at every library "story time."

"You don't have to watch the planes fly into the buildings," she reminded parents. Across Main Street from the library, flyers and posters quickly went up in the Superior Restaurant, one of Emmaus' two Greek diners, and in Shangy's, a popular beer distributor run by a family that emigrated from Iran decades ago. Martha's friend, Marge Iannace, told parents at the day care center she operated. Even Marge's husband, Paul, started spreading the word, far and wide. People listen to Paul. He's a state trooper.

Oct. 3 was almost three weeks away. Meantime, life went on with previously scheduled events. A few months earlier, in a moment of weakness, I had agreed to give a talk that fall on organic farming to a large group of food technologists in Maryland. It was a double bill. The other speaker was Mike McGrath, former editor of *Organic Gardening* magazine. Mike and I were old friends from our years together at Rodale. We were also neighbors, so we decided to carpool. There was just one condition — that I drive. Mike's as Irish as the Ring of Kerry, not Italian, but he talks with his hands. And Mike talks a lot.

That's not a bad thing, considering that he makes his living on the radio. He hosts "You Bet Your Garden" every Saturday at 11 a.m. on WHYY, the NPR station in Philadelphia. His show is syndicated in 23 states and heard nationwide on Sirius satellite radio. Mike bills himself on the Web as an "organic gardening entertainer."

Mike's a brash big-city boy, born and raised in the gritty Frankford section of northeast Philadelphia. To his loyal listeners, Mike is almost as much of a Philadelphia icon as Rocky Balboa's statue in front of the Philadelphia Museum of Art. His late father, Harold "Graff" McGrath, was a Philadelphia homicide detective. A frequent visitor at the McGrath home while Mike was growing up was then Police Commissioner Frank Rizzo. In the late '60s, Mike had hair down to his shoulders and, in Philly-speak, an "attytood" when Rizzo dropped by one day.

"Howya doing, hippie?" Rizzo asked as he punched Mike in the gut.

Mike slugged the commissioner in the shoulder. "I'm fine!" he said. "How are you today, *pig?*"

"Best thing you coulda done," Mike's father said later. He meant it.

It was a three-hour drive to our destination just south of the Mason-Dixon Line. We were almost there when Mike finally ran out of steam — and words. But, like most radio guys, he simply couldn't abide "dead air." So he asked me how things were going as a volunteer firefighter these days. Before I could answer, Mike said he didn't really get the whole "volunteer thing."

From his big-city perspective, Mike said, "A firefighter is a job you pay someone else to do." It's like being a cop, a teacher, a sanitation worker, or a bus driver. It's why people pay taxes. For him, it was something you could take for granted. When you pick up a telephone and call for help, firefighters come running, because that's their job.

Compared to Mike, I'm the original quiet man. I normally don't talk much about what I do as a volunteer. But he asked, so I unloaded on him. For the next 15 minutes, I told Mike all about our weekly fire practice and weekend training classes; almost falling through the floor in a townhouse fire; putting out bus and truck fires while "playing in traffic" on the Highway from Hell; sleeping at the firehouse; running with two volunteer fire companies and responding to hundreds of fire calls a year; missing work, meals, and sleep; cradling a dead child in my arms; pulling a neighbor out of a drainpipe in a pond during Hurricane Floyd; playing hide-and-seek with a suicidal gunman inside a burning building, and regularly scaring the bejesus out of my wife.

Silence. No snappy comeback. Finally, Mike said, "I can't imagine doing that."

Silence. No snappy comeback. Finally, I said, "I can't imagine *not* doing that."

Why not?

Mark Twain once wrote, *"The two most important days in your life are the day you were born and the day you find out why."* Today, then, would be the second most important day in my life. I had just realized something that had been haunting my subconscious for years: Answering fire calls is why I was put on this earth.

Fire calls were turning me into a totally new person, I realized. A better person, I hoped. No longer was I just a "spectator," an "impartial observer" with a reporter's notebook and a camera. I was an active participant in life, and a guardian of all life. By risking my life to help others, I was living life to its fullest. I knew, better than most, how incredibly fragile, fleeting and precious life really is. I knew that, at any time, it could all end in a split second ... in a moment of carelessness on the highway ... with a grease fire in the kitchen ... from a candle burning in the bedroom. Fire calls had changed me, and were continuing to change me, in the most fundamental ways — physically, emotionally, psychologically and even spiritually. I was never much for organized religion. But I was a firm believer in a God who watches over us and who works in often mysterious, sometimes miraculous ways. I played many roles in life — husband, father, photographer, reporter, editor, farmer, direct marketer — but the one that trumped them all was firefighter. I was a firefighter, heart and soul ... to the very end. It was an honor, a privilege, a blessing — and also a curse. "You gotta love it," as Chief Reiss liked to say. And I did.

Then I thought of the Bob Dylan song, "Tangled Up in Blue." And the words of a thirteenth-century poet rang true, only this poet was not Italian. He was Persian. His name was Rumi. He was a Sufi, a Muslim mystic. Something he once wrote touched my soul:

One dervish to another, What was your vision of God's presence?
I haven't seen anything. But for the sake of conversation, I'll tell you a story.

God's presence is there in front of me, a fire on the left, a lovely stream on
the right.
One group walks toward the fire, into the fire, another toward the sweet
flowing water.
No one knows which are blessed and which are not.
Whoever walks into the fire appears suddenly in the stream.
A head goes under on the water, that head pokes out of the fire.

Most people guard against going into the fire, and so end up in it.
Those who love the water of pleasure and make it their devotion are
cheated of this reversal.
The trickery goes further.
The voice of the fire tells the truth saying, I am not fire. I am fountainhead.
Come into me and don't mind the sparks.

If you are a friend of God, fire is your water.
You should wish to have a hundred thousand sets of mothwings, so you could
burn them away, one set a night.
The moth sees light and goes into the fire. You should see fire and go toward
the light.
Fire is what of God — is world-consuming. Water, world-protecting.

Somehow each gives the appearance of the other.
To these eyes you have now, what looks like water, burns.
What looks like fire is a great relief to be inside.

Fire and water, two of the four classical elements most common in my life. I don't know if Rumi ever fought a fire, but he captured the essence of battling the flames. I was never more relaxed, more completely alive, than when I was facing the flames with a firehose in my hands.

And, on TV, the planes kept hitting the buildings.

Oct. 3, 2001 — The big day was finally here! The Emmaus Public Library proudly presented "Hometown Heroes."

The title seemed melodramatic, even a little embarrassing. But if it could help our children handle the trauma of the terrorist attacks a little better, I was all for it. Besides, remembering my recent conversation with Mike and his not-uncommon notions of firefighters, maybe we could even teach some adults a thing or two about what we do.

My uniform was clean and pressed. Getting dressed, I took a little extra time to make sure my badge and other insignias were perfectly positioned. I slid a black elasticized band over the two crossed bugles in the center of my gold captain's badge before fastening the heavy clasp.

I was working 5 p.m. to 11 p.m. again at the Emmaus Fire Dept. The event didn't start until 6 p.m., so we had plenty of time. But we still rolled a pumper toward the library almost as soon as we punched in. We backed into the first slot in the library parking lot by the driveway in case we got a fire call and had to make a quick getaway. We opened all four doors on the pumper and started getting everything ready.

Up front was the driver's seat and all of the truck's controls. Beside it was the officer's seat with banks of radios and switches. The rear of the cab had two rear-facing jump seats, complete with air packs built into the back-rests, axes, pry bars and other tools. We opened the side and rear compartments so people could see our chain saws and other power tools, nozzles and hose adapters, booster hose, foam equipment, tool boxes, and more.

We pulled an extra air pack and mask. They went on the pavement beside the truck so people could pick them up to feel the weight, and even try them on, if they wanted. Next came the Indian tank, a 5-gallon backpack sprayer that we use to fight field and brush fires. "It's the world's coolest squirt gun," I tell the kids. In the right hands, it has a range of about 30 feet — just right for soaking brothers and sisters, moms and dads, the fire chief, and tonight, even the children's librarian. "Oops! Sorry about that, Martha!"

Some of us were more nervous than we are when responding to a fire call. Outside of the usual Fire Prevention Week activities, this was totally new to all of us. Our Fire Prevention talks were easy, a safety demo, pure and simple.

Question: "What should you do if you clothes catch fire?"

Answer: "Stop. Drop. And Roll."

Yes! And don't forget to cover your face with your hands so your face won't get burned.

Fire Prevention Week at the schools was commonsense fire safety that everyone needed to know. The kids always loved it. So did firefighters, especially those who didn't have to say anything. It amazed me how so many big, tough firefighters totally froze up in front of a bunch of third-graders. Safety talks at school were one thing. The kids had to be there. They were a captive audience. But did children, their parents and the rest of their families really want to leave the comfort of their homes at dinnertime just to see a bunch of fire trucks, cop cars and ambulances — in the middle of a national tragedy? You bet they did!

It was a beautiful fall evening, warm and sunny with a clear blue sky, much like that deadly day in September a few weeks ago. People didn't just trickle in. They positively poured in, flooding the library grounds from all directions. Soon, there was not a parking space left for hundreds of yards along Ridge Street. Across Main Street, the Superior Restaurant and Shangy's opened their parking lots for the overflow.

All of the Borough Council members were there. The mayor arrived on his Harley. Politicians agreed ahead of time: "No speeches." This was neither the time nor the place. The police chief and our state representative were there. At the last minute, Trooper Iannace arrived in his state police cruiser.

"Can you make room for me?" he asked Martha. Not a problem. A few veterans were there, too. Jay, a borough maintenance worker, brought some of his Marine gear from the first Gulf War.

Martha greeted everyone personally. Clipboard in hand, she meticulously counted heads (450, by the time the evening ended), while passing out little American flags and patriotic stickers and making everyone feel right at home. "They need to be here as much as I do," Martha said. "This is where we belong. It's like Memorial Day used to be when it was really Memorial Day and everyone wore poppies."

There were parents, grandparents, even some great-grandparents. Children arrived on foot or on Daddy's shoulders, in little red wagons and strollers, on bikes, scooters and skateboards.

There were library regulars, and others who didn't know where the library was until today. A group of Mennonite women and girls appeared in their long, plain pastel dresses with tight-fitting wrists and collars, white socks and sneakers, and traditional white prayer caps. They hefted the air pack, then followed some teens with spiky hair through the crew cab, trying out the jump seats before hopping off the other side of the truck, giggling.

"What's that black thing on your badge?" a little girl asked me.

"It's a ..." I started to say, "mourning band." Then I remembered my audience. "It means I'm sad for the firefighters in New York."

"Oh. Me, too."

Then there was the little old lady who asked if she could drive the fire truck, or at least try out the driver's seat. "Pretty please?" She stood about 5 feet tall. We boosted all 100 pounds of her up into the driver's seat, then put a fire helmet on her white head. She gripped the wheel with both hands, wailed like a siren and started bouncing up and down, whipping the big wheel back and forth. She was as giddy as a 12-year-old. "I've wanted to do this all my life!" she giggled. Great-grandma was 87.

After about an hour, I looked up from the Indian tank where I was coaching another budding marksman. I saw a mother practically dragging her little boy across the driveway. He was 5, maybe 6 years old. And it was obvious he really, truly did not want to be here tonight.

What his mother said next explained why. "It's OK, honey. See? The firemen aren't *all* dead."

Grandpa "Paga" George lifts 16-month-old grandson Hunter up into a fire truck, while 3-year-old Forest scrambles into a jump seat.

PHOTO BY MELANIE DEVAULT

CHAPTER THIRTY-FIVE

Battle of the Budget
(and a ghost story, of sorts)

Something strange is happening in the road up ahead. Traffic's backing up, slowing to a crawl at a main intersection. Then it stops. Is there a bad accident? No, don't think so. A fire truck sits on the side of the highway, but there are no flashing lights. There's no ambulance, no cop car. Just a few firefighters moving between the cars, talking with the drivers. They're wearing bunker gear, but no helmets. They hold the helmets in their outstretched hands. Fire boots, too.

We politely call the activity "fundraising," probably to save our dignity. The naked truth is the firefighters are begging. They're hitting up passing motorists for donations to help keep the local fire company going.

Curious that firefighters are reduced to panhandling when the non-profit National Volunteer Fire Council estimates that volunteer firefighters save American taxpayers $139.8 billion a year. Mighty curious.

But wait. It gets even curiouser. And curiouser.

In the mid-1970s, Pennsylvania had about 300,000 volunteer firefighters. By the late 1980s, that number was down to around 70,000. "Based on my travels around the state, we're probably closer to 60,000," Pennsylvania State Fire Commissioner Edward A. Mann said on May 23, 2013. "I don't think we can go any lower."

Yet we did. Just six months later, D. Robert Brady II, a local government policy specialist with the Governor's Center for Local Government Services testified before the Pennsylvania Senate.

"Our number one problem is the decreasing number of volunteers. Today, the number is estimated at 45,000 to 50,000 responders. If the trend continues and is not reversed, by 2020 there may be no volunteers left in Pennsylvania, or at least in large areas of the state," Brady said.

Benjamin Franklin must be spinning in his grave. Remember, Brady was talking about Pennsylvania, the place that many regard as the birthplace of volunteer firefighting with the founding of "Ben Franklin's Bucket Brigade" (the Union Fire Company) on Dec. 7, 1736.

Why the huge drop, and why the dire prediction?

"There are two reasons why people leave our business as volunteers," said Commissioner Mann. "They get tired of the lack of leadership, and everything associated with that, or they get tired of spending more time raising money to pay the bills than they do responding to calls. Some of these folks become professional bingo callers or professional fundraisers. But you ask them to go attack a fire and they wouldn't know which end of the hose to grab, because we're spending so much time doing fundraising that we don't have time to do the important things we need to do."

Brady agreed. "I, too, have never had a former volunteer firefighter or EMT tell me they quit because there was too much training. What I've heard is that they grew tired of the lack of leadership in the firehouse, or they spent more time raising funds to support the fire company than actually responding to emergencies," he testified.

The problems of "retention and recruitment" — keeping the good people we have, and attracting new volunteers — are not unique to Pennsylvania. "The causes of the problems are similar in all 50 states. No single region of the country is dealing with problems that are significantly different than those found in other regions," reported the United States Fire Administration (USFA). "On a regional level, the Northeast has seen the greatest decline in volunteers because it has traditionally been protected by volunteers more than other regions. Four states (New York, Pennsylvania, Delaware, and New Jersey) that have historically been served by large numbers of volunteers have all experienced a major volunteer decline.

"The volunteer emergency services ... is a tradition in danger of weakening and possibly even dying out. Many fire departments across the nation today are experiencing more difficulty with recruiting and retaining members than ever before," said the USFA in 2004.

"Fire departments can no longer count on the children of current members following in their parent's footsteps. Nor can they count on a continuous stream of community people eager to donate their time and energy to their local volunteer fire department. Adding to the problem, departments cannot rely on members staying active in the volunteer fire service for long periods of time."

In 1984, two years after I became a volunteer firefighter, the United States had a high of 897,750 volunteer firefighters. Our ranks bobbed around over the next few decades. Then, starting in 2008, the number of volunteer firefighters steadily declined for four years in a row. In 2012, it reached a two-decade low of only 756,400.

Money, or the lack of it, was high on the long and growing list of reasons for the steep decline. Start with the prevalence of two-paycheck families; add to that the national economic meltdown. More people were working two jobs just to make ends meet. They worked outside of the area where they lived and couldn't respond to daytime calls. Or, the boss just wouldn't let them leave work to handle the ever-increasing number of fire calls. There was no "spare time" to volunteer. Costs for fire companies soared. The price of chain saws and other products marketed to the "fire service" was routinely double or triple the normal price. Times were tough. Still are.

"There's a volunteer fire company in central Pennsylvania, in the northern tier of counties, that I visited recently. They have a dirt floor in the firehouse, and their big decision is whether to pay the electric bill or put fuel in the trucks," said Commissioner Mann, who regularly visits scores of fire departments all over Pennsylvania. In addition to his 13 years as state fire commissioner, Mann knows the challenges from 40 years of firsthand experience. The son of a volunteer firefighter, he grew up in the firehouse. He's a lifelong volunteer firefighter, and also a volunteer fire chief.

"In a nutshell, financial support for fire departments is all over the place," said the Commissioner. "Some local governments do very well in supporting their volunteer fire companies, while others do very little to support their fire companies.

"Pennsylvania's dependence on property taxes is problematic to begin with, and trying to fund local emergency services in the same manner complicates the situation even more. There are many communities in Pennsylvania that don't have large populations, which equates to a very small tax base. I recall talking with a government official in north-central Pennsylvania who explained that with a 3-mill fire tax they would not generate more than $2,000 in a year."

In another community without a fire tax, officials simply dipped into the municipal General Fund when the fire department asked for more money. "One local government official was upset," said Mann. "He felt the fire department was extorting money. He felt the 300 percent increase was blackmail. I finally asked him, '300 percent of what?' He then went on to tell me that they currently provided a $300-a-year contribution to the fire department!

"This is why I continue to say we need true partnerships between state, local governments and the emergency services, in order to create a toolbox of possible solutions. I believe this because what works for you won't work for others. In fact, even in the same county, what works in one place will not work in another. Bottom line is there is no easy answer to the problem and, while some local governments do a poor job of financing the fire department, there are some who do a decent job."

Since its founding in 1942, our volunteer fire department in the village of Vera Cruz has had money problems. The thrifty old Dutchmen who started the fire company built whatever they could, including our first two fire trucks. They bartered, made do, or went without until they could afford the few things they absolutely had to buy. They went slow, and tried to pay at each step along the way. But the plan didn't always work: At monthly meetings, the early treasurers often ended their reports by saying, "We're a little short this month, fellas. Can you help us out?" All of the firefighters dug into their wallets, the old-timers recalled with pride.

On average from 2008 through 2012, it cost $92,407 a year to operate the Citizens' Fire Company in Vera Cruz. Where did all of that money come from?

By far, the biggest pot of cash came from out-of-state insurance companies. In Pennsylvania, the "Foreign Fire Insurance Tax" charges insurance companies not incorporated in Pennsylvania a 2 percent tax on all fire insurance policies written in the Keystone State. In 2011, that tax brought in $111 million. Vera Cruz's share of that was $32,500.

But, there's a catch. The money does not go directly to the state's fire companies. Instead, it goes to "relief associations" that are totally separate legal entities. There are strict rules about what the money can — and can't — be used for. To assure compliance with all the do's and don'ts, the state audits relief association books every year.

There are six financial categories in the firehouse: 1) General Fund, 2) Relief Association, 3) Major Firefighting Fund, 4) Investment Fund, 5) Fire Police, and 6) Funeral Relief Fund. It gets complicated. Here, in order of importance, is how the income breaks down on the firefighting (General Fund) side of the budget battle:

1. Annual Mailing — The Citizens Fire Company simply would not exist without the goodwill and generosity of the residents of our fire district. Each year, the fire company sends out two appeals for donations. The mailings bring in an average of about $27,000 a year. But only about one-third of the households send in contributions. The rest of the residents get what some consider a "free ride," since we continue to make house calls regardless of whether someone helps the cause. (Elsewhere around the country, some fire departments charge an annual subscription or membership fee. If the fee is not paid and your house or business catches fire, the fire department will stand by ... and watch your buildings burn. I can't imagine doing that, but it happens now and then. There's always a huge public outcry afterward, and rightfully so. Firefighters who do such a thing don't deserve the title.)

To spread the cost of fire protection evenly and fairly among all property owners in our township, there's talk around the firehouse from time to time of seeking a fire tax. The Lehigh Valley has a steadily growing number of new arrivals moving here from New York, New Jersey and the Philadelphia suburbs because our taxes are lower and housing is more affordable here. Many in that group don't know we have an all-volunteer fire department. They seem to expect the same level of municipal services they enjoyed "back home," despite our lower cost of living. State law allows townships to levy a fire tax of up to 3 mills to provide an adequate and stable source of funding for fire departments and ease the fundraising burden on volunteers. But a fire tax might hurt response to the annual appeal for contributions, critics argue. Besides, Upper Milford Township prides itself on keeping taxes as low as possible. Any new taxes risk a taxpayer revolt, and political suicide for the elected officials who dare to defy decades of tradition and raise taxes.

2. Township "Contribution" — At least that's what it's called in the township's annual budget. In 2014, that amounted to $25,430. (Total was actually double that figure because Old Zionsville, the other volunteer fire company in the township, received the same amount as Vera Cruz.) The township also paid $9,500 for workers' compensation insurance for the volunteers.

On the one hand, property taxes for 2014 in Upper Milford Township are minimal, 0.171 mills. Translating that into dollars and cents, township real estate taxes cost most property owners about as much as two large deluxe pizzas a year. On the other hand, our East Penn School District has a property tax rate of 46.75 mills. That equals enough to buy a good used car every year.

So, how do volunteers make up the difference, year after year? Any way we can.

Long gone are the days when passing the hat at a monthly meeting can keep the fire company from going over the fiscal cliff. Also gone are the days when volunteers are numerous enough — and young enough — to cook breakfasts for the community in the Social Hall or collect truckloads of household treasures and haul them to the firehouse for auction at white elephant sales. (Never mind the "white elephants" that don't sell and end up being hauled home to gather dust or rust.)

3. Rental House — The fire company owned an old two-and-a-half story house directly across the street from the firehouse. Rent brought in about $12,000 a year. But the mortgage ran about $5,700 a year, while maintenance costs were anywhere from a few hundred dollars to nearly $4,000 a year. In 2009, the year the rental house needed a new roof and we missed one month's rent while the house stood vacant, the "net" income didn't even cover the fire department's annual telephone bill. We finally sold the rental house in 2013. The proceeds paid off loans on our rescue squad and fire police trucks.

4. Grants — Mostly from state sources, grants average about $11,500 a year. Once a decade or so, a federal grant may pay to replace worn-out bunker gear and air packs that are nearing their expiration dates.

5. Pennsylvania Turnpike — Citizens' Fire Company has a long-standing contract to provide fire protection on part of the Northeast Extension of the Turnpike that runs right beside the firehouse. Average annual Turnpike income — for regularly putting our trucks and volunteers in harm's way an average of 31 times a year — is $6,976. The Turnpike pays a flat fee of $225 per fire call. We haven't had a raise in more than 25 years.

6. Games of Chance — Feel Lucky? Vera Cruz doesn't have a casino. The nearest one is miles away in Bethlehem, where The Sands occupies part of the old Bethlehem Steel foundry. But we do have $5 drawings in the Social Hall four times a year. Besides selling some 300 to 350 tickets in advance of each fifty-fifty drawing, the effort involves an army of volunteers cooking cheese steak sandwiches, perogies and hot dogs and selling strip tickets to the crowd for chances to win booze or whatever door prizes we can scrounge from local businesses. The $5 drawings bring in an average of about $3,340 a year. A state Small Games of Chance license costs the fire company $100 a year. That's not too bad, but new Department of Revenue reporting requirements will soon create a lot more work for Treasurer Kris Kellar, who after six years of running the drawings pleads at every monthly meeting for someone else to take over the drawings. Please!

7. Sandwich Sales — The year 2012 saw the end of the monthly ham and cheese sandwich sales, which had been bringing in only about $2,000 a year. After sandwich sales dropped by two-thirds in 2011, members voted to suspend the traditional project. There just weren't enough volunteers with the free time to sell, make and deliver hundreds of sandwiches every month.

In its place, after much discussion, volunteers finally voted in 2013 to try "third-party billing." With the blessing of the township's board of supervisors, an outside company working on commission began billing insurance companies for the time spent and materials used cleaning up after auto accidents, spills of hazardous materials, and various other calls. Expected payment rate is about 50 percent. The billing company charges a 15 percent commission on whatever is collected.

8. Ladies' Auxiliary — This dedicated group of women sells pizzas and shoofly pies to earn money for the fire company. Income averaged about $1,700 a year. In 2010, that was enough to cover the cost of putting fuel in the fire trucks, with $46 to spare. In other, busier years, the fuel bill was nearly double what the Auxiliary raised.

9. Social Hall Rental — The social hall that the firefighters built back in the 1950s is for rent for birthday parties, wedding receptions, family reunions, dances, and even wakes. Rental income grosses an average of $1,127 a year. But it costs at least $50 to clean the hall after each event. The roof, heating and air-conditioning, and water systems are old and in constant need of repairs.

10. Dues — Yes, we have annual dues. Volunteers have to pay $4 every year to belong to the Citizens' Fire Company of Upper Milford Twp. Dues bring in an average of $507 a year. On paper, that looks good. Real good. At $4 a pop, it means Vera Cruz has about 126 members. Many community members have joined just to support the fire company, and also to receive the "member discount" on renting the social hall. There is also a modest "death benefit" for those who qualify. The roster of active firefighters lists only a couple dozen names. And, depending on when the fire siren goes off, only about one-third of those actually climb on a fire truck.

Dues do not translate into fancy uniforms and badges. The fire department doesn't even issue a uniform shirt. You want a shirt and a badge so you don't look like a bum in jeans and a T-shirt at funerals, parades and other special events? Fine, dig into your own pocket and come up with $100. How about a light bar for your car? There might be a few hand-me-downs hiding around the firehouse, but most volunteers shell out a couple hundred bucks for emergency lights.

11. Reflective Address Signs — We make, sell, often deliver and sometimes install reflective house number signs, both to raise money and to make houses in the country easier to find when we have a fire call. That enterprise grosses an average of $396 a year.

12. T-shirts R Us — Sales of fire department T-shirts and sweatshirts bring in an average of $198 a year.

13. Bank Interest — For 2012, our interest on the General Fund totaled a whopping 81 cents. But, boy, was the bank quick to charge the fire company "service fees" when we didn't maintain a proper "minimum balance" in our checking account.

No matter how much money the fire company earns, it's never enough. So members are always asking, "What else can we do to raise money?"

The list seems endless, limited only by imagination and the willingness of volunteers. Fundraisers around the country include carnivals, raffles of everything from shotguns to hunting trips, pork and sauerkraut dinners, bake sales, parties with wide-screen TVs for major sporting events like the Daytona 500, World Series, Kentucky Derby, and the Super Bowl, basket bingo, comedy nights (the raunchier the better), poker runs, fire department calendars with "hot" female and male firefighters (often wearing fire helmets and little else), flower and plant sales, a car wash at the firehouse, craft fairs, selling firehouse BBQ and hot sauce, golf tournaments, and more. When all else fails, the tankers can fill swimming pools and hot tubs with water for a modest fee. Trouble is, the pool of volunteers available and willing to do all of the above is drying up. So we try new ideas whenever we can. It doesn't hurt if it's something we can have a lot of fun with.

"How about a haunted hayride?" someone said. "Whitehall just did one. Made a lot of money!"

Oh, yeah! Firefighters Jim and Kris Kellar immediately volunteered the use of their 60-acre farm.

"Cool! Perfect!" everyone said. It's a natural! The old farmhouse there really is haunted!"

At least that's what the Kellars' then 11-year-old daughter, Kourtney, said. Alone in the empty stone farmhouse, built in 1845, she and others had heard voices. A man and woman were yelling at each other. The argument quickly built in volume and violence, until ... "Bang!" A door slammed. Then all was quiet.

Few people in Vera Cruz doubted the story. "Ghost stories" are common hereabouts. Late-night strollers swear they still see the spectral "Lady in White" walking the trail over South Mountain to Vera Cruz. Local legend says she was the teenage housekeeper at an old stone house east of the village. Way back in the early 1920s, the girl vanished without a trace. Years later, word spread about a nasty brown stain — the color of dried blood — mysteriously appearing on the basement floor of the old house. And every time someone scrubbed the basement floor, the stain eventually reappeared, old-timers said. In other area homes, family treasures would mysteriously disappear for weeks, then suddenly reappear, but only after the owner had yelled and screamed about not being able to find things. Nearly everyone in the area has a ghost story of sorts, or so it seems. (Of all the holidays, the favorite of the Pennsylvania Dutch seems to be Halloween. It's the only event that rates an annual parade in Vera Cruz and many surrounding small towns.) To top it off, the long-neglected Mates farm that the Kellars bought really looked like a set for a horror movie.

Yes, a haunted hayride was just the ticket. So, as firefighters often do, we gave it our all, and then some. The organizers laid out a mile-long "spook loop" around the farm. We lined up body snatchers, chain saw-weilding killers, mad scientists with an outdoor laboratory full of "body parts," assorted zombies, ghosts and goblins galore, flying monkeys, and much more. We even signed up the Grim Reaper.

The first and most necessary equipment was, of course, tractors and haywagons. Firefighters who lived nearby, brothers Gary and Arnie Mohr, Chief Tapler and I, all volunteered our tractors, and ourselves as drivers. We didn't want to miss any of the freaky fun! The tractors were mostly tricycle-type Farmalls from the 1930s through the 1950s. Reddish, Great Pumpkin orange and rusty, they were perfect Halloween tractors. My green and gold John Deere 1050 from the early 1980s was the oddball. It was the only diesel and the only tractor with a rollbar and a seat belt. The tractors were all cranky at times. Good thing Jim was also a master mechanic.

The fiends in charge of the fun customized the haywagons with wooden siderails for safety and tape players and hidden stereo speakers for fright. The sound systems broadcast bloodcurdling screams, ghostly groans and moans, and maniacal laughter. A clicker in the tractor driver's pocket controlled the sound effects. Next, strategically placed around the fields, woods and outbuildings, came spotlights, heavy-duty battery packs, Porta-Johns, generators, a fire pit, picnic tables, and food. Lots and lots of food: Firefighters' families freely contributed homemade and store-bought tossed salad, pasta salad, pepperoni salad, barbecue chicken, slowly simmered sausages with onions and peppers, hamburger barbecue, perogies, hot dogs mit kraut, and much more. There was no beer, at least not for the volunteers, until after the hayrides, but we had lots of pop, coffee and hot chocolate for the customers.

The course started out in a level area behind the old Mates farmhouse. Once a haywagon was loaded, the tractor driver would ease it up and over the steep railroad crossing into a cornfield. The wagons creaked and wobbled precariously. Passengers screamed, and they were not even to the first fright yet.

It was night. We were driving without lights. Only a glow stick every hundred yards or so on the ground marked the way. The corn towered above us. Suddenly, a body snatcher burst out of the corn on the left. He ran right up to the wagon. Before anyone could react, the ghoul hauled a young girl over the siderails. He threw her over his shoulder and darted back into the darkness, carrying the kicking and screaming girl. The remaining passengers huddled together for protection. They didn't know that the "victim" was part of the show.

When the wagon came to the railroad tracks again, it was an easy, flat crossing. Everyone relaxed. But just as the haywagon straddled the tracks, the tractor's engine suddenly died. The driver cranked the starter again, and again. Then a blinding light hit the haywagon. It was a spotlight, the face-melting 2 million candlepower headlight of an oncoming locomotive. The light was only 100 feet away! Dual air horns from a real locomotive ripped through the night. Everyone screamed in real terror, convinced that in seconds they were all going to die under the wheels of a lunatic locomotive.

Then the air horns fell silent. The spotlight went out. The tractor engine fired right up. The wagon lurched forward. Everyone relaxed, but only a little. Nerves were getting raw, and our passengers still had a long, dark ride ahead of them.

As we reached the dark woods, a chain saw roared to life. Suddenly, ghouls were everywhere. Growling and howling, they beat on the sides of the haywagon with baseball bats and pipes. A madman in a hockey mask charged the wagon with a chain saw roaring at full throttle. There was no chain on the saw, but our passengers didn't know that. They all scrambled toward the center of the wagon for safety.

Rounding another bend, the girl taken by the body snatcher reappeared. Or, at least her body did. It hung limply, spread-eagle on X-shaped timbers ringed by spotlights in a clearing in the corn. (Our "victims," played alternately by Kourtney Kellar and her cousin, Sierra, were never harmed. But their acting was so good and the stage setting so real that one young passenger refused to leave at the end of the ride until he saw the kidnapped girl again in person, just to make sure she was really safe.)

As the woods closed in on both sides to form a dark canopy over the narrow, winding wagon trail, ghosts and goblins screamed from perches just above the passengers' heads.

Tractor drivers had specific instructions to drive right up beside one of the last treelines, and go slow. As we came in close and throttled back the tractors, flying monkeys on heavy ropes swung out of the trees. Screaming like demons from the pit, they zoomed toward the passengers' heads. Everyone ducked. A few even dove headfirst into the straw in the wagons to hide.

At the end, people couldn't wait to get off of the wagons. Finally, they were safe. Or so they thought. But first they had to get past Father Time (Fire Police Officer Matt Fatzinger), The Grim Reaper (Kris Kellar, eyes aglow with red zombie contacts, a ghostly white face in a hooded robe) and through the Haunted Woods.

The scene repeated itself on Friday and Saturday nights through much of October for three years. There were also a couple of more leisurely and relaxing foliage rides through the woods and fields on Saturday afternoons.

The minimum staffing to run the haunted hayride was 24, a full two dozen volunteers. "Thirty-six is even better," Kris said. "When you don't have enough people, it's kind of lame." With an average of 30 people working four hours each hayride, that totaled 720 volunteer hours per year, or 2,160 hours over the three years. It was no wonder we could only muster a skeleton crew to do a single hayride on the fourth and final year. The body snatchers, flying monkeys, tractor drivers and hosts had simply burned out. As much fun as the haunted hayride may have been, it just was not sustainable.

Financially, though, we considered it a huge success. The event took in a total of $10,128.29. Expenses were only $2,490.07. That translated into a "profit" of $7,538.22. Too bad the cost of outfitting one firefighter with new bunker gear and an air pack was about $7,800.

The haunted hayrides are just a memory now. Jim and Kris are almost done restoring the old farmhouse. Whatever ghosts hang around the old Mates farmhouse seem happier these days: Kris and Jim don't hear them arguing, anymore. But, at monthly meetings, we still hear an occasional groan in the spirit of the early fire department treasurers:

"We're a little short this month, fellas. Can you help us out?"

And, while we're at it, will someone take over the $5 drawings from Kris? Please!

CHAPTER THIRTY-SIX

All in the Family

"Yeah ... what happened next?" asked the man next to me at the bar. He was sitting on the edge of his chair. We were tipping back our second Samuel Adams Boston Lagers from brown, longneck bottles at a cheap motel bar in far western Pennsylvania. The questioner was Ira Glass, host of the popular NPR radio program "This American Life." The show aired on more than 500 public radio stations each week. It had some 1.7 million loyal listeners. But, not being a NPR regular, I didn't know about Ira or his show until his producer called out of the blue and asked me to be a part of an episode that ended up with the title "Farm Eye for the Farm Guy (Episode #273, first aired on Sept. 24, 2004)."

It was a makeover show in the style of the then popular "Trading Spaces," "Extreme Makeover," "The Swan," or "The Queer Eye for the Straight Guy." I was the "farm eye." The "farm guy" was a wannabe farmer, a former photographer who bought 75 acres in the boonies and dreamed of being a vegetable farmer. But, because he had a bad back, field work was difficult. Plus, he stayed up most of the night tweaking photographs on his computer. Then he slept until noon. He and his wife worked their butts off washing a few bags of lettuce, leaf by leaf, and couldn't understand why they only made $15 at the farmers' market. Rent for their booth was at least $7, so they were losing their shirts. (Soon after the show aired, the "farm guy's" Korean-born wife moved to New York City, where she went back to work in the fashion industry. He stayed on the farm and stuck with photography, but eventually went back to college and ended up teaching photography at the University of Florida.)

After a long afternoon of taping and tromping around the farm guy's fields in the hot summer sun, Ira and I were recovering and ruminating at the bar. Ira wanted to talk small farming. I was trying to interest him in doing a show on the secret life of volunteer firefighters. The trigger was the red light on the top of my pickup truck. When Ira asked about it, there was not a flicker of understanding of what volunteer firefighting involved. Like most Americans, Ira was totally clueless.

Ira was nibbling on the idea of a firefighter segment, but he wasn't biting. So, later, I took the extreme literary liberty of drafting a script of how such a show might go. Back home at my computer keyboard, I channeled Ira's unique, distinctive voice and herky-jerky delivery. Why not? "This American Life" also aired in Canada and Australia. It won nothing but the highest honors for broadcasting and journalistic excellence. *The American Journalism Review* said it was "at the vanguard of a journalistic revolution." Just the place to tell folks what being a volunteer firefighter was really all about. I e-mailed the script to Ira in Chicago. But, again, he didn't bite.

Then it hit me. This was radio. Radio needed sound, and lots of it. Mere written words just wouldn't do. So I started carrying a microcasette tape recorder in one of the radio pockets of my bunker coat. And extra tapes and extra batteries in a plastic bag so that they didn't get soaked on fire calls when I did. I taped everything. The electronic squealing of my pager on initial dispatch, and the dispatcher's deadly calm but haunting voice message: *"Stations 28, 7, 30 ... Buckeye Pipeline ... gasoline transmission pipeline struck."*

"Oh, shit!" I said with the tape rolling. The sprawling tank farm was the absolute worst nightmare in our fire district. The recorder captured the wailing of the fire siren atop the Social Hall across the road from the engine room, the sound of overhead doors going up, the rumble of the diesel engines on the fire trucks clattering to life. The tense voices of firefighters yelling and swearing as we poured into the engine room and scrambled into our bunker gear. Officers barking commands. Radio transmissions to and from everyone involved in today's fire call:

"14-inch gasoline transmission pipeline cut by backhoe operator ..." A fountain of pressurized gasoline shot 40 feet into the air, then poured down on a backhoe — with the engine running. The operator quickly bailed out. He and other frantic workers were running around in the potentially deadly deluge as gasoline rained down on them and the pumping station's electrical equipment.

"Engine 2812 responding ..." "Engine 712 responding ..." "Second alarm ..." "Notify Lehigh County Emergency Management, and HazMat Team ..." "Hit the hydrant ..." "Lay a 4-inch supply line ..." "Close Buckeye Road ..."

We were lucky, this time. No gasoline ignited. There was no fire, no explosion. And no radio show. The quirky ending that was the trademark of Ira's popular show just wasn't there.

"What happened next?" Ira's question haunted me, not because the answer was so elusive, but because it was so obviously simple. While it's true that fire calls come in an endless variety, and each is completely unique, the ending is always exactly the same: We regroup, then we do it all over again. If we're lucky.

"Let's get those trucks back in service!" yells Emmaus Chief Reiss.

It's a little past 6 a.m., half an hour until sunrise on an April morning. Time for most of us to get up. Time to go to work soon. But we're already 5 hours into a fatal fire call, and we still have 2 hours of work left to do.

How did we get here? Hit the rewind button. This fire call comes in about 1:15 a.m. Emmaus and Salisbury Township firefighters are already out on an automatic fire alarm at Lehigh Valley Hospital Center. Then an Emmaus cop on routine patrol spots flames near the top of South Mountain. He immediately radios for help. The blaze is easy to see. There are few leaves on the trees yet. It's a big old house on Rockcliff Road several miles away and more than 150 feet above the valley floor. Flames billow from the home of Kenneth K. and Faith Fegley. The fire's like a lighthouse beacon lighting up the eastern sky.

As the cop races to the scene, Faith Fegley scrambles out of a bedroom window in her burning house. She runs into the night, screaming. Her nightclothes and hair are on fire. With burns over 50 percent of her body, she's already in shock by the time she reaches a neighbor's back porch. The neighbors usher her inside. The cop radios for an ambulance.

The cop and neighbor rush back to the burning house. Faith's husband, Kenneth, is still somewhere inside. But there's nothing the men can do for him. Thick, black smoke, intense heat and flames keep them from going inside to search for Fegley. They hear things popping in the house.

An Emmaus pumper is first on the scene. Emmaus Firefighter Todd Garloff bravely battles his way into the blazing bedroom. He actually has a hand on Fegley, according to *The Morning Call*, but it's too late. His yellow bunker gear turns black, as fierce flames drive him out of the house, empty-handed, with burns on his face around his air mask.

I'm in a jump seat on Emmaus' second pumper. After zooming across town, we suddenly stop at the base of South Mountain on Second Street, just inside the borough boundary. "Why are we stopping here?" I wonder. We're at the fire hydrant closest to the burning house. It's the very last one in the borough, and more than half a mile from the fire. We're dropping supply hose. On top of the mountain, they're out of water. With the help of other engines, we lay more than 3,500 feet of hose up the winding mountain road and down the long lane.

When we arrive, we quickly knock down the fire in and around the bedroom, but it's too late for Kenneth Fegley. The coroner pronounces him dead about 2 a.m. Chief Reiss and I are in the bedroom with the coroner.

As other firefighters battle flames in the rest of the house, we gently lift and turn the body on the bed as the coroner makes his preliminary examination. He finds scorched ammunition here and there in the bedroom. Exploded ammunition, .22-caliber long rifle casings, explain the earlier popping sounds. There's nothing suspicious about the body.

The dead man is related to Chief Reiss by marriage. The chief doesn't go into detail. I don't pry. It's neither the time nor the place, and it doesn't really matter, anyhow. The coroner finishes his grim work. We ease Fegley's body into a metal rescue basket, then slide the basket through the window frame and down a metal ladder to other firefighters. I go back to fighting the fire.

"How many air bottles have you gone through?" a medic asks later, as I kneel in the side yard. Another firefighter is securing a fresh air bottle to my air pack frame. The medic's checking vital signs. Anyone whose pulse or blood pressure is too high automatically goes to rehab. Two air bottles also earn an automatic time out in rehab.

"Just one bottle. This'll be my second," I say. It's a lie. Actually, this will be my third air bottle. I'm not about to warm the bench in rehab, though, not when the house is still burning. Not when the man of the house is dead, his wife's in critical condition at the hospital, and now two firefighters are injured. I have to stay in the fight, try to even the score, if that's possible. It's not. Tonight, we fight a losing battle. Fire guts the two-story frame home. It's filled with books and magazines, mostly on railroading. Fegley, 62, retired as a railroad conductor just weeks before the fire. His first pension check arrived the day before the fire. Eventually, parts of the first and second floors collapse into the basement. That's going to make finding the cause of the fire difficult. But investigators eventually find the culprit, an overloaded fusebox. On the kitchen table, they also find Chief Reiss' anniversary present to the couple — two smoke detectors, still in their original boxes.

What happens next? The same thing that always happens. We go home.

This fire's in neighboring Salisbury Township. Their pumpers and crews will stay on the scene, mopping up the hot spots. We drain and roll up our hoses, pack up our other gear and head back to the firehouse.

"Get those trucks back in service!" barks the chief. "Attack truck, first!"

We have hundreds of feet of filthy, stinking hose to wash. Clean, dry hose needs to go on the trucks. Air packs and air masks need washing. There are air bottles to refill, fire trucks to wash, inside and out. Despite that, they'll still smell like smoke for days. So will we. Soiled bunker gear goes into a large, commercial-scale washing machine. We need to clean and oil chain saws, disinfect rescue and medical equipment, clean and check ladders, ropes and other gear for damage. Radio batteries need changing. Trucks need refueling. This is going to take hours.

All I really want to do is crawl up on the hose bed of a pumper and go to sleep. When you're physically and emotionally exhausted, the long folds of canvas-covered hose make a surprisingly comfortable bed. Instead, I grab another cup of coffee, and keep washing hose.

My family can't really understand it. All through his 80s, my father keeps urging me to quit the fire department. "You should think of your family, son," he pleads. I do, Dad. Family is all I can think of, every time there is a fire call. The people we help are part of someone's family. I don't know whose family, and it doesn't matter. They're all family.

While we're waiting for the ambulance to arrive at the crash scene on a rainy night on the Turnpike, I'm holding the trembling hand of a frail old woman. She's someone's mother. She could be my mother. The little boy in my arms is someone's son. He could be my grandson. The man thrashing about in the pond during a hurricane is someone's husband and a father. He could be my brother. The woman reported trapped inside the burning house is someone's daughter. She could be my daughter. I may not know any of them. But the same thing, or worse, could just as easily happen to a member of my family or your family. And, if it ever does, I know that kind, caring strangers will immediately drop whatever they're doing. They'll put their daily lives on hold and rush to do everything they can to help.

As I keep wrestling wet hose out of the washer, Bob Rodale's long-ago words about leaving work for fire calls come back to me: "Do what you have to do, George. It might be *my* house. It might be *your* house." We never know when or where there will be another fire call. But we know for sure there will be a next.

There's a fire call somewhere in the United States every 23 seconds. Now do the math. That's roughly three fire calls every minute. Times 60 minutes, that's about 180 fire calls every hour — 24 hours a day — 7 days a week. Fire calls never take a day off. In one year, it adds up to almost 1.6 million fire calls. That's why, no matter what, we always have to be ready ... for the next fire call.

THE END

A Flag from Ground Zero

On the surface, *"Fire Call!"* may seem to be the stories of one firefighter. But deep down, this book is really the story of all firefighters, everywhere. Only the details change with each fire call.

That thought was always in the back of my mind as I wrote and endlessly rewrote *"Fire Call!"* over the years. But that gut feeling never completely crystalized until I met a fellow firefighter on the other side of the world. It was in his modest firehouse in Laguna Verde (Green Lagoon), a dusty village on the Pacific coast of Chile about 70 miles west northwest of the capital city of Santiago.

What took us to Chile? Melanie and I were finally visiting our son, Don, and his very pregnant wife, Bree. The kids, both adventurous language teachers, were homesteading off the grid in the steep, piney hills outside of the village. "Think Big Sur in the 1950s, Dad," is how Don described it. The area is known for its secluded beaches and miles of old logging roads that snake back into the rugged coastal mountains. A building boom was sweeping the area as several large landowners began selling off reasonably priced lots. It was a chance to take advantage of Chile's stable economy and the desirable location near large cities and popular resort areas. People from nearby Valparaiso and even Santiago were quickly building thousands of vacation or second homes in the country's outback.

As a father and a firefighter, that worried me greatly because, just like in California's Big Sur, the biggest danger to life and property around Laguna is wildfire. Living in a dense pine forest is risky enough. But then bulldozers come to clear winding roads and remote building lots. The machines push uprooted pines into huge piles wherever it's convenient. The piles quickly become dry as tinder, with the potential explosive force of solid gasoline. The forest floor is covered with a thick carpet of dry pine needles. Gypsy loggers with portable sawmills leave huge piles of tree trimmings and slabwood on the steep hillsides.

That's not good because many people in the area heat their homes with wood. They cook on wood fires, often outdoors. A lot of people there smoke.

Onshore winds are constant, often strong and unpredictable, frequently coming from all directions as they bounce around the coastal canyons.

Also, as in California, there is the ever-present threat of earthquakes. Chile is the most earthquake-prone country in the world. Chile's 9.5 Valdivia earthquake in 1960 was the most violent earthquake on record. The most common hazard after any earthquake? Fire.

So when the kids first started clearing their land and building a little house almost 2 miles from the nearest paved road, I strongly suggested that they make contact with the local fire department. At least get on its radar. Firefighters need to know — ahead of time — that someone is living way back in the woods at the very end of an unmapped dirt road.

The kids probably thought I was nuts, but they humored old Dad. They learned the location of the nearest firehouse, which is more than many people do. Then they stopped by the firehouse and schmoozed. In the process, they learned that all of the local firefighters — and nearly all of the firefighters in the entire country — are volunteers.

Don and Bree didn't think much more about the threat of wildfires until the middle of February 2013. Then they suddenly became believers. A construction worker cutting steel panels with a welder's torch accidentally set the woods on fire in the hills above Laguna. The weather was hot and dry. It was the height of the summer holiday season in the Southern Hemisphere. Strong, changing winds drove flames deep across the rugged countryside ... right toward the couple's little house in the forest.

"It was crazy, because it was really close to our house," said Bree. "Firefighters responded quickly, and it was amazing to see. We got on top of our house and watched as the planes and helicopters flew over us. It was really nuts. Don was going crazy trying to chop down all the trees close by our place, just in case the fire got too close. We were lucky they got it out so quickly."

The kids were all packed, ready to bug out when the winds changed again and pushed the fire away from them. Yes, they were lucky. The fire destroyed more than 100 nearby homes and forced 1,200 people to flee. Firefighters were lucky, too. Just the year before, similar conditions in Patagonia in southern Chile spawned nearly 50 wildfires that killed six firefighters when winds suddenly shifted. Melanie and I followed it all nervously through Facebook, e-mail and CNN.

Our trip to Chile was the first real vacation for Melanie and me in six years. It was early February, a time when nothing was growing on our farm in the Northern Hemisphere. It was also easier for us to get away because I had retired from the fire service the year before. That was a tough decision, but the time was right. With both of us in our 60s, and after 30 years with more than 5,000 fire calls (47 years if you count 22 years with Emmaus AND 25 with Vera Cruz), I figured I owed my wife a life in our "golden years." So, with a heavy heart, I hung up my helmet and bunker gear for good at the end of 2012.

One of the first places Don and Bree showed us in Laguna Verde was the firehouse. It was a quaint adobe and log building from the mid-1800s. The parking lot was empty, as you might expect at a volunteer firehouse in the middle of the day. But as our tires crunched on the gravel driveway, a lone firefighter came out of the building to see what was up.

His name was Rafael Valesquez, or "Rafe," for short. For 30 years he had been a firefighter in Talca, a city of 200,000 about 160 miles south of Santiago. He didn't go into any detail about his work there. He didn't have to. With 30 years on the job, I knew he'd pretty much seen and done it all.

Instead, he was most eager to show us his firehouse and the only fire truck there at the time. It was a large Mercedes tanker with a "porta-pond" on one side. He apologized for not having a pumper to show. But the pumper was in the repair shop. It had been rear-ended the day before by a kamakazi-like transit bus.

Laguna Verde's fire company has 24 members. For the most part, they're all volunteers. Rafe was the exception. He said he was at the firehouse today because he was a driver being paid to make sure the truck would get out when there's a fire call. Sounded vaguely familiar. Having a paid driver on standby during the day is becoming more and more common everywhere as the ranks of volunteers shrink.

About 5 minutes into the tour, I gave Rafe a uniform patch from the Vera Cruz fire department in faraway Pennsylvania. It was nothing fancy, just a simple Maltese cross shape with red embroidery of a "fire scramble" (crossed axes, a ladder, helmet and fire hydrant) on a plain white background. Did he have an extra patch for his department handy?

His department has a really stunning patch. It's bright gold on a shamrock green Maltese cross, as befits a fire company named after the son of an Irish immigrant. "Pump Libertador Bernardo O'Higgins Riquelme," or company number 16, as it's also known, honors one of the fathers of Chilean independence from Spain. Bernardo O'Higgins (1778-1842) was celebrated as a freedom fighter throughout Chile, much of South America and even in his ancestral homeland of Ireland.

Although the sprawling Valparaiso fire district was founded in 1851, Rafe's Station 16 is the newest station in the district. It was founded in 2002 because of the growing number of wildfires in the area. Rafe said the next most frequent call was "rescues," usually on the narrow, steep and winding mountain roads. Sounded eerily familiar.

Names of other companies in the district reflected the steadily growing population and cultural diversity of the area. Station 2 honored Germany; 5 and 8, France; 7, Spain; 11, Great Britain; 12, Switzerland; and 15, Israel. Station 16 planned to build a new, thoroughly modern firehouse on land it had on free loan for 50 years. All they needed now is money, lots of money. Sounded familiar, too.

Alas, Rafe didn't have a spare patch. He dropped his eyes to the floor when I asked about a swap. His captain kept the patches locked away. You see, Rafe explained, members of his department have to buy all of their own patches, emblems — and uniforms. Sounded really familiar.

No problem, I said. I forgot all about it, but Rafe didn't. Halfway through the tour, somewhere between the kitchen and the bunkroom, Rafe stopped in the middle of the hallway. He fished in his back pocket and pulled out his wallet. It was a long, leather chain wallet, well worn, and dark with age. From deep inside, he pulled out a small embroidered patch, and handed it to me. It was a Chilean flag, a single white star in a blue field

International Brotherhood — Laguna Verde Firefighter Rafael Valasquez presents George with a Chilean flag patch, all that was left of his gear after Rafe worked the 2010 Chilean earthquake that killed more than 500 people.

PHOTO BY MELANIE DEVAULT

flanked on the right by one broad white stripe and below by one red stripe. Little bits of yellow thread hung from the edges of the patch.

"Thank you! Muchas gracias!"

But it was more than just a flag patch. Much more. The patch was all that was left of the gear Rafe wore during rescue and recovery operations after the 2010 earthquake that killed more than 500 people in Chile. With a magnitude of 8.8, it was the sixth strongest earthquake ever recorded. The quake ravaged his old hometown, where he was sent to work for rescue and recovery. The quake triggered a tsunami that wiped out several coastal villages in Chile and prompted tsunami warnings in 53 countries around the Pacific. Tsunami waves caused minor damage in San Diego, California, USA, more than 5,000 miles to the north, and caused millions of dollars worth of damage in Tohoku, Japan, more than 10,000 miles away on the other side of the Pacific. It was a monster quake that blacked out 93 percent of Chile for days. Don and Bree and their trembling dog, Japhy, rode out the 3 minutes of intense shaking in a doorway of their fourth-floor apartment in the old "Bohemian" section of Santiago.

Like New York City firefighters working the piles of rubble at Ground Zero after the collapse of the Twin Towers, Rafe spent weeks after the quake doing anything and everything Chile's firefighters had to do to help put his country back on its feet. The work meant so much to him that he carried the patch with him every day for 4 long years.

When saying good-bye, firefighters in the United States usually tell each other, "Be safe!" That didn't translate easily or well into Spanish, so we mumbled our way through a clumsy parting. Then, after we were back on the road, Don and Bree translated more of what Rafe had said about his flag. I was stunned, absolutely amazed that he would give such a deeply personal keepsake to a total stranger.

Rafe's patch means a lot to me, too. That's why it now hangs on the wall by my computer ... right beside Georgie's fire/rescue patch from Baghdad International, a small pennant given me by a Russian firefighter who lost a good friend at Chernobyl and designer Karen Simon's "Rise Above" poster of the Twin Towers on an American flag background. They're priceless treasures.

All I can offer in return is a humble, heartfelt blessing: Go with God, brothers and sisters. "Vaya con Dios, hermanos y hermanas." Be safe wherever future fire calls may lead you.

ACKNOWLEDGMENTS

There once was an assistant managing editor at *The Morning Call* in Allentown, Pennsylvania, who was known in the newspaper composing room as the "Picky Little Shit," or "PLS," for short. He could spot a typo a mile away. When Randall Murray began prowling the composing room and reading proofs as Home Section editor, he quickly became known as "PLS2." He wore the title like a badge. Thank you, Randall, for taming what you once described as "War and Peace — in Flames!"

Other superstars are our long-time neighbor and friend, designer Ken Kleppert, who consistently went above and beyond the call of duty and turned a pipe dream into a work of art, and memoir meister Joe Kita, who knows the difference between cellophane and a winning lottery ticket.

The Borough of Emmaus will always have a special place in my heart. I am especially indebted to the late Martha Vines, Emmaus Library children's librarian. Our "Hometown Heroes" day every Sept. 11 won't be the same without you. Then there is former Emmaus Councilman Mike Waddell, Ph.D., and his wife, Linda, our longtime neighbors and friends, who were blown away to learn what their next door neighbor did as a volunteer firefighter in our small town. Thanks for pouring over the original manuscript.

This book simply would not exist without all of the men and women, past and present, of the Emmaus Fire Department. I owe special thanks to Fire Chief Robert Reiss, officers Kenny Young, Dean Seibert, Victoria Schadler, and Roscoe Schmick, and firefighters Randall Murray (again!), Bob Grantham, Ed Litzenberger, Keith Frankenfield, James Reiss, Glenn Lauer, Todd Garloff, Bill Springer, brothers Wayne and Dave Ernst, Miles Engleman, Randy "Moose" Miller, Eric Loch, Hunter Hendricks, Steve Knauss, and Craig Wolter. Then there are the very special fire police, Warren Godusky, Jeff Kuhns, Jan Harmony, and Janice Engleman. All of you always had my back. Same goes for Vera Cruz firefighters Brian Kleppinger, Kris Kellar, Jim Kellar, Jason Tapler, Gary Mohr, Cyrus Mohr, and Carl Schell, plus our fire police, Capt. Jason Welter, Lt. Roxy Fatzinger and her husband, Matt. Medics who watched over me include Emmaus Ambulance Chief Mike Nonnemacher, his wife, Donna, and Devin

Neitz and Macungie Paramedic Chris Greb. Then there's every firefighter's best friend, Pennsylvania State Fire Commissioner Edward A. Mann.

Robert Rodale, the late chairman of Rodale Press, generously allowed responding to fire calls to be part of my job description. We need more community-minded business leaders like Bob. Many thanks also to the old Rodale mafia, Mike McGrath, ace photographer Mitch Mandel, copyeditor Alice Perry, and Web marketing guru Fred Zahradnik.

For historic photographs, I'm indebted to Rose Parry of the Upper Milford Historical Society, and Andrew Kerstetter of the Emmaus Historical Society. Photographer Jim Marsh graciously contributed more modern images.

"Gross dank" to my Pennsylvania Dutch friends, Brian Moyer, Doris Mory, Carl and Jean Meck, and farmers Beth and Dave Rice. Keith Crotz, the American Botanist in Illinois, always kept the faith, as did Cass Peterson.

In the "Permissions Department," thank you to Little, Brown and Company for permission to reprint from "FIREHOUSE" by David Halberstam, 2002; to former New York City Firefighter Dennis Smith for permission to reprint from his 1972 firefighting classic, "Report From Engine Co. 82"; and Glenn J. Kashurba, M.D., author and publisher, for permission to reprint from his Flight 93 oral and pictorial history, "Courage After the Crash," SAJ Publishing, 2002.

To my children, Donald and Ruth, who lived much of this, too. And to your children. May you teach your children well. Finally, there's the most important person in my life, my wife, Melanie. A "faithful, judicious, and painstaking editor," as Mark Twain once wrote of his wife. I didn't always follow your suggestions, but you were right more often than not. We fell for each other on the night police beat. Newsroom gossips said we wouldn't last 6 months. Almost 40 years, two coups, and more than 5,000 fire calls later, we're still "two kids playing house." Don't know why you put up with me, but I'm glad you do. Must be love.

What else can be done to ease the burden on our volunteers? Plenty. The USFA, NFPA and other agencies that have studied the fire service for decades say there is a lot you can do to help your local volunteer fire department, even if you never want to go near a burning building or put on an air pack. Here are just a few of the non-combat jobs that need filling to keep even more volunteer firefighters from burning out:

* Grant writer
* Fundraiser
* Publicist
* Bookkeeper
* Mechanic
* Nurse
* Attorney
* Physical fitness/lifestyle coach

* Groundskeeper
* Historian
* Recording secretary
* Photographer
* Cook
* Electrician
* Online manager
* Chaplain

If nothing else, you can at least write a bigger check the next time your fire department has a fundraising drive. Or, you can follow Lillie Coit's example and remember your local volunteer fire department with a generous bequest in your will. What better way to do something really good for your community long after you're gone. Monuments like Coit Tower in San Francisco are rare, but maybe a new fire station would be named in your honor. You never know what may happen ... when you answer a fire call.

Made in the USA
Middletown, DE
18 January 2015